MW00985634

DESTROYING WORLD ORDER

DESTROYING WORLD ORDER

U.S. Imperialism in the Middle East
Before and After September 11

by

Francis A. Boyle

CLARITY PRESS, INC.

© 2004 Francis A. Boyle

ISBN: 0-932863-40-X

In-house editor: Diana G. Collier

Cover photo: AP/World Wide Photos

ALL RIGHTS RESERVED: Except for purposes of review, this book may
not be copied, or stored in any information retrieval system, in whole or in part,
without permission in writing from the publishers.

Also by Francis A. Boyle:

World Politics and International Law (1985)
Defending Civil Resistance under International Law (1987)
The Future of International Law and American Foreign Policy (1989)
The Bosnian People Charge Genocide (1996)
Foundations of World Order (1999)
The Criminality of Nuclear Deterrence (2002)
Palestine, Palestinians and International Law (2003)

Library of Congress Cataloging-in-Publication Data

Boyle, Francis Anthony, 1950-
   Destroying world order : U.S. imperialism in the Middle East before and after
September 11 / by Francis A. Boyle.— 1st ed.
      p. cm.
Includes bibliographical references and index.
ISBN 0-932863-40-X
1. Middle East—Relations—United States. 2. United States—Relations—
Middle East. 3. Imperialism. 4. Persian Gulf War, 1991. 5. War on Terrorism,
2001- 6. Iraq War, 2003. I. Title.
   DS63.2.U5B69 2004
   327.73056'09'049—dc22
                                        2003027096

The Publisher gratefully acknowledges the contribution of
Arthur Clark
to the production of this title.

CLARITY PRESS, INC.
Ste. 469, 3277 Roswell Rd. NE
Atlanta, GA. 30305

http://www.claritypress.com

Dedication

In Honor of Ramsey Clark

I would like to dedicate this book to my friend and colleague, Ramsey Clark, whom I have followed (for the most part) during the past two decades on our mutual quest for peace, justice, human rights, and democracy around the world, and especially here in the United States of America. Defending the poor, the oppressed, and the downtrodden. Unfortunately, I do not believe that I can personally measure up to the task of trying to honor Ramsey. Therefore, I believe it would be better for someone else besides me to say a few words in his honor. And I have just the right person—the late Sean MacBride, Irish Nobel Peace Prize Laureate and former Chief-of-Staff of the Irish Republican Army.

I think both Ramsey and I would agree that perhaps the greatest man we have ever known was Sean MacBride, whose profound impact upon me has been duly recorded elsewhere. Sean was one of the great historical figures of the twentieth century. And I am sure that Ramsey would also be the first to agree that Sean was the most principled and courageous person it has ever been our pleasure to know. Indeed, it never ceases to amaze me that when I travel around the world, oppressed peoples everywhere still possess an enormous degree of respect, admiration, gratitude, and genuine personal affection for Sean MacBride despite the fact that he has been dead now for over fifteen years. They feel the same way about Ramsey.

In August of 1987, Sean and I were attending an international conference of lawyers against nuclear weapons for the purpose of founding an international organization to achieve the objective of eliminating nuclear weapons from the face of the earth. At the time, one of Sean's great fears was that the organization would be dominated by the lawyers from the United States and the Soviet Union to the effective exclusion of meaningful input from lawyers all around the world, and especially from Third World countries. Sean believed that it would be unprincipled, imprudent, and counterproductive to have lawyers living in the world's two nuclear superpowers placed in charge of eliminating nuclear weapons. As he saw it, that would be akin to putting the foxes in charge of the chicken coup.

In order to prevent this from happening, Sean strongly believed that Ramsey Clark should be invited to play a prominent role in the founding of this organization. Without even bothering to discuss the issue with him, Sean instinctively knew that Ramsey would agree with him on this important matter of principle and politics, which he later did. A special executive meeting of this proposed organization convened to discuss these and many other issues as well. There Sean put forth Ramsey's name.

Sean's proposal immediately provoked sharp objections from most of the American lawyers sitting around the table. They argued that Ramsey Clark was generally perceived to be too radical, without credibility, marginalized, and without much of a following. These ad hominem attacks upon Ramsey precipitated a fairly sharp response from Sean and me. After about 30 minutes of fairly vigorous debate on this subject, we all agreed to take a break from the discussions in order to allow tempers to cool.

As we strolled down the hallway from the meeting room, I turned to Sean and said: "You know, all their objections to Ramsey Clark are total nonsense. Ramsey is a hero to tens of thousands of people in the peace movement here in the United States as well as around the world, myself included."

At that point, Sean turned to me and said: "You're right, Francis. And Ramsey Clark is one of my heroes too!" Sean then proceeded to tell me the story of when they were both in Hanoi together on a fact-finding mission to oppose the U.S. aggression and genocide against Vietnam while American B-52 bombers were mercilessly pounding that city with their "ordnance." They had to take cover in bomb shelters on more than one occasion. Many years later, Ramsey would repeat this heroic performance during February of 1991 when he travelled to Iraq on a fact-finding mission while those same U.S. B-52 bombers were mercilessly obliterating the cities and people of that poor country. Plus ça change, plus ça reste la même chose.

Sean concluded his story by giving the following instruction to me: "Now you go back into that room and tell those American lawyers that Ramsey Clark is one of my heroes!" He then walked off to his hotel room, obviously fatigued by these needless mental exertions. He had less than five months to live. He died just before he was to meet with U.N. Secretary General Javier Perez de Cuellar for the purpose of establishing his truly international organization of lawyers from around the world in order to eliminate nuclear weapons from the face of the earth.

In any event, pursuant to Sean's instructions, I returned to that room by myself in order to argue the case for Ramsey's inclusion. Of course, Sean's ringing endorsement of Ramsey did not make any difference to the American lawyers sitting around that room—for they also believed that Sean MacBride himself was too radical, marginalized, and without a following.

Be that as it may, both at the time and in retrospect, I was and am still struck by the fervor of Sean MacBride when he emphatically told me that Ramsey Clark was one of his "heroes." I think that even Ramsey would agree that no greater tribute could ever be paid to him by anyone. Someday I shall be most honored and pleased to learn that those in power consider me to be as radical and marginalized as Ramsey Clark and Sean MacBride. My heroes.

Table of Contents

Foreword

American Imperialism

It has become a truism to state that September 11, 2001 "changed everything" as well as that "nothing will ever be the same again." In fact, little has changed in the imperialist tendencies of American foreign policy since the founding of the United States of America in 1789. The fledgling United States government opened the 19th Century by stealing the continent of North America from the American Indians, while in the process ethnically cleansing them, and finally deporting the few pitiful survivors by means of death marches à la Bataan to bantustans (a.k.a. reservations) as a first instance of America's self-styled "manifest destiny." The imperial government of the United States of America opened the 20th Century by stealing a colonial empire from Spain, (Cuba, Puerto Rico, Guam, Philippines), then inflicting a near genocidal war against the Filipino people, while at the same time purporting to annex the former Kingdom of Hawaii while subjecting the Native Hawaiian people (the Kanaka Maoli) to genocidal conditions[1] —all in the name of securing America's "place in the sun."

Now, the 21st Century witnesses the effort of the imperial government of the United States of America to steal a hydrocarbon empire from the Muslim states and peoples surrounding Central Asia and the Persian Gulf under the pretexts of "fighting a war against international terrorism" (Afghanistan) and "eliminating weapons of mass destruction" (Iraq).[2] For the past 215 years the imperialist foreign policy of the United States of America has been predicated upon racism, aggression, genocide, ethnic cleansing, crimes against humanity, war crimes, and slavery. At the dawn of the third millennium of humankind's parlous existence, nothing has changed about the imperialist operational dynamics of American foreign policy. Plus ça change, plus ça reste la même chose.

While this Foreword permits neither the time nor the space to review the past 215 years of imperialist American foreign policy around the world, suffice it to say that the historical development of the American Empire reflects and confirms the trenchant analysis of the origins of both the Roman Empire and the Alexandrian Empire as "great robber bands" that was set forth by Saint Augustine of Hippo in Book 4, Chapter 4 of his monumental *The City of God*:[3]

> Kingdoms without justice are similar to robber barons. And so if justice is left out, what are kingdoms except great robber bands? For what are robber bands, except little kingdoms? The band also is a group of men governed by the orders of a leader, bound by a social compact, and its booty is divided according to a law agreed upon. If by repeatedly adding desperate men this plague

grows to the point where it holds territory and establishes a fixed seat, seizes cities and subdues peoples, then it more conspicuously assumes the name of kingdom, and this name is now openly granted to it, not for any subtraction of cupidity, but by addition of impunity. For it was an elegant and true reply that was made to Alexander the Great by a certain pirate whom he had captured. When the king asked him what he was thinking of, that he should molest the sea, he said with defiant independence: "The same as you when you molest the world! Since I do this with a little ship I am called a pirate. You do it with a great fleet and are called an emperor."

The United States of America has succeeded to the imperial mantles of Rome and Alexander. It has become the Emperor of the world. The "seven fleets" of the United States of America can now terrorize all the states and the peoples of the entire world at will. The imperial U.S. power elite proudly boast of America's planetary hegemonial imperialism: Long live Pax Americana![4] In light of its preponderance of force, the United States of America has the sheer audacity to claim that those who resist its imperialist hegemony are "terrorists" and "criminals." While there very well might be some "pirates" lurking out there somewhere in the Third World, the United States of America has always aspired to the role of Alexander. Today, we are he!

Saint Augustine's descriptions of the formation of the Roman and Alexandrine empires presciently described the historical origins of the United States of America as a great robber band. Gangs of European robbers, marauders, and freebooters governed by leaders with social compacts (e.g., William Bradford and the Mayflower Compact) sailed over to North America in order to steal the land from the indigenous Americans. They ethnically cleansed these lands by means of genocide and, as humankind as a whole grappled to restrain state lawlessness, by what would come to be expressed in international law as crimes against humanity and war crimes, and then deported the few remaining survivors to what they euphemistically called "reservations." This great band of European colonial robbers carved up the booty among themselves by means of laws and then later under the rubric of their so-called "Articles of Confederation" of 1781. This plague of desperate European imperial robber barons was so successful that they were able to establish the imperial Republic of the United States of America by means of a Constitution in 1787,[5] which ratified, condoned, and "legalized" after the fact their multifarious aggressions, genocides, crimes against humanity, ethnic cleansing, war crimes, and thievery of North America, including the kidnapping, mass deportation, subjugation, and exploitation of millions of Africans to work these stolen lands as slaves.[6] For the past 215 years, the successors to Saint Augustine's great band of robbers, freebooters, and criminals have pillaged and plundered the entire world under their chosen pseudonym—the United States of America, ". . . not for any subtraction of cupidity, but by addition of impunity. . . ."

In this regard, I have detailed the United States government's international crimes inflicted upon American Indians, African Americans, Native

Hawaiians, Puerto Ricans, and Mexicanos in my *Indictment of the Federal Government of the United States of America for the Commission of International Crimes and Petition for Orders Mandating its Proscription and Dissolution as an International Criminal Conspiracy and a Criminal Organization* (18 September 1992). At the request of my client the American Indian Movement (AIM), I drafted, filed, served, and prosecuted this *Indictment* in my capacity as Special Prosecutor of the Federal Government of the United States of America before the International Tribunal of Indigenous Peoples and Oppressed Nations in the United States of America, which convened in San Francisco from October 2-4, 1992 for the purpose of commemorating the 500th anniversary of Christopher Columbus's invasion of the Indigenous Western Hemisphere.[7] I will not review here the sordid history of the racist and genocidal American imperial atrocities perpetrated against the Indigenous Peoples, enslaved Africans, Puerto Ricans, annexed Mexicanos, and Kanaka Maoli.

        As for this great band of robber barons' belligerent opening of the twentieth century, my *Foundations of World Order: The Legalist Approach to International Relations 1898-1922* published by Duke University Press in 1999 has already dealt with Imperial America's theft of the colonial empire from Imperial Spain under the guise of the United States obtaining its "place in the sun." As explained therein, Imperial America's theft of the Spanish empire in the supposedly "Pacific" Ocean made war with Imperial Japan inevitable and thus produced Imperial America's precipitation into the Second World War, as President Franklin Roosevelt had desired and planned.[8] So too, today's theft of a hydrocarbon empire from the Muslim states and peoples of Eurasia by the successors to the great band of robbers (a.k.a. the succeeding governments of the United States of America) will someday make the Third World War inevitable. The purpose of this book is to explain what happened and why—and what can be done to stop this oncoming Third World War.

Founding World Order

        The above-mentioned book provided the first comprehensive analysis of the history of American foreign policy towards international law and organizations from the Spanish-American War in 1898 through the foundation of the League of Nations and the Permanent Court of International Justice as of 1922. This essentially pre-World War I American legalist approach to international politics sought to create an actual "regime" of international law and organizations that would prevent, reduce, and regulate the transnational threat and use of force in international relations. In particular, the pre-World War I American legalist war prevention program for world politics consisted of obtaining the following concrete objectives: (1) the creation of a general system for the obligatory arbitration of disputes between states; (2) the establishment of an International Court of Justice; (3) the codification of important areas of customary international law into positive treaty form; (4) arms reduction, but only after, not before, the relaxation of international tensions by means of these and other legalist techniques and institutions; and (5) the institutionalization of the practice of convoking periodic peace conferences for all states in the recognized international community. In addition, a subsidiary element of this pre-World War I American legalist war prevention program for world politics was to strengthen the well-established international legal institution of neutrality and the humanitarian laws of armed conflict in order to further isolate the bulk of the international community, and especially the United States, from some future war in Europe that might erupt despite the enactment of these preventive legalist devices.

The fifth legalist objective of creating some mechanism for the convocation of periodic international peace conferences was attained and far exceeded by the creation of the League of Nations. Nevertheless, for reason explained in the above book, the United States government never joined the League nor its related Permanent Court of International Justice. Moreover, after the definitive repudiation of the Treaty of Versailles by the United States Senate, no further attempt was made by the United States government to join the League on some other terms. And despite repeated attempts by its American legalist supporters, the United States never joined the Permanent Court either.

The dominant interpretation among historians, political scientists, and international lawyers is that during the period between the First and Second World Wars, the United States government simply retreated to its traditional foreign policies of isolationism in peace and neutrality in war vis-à-vis the rest of the world that went all the way back to President George Washington's Farewell Address. To the contrary, during the interwar period, the United States government continued to pursue a foreign policy based upon the active promotion of international law and organizations for the rest of the world. In this regard, there was a remarkable degree of continuity between American legalist foreign policy during the 1898-1922 era and the interwar period of its history.

One of the overall objectives and dilemmas of American foreign policy during the period between the First and Second World Wars became how to advance the perceived vital national security interest of the United States in promoting international law and organizations around the world without participating in the League of Nations. This interpretation of American interwar diplomacy can account for the Kellogg-Briand Peace Pact, the Stimson Doctrine, the Washington and London Naval Conferences, U.S. Neutrality Legislation, numerous Inter-American Peace conferences, etc. The United States government simply continued to pursue its legalist approach to international relations that was classically defined and articulated during the pre-World War I era into and throughout the interwar period, though without dealing with the League.

Despite the fact that the United States government was hindered by its non-participation in the activities of the League, America nevertheless sought to trump the League by promoting a new concept of international law and politics: the outlawry of war. As explained in the above-mentioned study, that principle of international law and politics goes all the way back to a series of Inter-American Peace conferences held before the First World

War. This idea would be resurrected by the United States government and ultimately enshrined in the Kellogg-Briand Peace Pact of 1928 that outlawed war as an instrument of national policy. This would later be followed up by the Stimson Doctrine of 1931 whereby the United States government refused to recognize any legal results flowing from a violation of the Kellogg-Briand Peace Pact with respect to the Japanese invasion of China. The principle announced by the Stimson Doctrine would ultimately be endorsed by the League of Nations Assembly.

The outlawry of war would later be enshrined into article 2(4) of the United Nations Charter, the cornerstone of the post-World War II world order: "All Members shall refrain in their international relations from the threat or use of force against the territorial integrity or political independence of any state, or in any other manner inconsistent with the Purposes of the United Nations." Immediately after the culmination of the Second World War, some of the major Nazi war criminals would be tried, convicted and sentenced to death by the Nuremberg Tribunal for waging an aggressive war or a war in violation of international treaties such as the Kellogg-Briand Peace Pact. Thereafter, the Nuremberg Charter, Judgment, and Principles would become yet another pillar of the post-World War II legal and political world order.

Membership in some international organization for the maintenance of international peace and security would not again become a formal objective of American foreign policy until after U.S. intervention into the Second World War. On October 30, 1943, the United States, the United Kingdom, the Soviet Union, and China proclaimed the Moscow Declaration, which recognized "the necessity of establishing at the earliest practicable date a general international organization, based on the principle of the sovereign equality of all peace-loving States, and open to membership by all such States large and small, for the maintenance of international peace and security."[9] The Moscow Declaration would eventually result in the creation of the United Nations Organization in 1945. Thus under the impetus of the Second World War, the United States government returned to pursuing the vision of world order that had been designed, articulated, and substantially implemented by American international lawyers during the first quarter of the twentieth century by founding both the United Nations Organization and its International Court of Justice. Yet today the Bush Jr. administration is striving mightily to destroy the very foundations of the international legal order that previous U.S. administrations had patiently but tenaciously constructed during the past 100 years of American foreign policy towards international law and organizations despite their imperialist tendencies.

Destroying World Order

Chapter 1 begins *in medias res* with the 1979 revolution in Iran spearheaded by the Ayatollah Khomeini, which overthrew the U.S. imperial puppet known as the Shah of Iran. "International Crisis and Neutrality: U.S. Foreign Policy Toward the Iraq-Iran War" addresses the resultant "tilt towards Iraq" and its brutal leader Saddam Hussein by the allegedly "liberal" human rights-oriented Carter administration acting under the inspiration of Zbigniew Brzezinski. In a grotesque perversion of its publicly purported policy orientation, the Carter administration encouraged Saddam Hussein to invade Iran in September of 1980, resulting in a post-World War II conflagration that produced over one million casualties for both sides.[10] The so-called "Iranian hostages crisis" of 1979-1981, a further by-product of the Iranian revolution, served as a sideshow that would lead to Carter's defeat by Ronald Reagan in the 1980 U.S. presidential election.[11] Not surprisingly, the Reagan administration continued Carter's "tilt" towards Iraq and Saddam Hussein against Iran and in violation of fundamental principles of public international law. Whether consisting of Liberal Imperialists (Carter et al.; Clinton et al.), Conservative Imperialists (Bush Sr. et al.), or Reactionary Imperialists (Reagan et al.; Bush Jr. et al.), American administrations without exception believe in Imperial America's "manifest destiny" to rule the world. They are emperors all!

Divide et impera was an imperial strategy that the racist American power elite learned from Rome and applied inter alia to Iraq and Iran. Later on the Clinton administration would euphemistically call this Iraq-Iran policy "dual containment." But with respect to stealing Persian Gulf oil, the scenario was always the same going back at least to the Nixon/Kissinger regime: encourage Iraqis and Iranians to kill each other off by means of weapons sold to them at inflated prices, then claim the hydrocarbon prize. It is a scenario that could have been taken right out of that classic film *Yojimbo* (1961) by the revered Japanese director Akira Kurosawa and starring the great Japanese actor Toshiro Mifune as a rogue samurai-for-hire during Imperial Japan. More colloquially, the Italian director Sergio Leone would later plagiarize the script, put its plot into the 19th Century Imperial American "West," and produce the hit movie *A Fistful of Dollars* (1964) starring tough-guy Clint Eastwood. Today American foreign policy is in the charge of a *faux* Texas cowboy *cum* failed oil baron pretending to be *Dirty Harry* (1971).

Chapter 2 relates the unfolding tragedy and atrocity of the Bush Sr. war of decimation against Iraq in 1991. Based upon work I performed as Counsel to The Commission of Inquiry for the International War Crimes Tribunal that was organized and chaired by former U.S. Attorney General Ramsey Clark, [12] it details the criminal charges under international law that we collectively developed against the Bush Sr. administration. The final results and documentation of the Commission and Tribunal have been published in Ramsey Clark's book *The Fire This Time: U.S. War Crimes in the Gulf* (1992).

Chapter 3 concerns the case of Captain Doctor Yolanda Huet-Vaughn, which is included here because it is of vital significance today for situations which will undoubtedly arise requiring the defense of U.S. military personnel who refuse as a matter of conscience and principle to engage in U.S. wars of aggression in Iraq and elsewhere around the world in the future. While Gulf War I raged on and the Bush Sr. administration ferociously inflicted genocide, crimes against humanity, and war crimes against the Iraqi people, I was honored to serve as Counsel for the defense of Captain Dr. Yolanda Huet-Vaughn, who was court-martialed for desertion by the United States

Army for refusing to participate in this slaughter as a matter of principle, and faced five years in a military prison for her heroic act of conscience. The U.S. Army's persecution of Captain Dr. Huet-Vaughn proved the old adage that "military justice is to justice as military music is to music." To make a long story short, we got her out of medium security at the Fort Leavenworth, Kansas Prison after eight months. How we achieved this remarkable result is fully explained in this chapter.

Captain Dr. Yolanda Huet-Vaughn is America's equivalent to Vaclav Havel, Andrei Sakharov, Wei Jingsheng, Aung San Suu Kyi, and others. We Americans like to delude ourselves into believing that there are no "prisoners of conscience" or "political prisoners" in the equivalent of the Gulag Archipelago run right here in the United States by the United States government. In fact, there are many.[13] Captain Dr. Huet-Vaughn is among the most courageous. She is the archetypal American Hero whom we should be bringing into our schools and asking our children to emulate, not those wholesale purveyors of violence adulated by the government, the power elite, the news media, and the entertainment industry.

During the course of this litigation we raised on behalf of Captain Dr. Huet-Vaughn the criminalities surrounding what later came be known as the Gulf War Syndrome that currently afflicts over one-fifth of the half-million U.S. (and U.K.) veterans who participated in Bush Sr.'s Gulf War I and undoubtedly will afflict U.S. (and U.K.) veterans of Bush Jr.'s Gulf War II. The Pentagon still denies that there is such a thing as the Gulf War Syndrome in order to cover up its own criminality. After my 6 May 1991 expert testimony given in the Article 32 Hearing for Captain Dr. Huet-Vaughn, it was publicly revealed that the Reagan/Bush Sr. administration had knowingly authorized numerous shipments of weapons-specific biological agents to Iraq in wanton violation of the 1972 Biological Weapons Convention, obviously in the hope and expectation that Saddam Hussein would develop and use biological weapons against Iran.[14] So Iraq and Saddam Hussein actually obtained their biological weapons courtesy of the Reagan/Bush Sr. administration. Secretly knowing this fact, the Bush Sr. administration then forced U.S. Armed Forces being deployed for Gulf War I to take experimental medical vaccines in an effort to counteract these bioweapons, an effort which was nonetheless in violation of the Nuremberg Code on Medical Experimentation.[15] In other words, the highest level officials of the Bush Sr. administration—some of whom currently work for Bush Jr. (e.g., Vice President Cheney, then Secretary of "Defense")—inflicted a Nuremberg Crime against our own U.S. troops in yet another instance of the class warfare perpetrated by the racist U.S. power elite upon the poor Blacks, Latinos, and Whites who predominantly participated in Gulf War I. Tragically, the same will prove true for the Bush Jr. administration's Gulf War II.

While working to defend Captain Dr. Yolanda Huet-Vaughn, during the summer of 1991 I was contacted on behalf of some mothers in Iraq whose children were dying at astounding rates because of the genocidal economic sanctions that had been imposed upon them by the Security Council in August of 1990 at the behest of the Bush Sr. administration. They requested that I do something in order to save these innocent children from perishing in agony before their mothers' very eyes. Using the format of the *Writ for World Habeas Corpus* that had been previously provided to me by my friend and colleague, the late Luis Kutner, Esq. of Chicago, Illinois, I filed a *Complaint* on behalf of the 4.5 million children of Iraq against President George Bush Sr. and the United States of America with the United Nations Organization, dated 18 September 1991, which can be found in Chapter 4.[16]

Despite my best professional efforts working on behalf of my clients *pro bono publico*, the grossly hypocritical United Nations Organization adamantly refused to act to terminate these genocidal sanctions and thus to save the dying children of Iraq. The United Nations' own Food and Agricultural Organization (FAO) Report of 1995 estimated that these genocidal economic sanctions against Iraq had killed about 560,000 Iraqi children since they were first imposed in 1990.[17] In regard to these murdered Iraqi children, later U.S. Secretary of State Madeline Albright was interviewed on the CBS Television Network on 12 May 1996 by correspondent Leslie Stahl. The transcript of this interview provided by CBS News itself reads as follows:[18]

> Stahl: (Voiceover) If the Iraqi people place any blame on Saddam Hussein, they're afraid to say so. And there is no longer much hope that the sanctions will inspire the people to rise up and topple the government. Now people are just trying to get by because one of the side effects of the sanctions has been inflation, which has jumped as high as 3,000 percent. To make ends meet, Iraqis are selling everything they can. Flea markets have sprung up on the streets, where families can sell their furniture, clothes, anything they can to make a few extra dinars. Most Iraqis are suffering.

> We have heard that a half a million children have died. I mean, that's more children than died when-wh-in-in Hiroshima. And-and, you know, is the price worth it?

> Ambassador Albright: I think this is a very hard choice, but the price—we think the price is worth it.

This shocking statement by the later U.S. Secretary of State provides proof positive of the genocidal intent by the United States Government against Iraq and its people as defined by and in violation of Genocide Convention Article II: "In the present Convention, genocide means any of the following acts committed with intent to destroy, in whole or in part, a national, ethnical, racial, or religious group, as such. . . ." Certainly a half-million dead Iraqi children that the later U.S. Secretary of State specifically intended to destroy as such, and did indeed destroy as such, constitutes a very important "part" of the Iraqi people. These half-million dead children were the very future of the people and state of Iraq.

This Albright statement is what criminal lawyers call a classic "Admission Against Interest." This Statement by the then Ambassador and later U.S. Secretary of State, then acting within the scope of her official duties and speaking in the name of the United States government, could be taken to the International Court of Justice in The Hague and filed to prove that the United States of America possessed the *mens rea* (criminal intent) necessary to commit the international crime of genocide. Under both international law and U.S. domestic law, to be guilty of a crime a person or a state must possess the requisite *mens rea* at the same time that he or she or it commits the criminal act (*actus reus*). With respect to these genocidal economic sanctions against Iraq, the *actus reus* for the U.S. government and its officials committing the international crime of genocide is set forth in Genocide Convention Article II (c): "Deliberately inflicting on the group conditions of life calculated to bring about its physical destruction in whole or in part." The 500,000 dead Iraqi Children, as conceded and approved by later U.S. Secretary of State Albright, constituted a substantial "part" of the People of Iraq. Albright incriminated both herself and the United States of America at the same time, apparently without thought as to any future international legal determination of her culpability. Such is the arrogance of the powerful—which is usually the source of their downfall.

The United States and the United Kingdom obstinately insisted that the genocidal economic sanctions imposed against Iraq remain in place until after the conclusion of the internationally illegal Gulf War II perpetrated by Bush Jr. and Tony Blair. Then, on 22 May 2003, the United States and the United Kingdom procured U.N. Security Council Resolution 1483 lifting these genocidal economic sanctions, not with a view to easing the decade-long suffering of the Iraqi people, but rather so as to facilitate their unsupervised looting and plundering of the Iraqi economy and oil fields in violation of the international laws of war as well as to the grave detriment of the Iraqi people.

Delivered as the *Dr. Irma M. Parhad Lecture* before the Faculty of Medicine at the University of Calgary in Canada on March 13, 2001, my "Humanitarian Intervention Versus International Law" address acquired contemporary relevance when, in a classic case of bait-and-switch, Bush Jr. and Blair could not produce the alleged weapons of mass destruction that had provided the fraudulent pretext for a war of aggression against Iraq for oil and on behalf of Israel, and switched their public justification for the war on Iraq to the hoary but long-discredited doctrine of "humanitarian intervention." Ironically, the late Dr. Parhad, in whose honor I gave this endowed lecture, was of Iraqi descent. Indeed, as explained in what is now Chapter 5 in this book, what has been needed all along is real "humanitarian intervention" by the international community of states for the purpose of saving the long-suffering people of Iraq from the longstanding depredations inflicted upon them by the United States and the United Kingdom. Their agony and torment continues!

Chapter 6 contains the Special Introduction to my book *The Criminality of Nuclear Deterrence: Could the U.S. War on Terrorism Go Nuclear?* (Clarity Press: 2002), entitled "George Bush, Jr., September 11, and the Rule of Law," which deals comprehensively with the Bush Jr. war of aggression against Afghanistan during 2001-2002.

Chapter 7, titled "The Bush Jr. Administration's War of Aggression against Iraq", covers the period 2002-2003. The reader is asked to carefully consider this fact: The Bush Jr. administration waged two major wars within two years of each other against two separate countries that are almost half a planet away from the United States of America. This could not have been accomplished without the most meticulous planning and preparatory work over several years by what the former Soviet Union used to call their "power ministries": the Pentagon, CIA, NSC, NSA, DIA, NRO, etc. It is inconceivable that the United States of America could launch two wars in close succession to steal, control, and dominate two-thirds of the world's hydrocarbon resources unless there were preexisting, tested, "gamed," and well-honed war plans and military preparations that went back for quite some time. And of course, if the war plans and preparations preceded September 11, then that tragedy could hardly be regarded as their cause; the true motivation had to precede them.

In point of fact, the racist U.S. power elite and its governments had been continuously planning, preparing, and conspiring to steal the Persian Gulf oilfields since the time of the Nixon/Kissinger regime in reaction to the 1973 Arab oil embargo of Europe and the United States because of their support for Israel. A combination of oil and Israel can be seen to account for most of U.S. imperial policy towards the Middle East before and after 11 September 2001, dating back at least three decades to the 1967 Israeli aggressions against the surrounding Arab states and peoples for *lebensraum* with American support under the Johnson administration.[19] The policy has been little mitigated irrespective of the American regime in place: Johnson, Nixon, Ford, Carter, Reagan, Bush Sr., Clinton, and Bush Jr.

With the public onset of the Bush Jr. war of aggression against Iraq in late August of 2002, my assessment of the situation was that the Bush Jr. administration was pursuing roughly the same diplomatic, political, military and propaganda strategy that the Bush Sr. administration had followed against Iraq starting in August of 1990. So on the first available occasion, which was before a peace rally held here at the University of Illinois Urbana-Champaign campus on 7 October 2002, I launched a National Campaign to Impeach Bush, Cheney, Rumsfeld, and Ashcroft for the substantive reasons set forth in Chapter 8. Draft articles of impeachment are included. At the time, it seemed to me that Bush Jr.'s call for a preventive war against Iraq required a preventive impeachment campaign in response against the highest level officials of the Bush Jr. administration with a view to preventing the war. Since that time, Ralph Nader, Senator Bob Graham of Florida, then a candidate running for the U.S. presidential nomination of the Democratic Party, the National Green Party, and the City of Santa Cruz, California, inter alia, have publicly called for the impeachment of President Bush Jr. There is no indication that the most recent wars against Afghanistan and Iraq mean the end of the Bush Jr. administration's imperial adventures—despite the fact that the record-breaking spending they require would seem to impose an insurmountable limitation to American hubris.

Prologue

In 1898 the United States deliberately chose to emulate the imperial countries of the Old World and set out to become a major global power by performing a series of naked acts of military, political, and economic expansion in order to seize its self-proclaimed "place in the sun" by means of raw and brutal force. Since that time, America has struggled to come to grips with the irreversible consequences of those fateful decisions, which directly contradicted several of the most fundamental normative principles in its 1776 Declaration of Independence and in its 1787 Constitution as subsequently amended, on which the United States was supposed to have been founded. During this era of pursuing hegemonic imperialism, the promotion of international law and international organizations has usually provided the United States with the means for reconciling the idealism of American values and aspirations with the realism of world politics and historical conditions. The U.S. government's resolute dedication to pursuing a legalist approach to international relations has proved to be critical for the preservation of America's internal psychic equilibrium, which in turn has historically been a necessary precondition for the preservation of its international standing.

Both well before and immediately after the First World War—as well as immediately after the Second World War—the United States established an excellent track record for pioneering innovative rules of international law and novel institutions for the peaceful settlement of international disputes. Drastic departures from this tradition of U.S. legalist diplomacy in order to follow instead a foreign policy based essentially on Machiavellian power politics produced only unmitigated disasters for the U.S. government both at home and abroad. In the case of the Bush Jr. administration, it could very well produce a Third World War. The choice is up to the citizens of the United States of America.

Unless and until the ordinary people of America rise up to challenge the elemental lawlessness of the Bush Jr. administration, the future of the human race will be determined by those Machiavellians who occupy positions of power and influence in America's government, its sycophantic think-tanks, its prostituted universities, and its corrupted news media. We must mobilize the common people of America to save humanity from these so-called experts. Only then can we expect to see some fundamental changes in the nature of the predicament created by the Bush Jr. administration's nihilistic international lawlessness that confronts America and the world today.

I believe that most of the American people are basically unaware of the gross violations of international law that are being perpetrated in their name by their own government on a day-to-day basis. Once they have been informed, however, they become clearly outraged and have usually decided to do something to stop the elementally lawless behavior of successive U.S. administrations around the world. For example, during many of the civil resistance protest cases I have worked on during the past twenty-one years, the jury will acquit the defendants of all or some of the criminal charges and then afterwards be interviewed by representatives of the local news media.[20] Routinely it has been the case that several members of the jury will publicly state that they were "shocked" to discover that the United States government was committing such gross violations of international law, and that this factor had led them to acquit the defendants. Moreover, some of the jurors will state that they had been so "radicalized" by the trial that they thought they themselves should go out and start to protest in order to do something about the situation!

In any event, many of the jurors who are permitted to hear and consider our international law arguments in defense of civil resistance protesters invariably reach the conclusion that in light of the international criminal activities by the Reagan/Bush Sr./Clinton administrations with respect to nuclear weapons, Central America, South African apartheid, the Middle East, etc., the defendants did what they had to do in order to stop them. I submit that this is precisely the same type of reaction that most American people will have when properly informed and educated about the relevance of international law to the criminal misconduct of foreign policy by the Bush Jr. administration or, for that matter, by any successors. The pernicious thesis incessantly propounded by political "realists" that for some mysterious reason a democracy is inherently incapable of developing a coherent and consistent foreign policy without Machiavellianism simply reflects their obstinate refusal to accept the well-established primacy of law over power in the American constitutional system of government, and most importantly, in the hearts and minds of the common people of America. The future of American foreign policy lies in the hands of the American people—not the bureaucrats, legislators, judges, lobbyists, think-tanks, pundits, professors, and self-styled experts who inhabit Washington, D.C. and New York City.

We must take and state our compelling case for obeying international law directly to the common people of America. Based upon my extensive experience of having done this for the past twenty-five years, the vast majority of American people will readily agree with the proposition that the United States government should possess a firm commitment to promoting the Rule of Law both at home and abroad. An enormous amount of work needs to be done explaining to the American people both why and how the Rule of Law must and can prevail in the daily conduct of U.S. foreign policy. But I personally have always found a very warm reception for international law arguments among ordinary Americans irrespective of their political persuasions. As far as most U.S. citizens are concerned, invoking the Rule of Law is as paradigmatically American as God, Motherhood, and Apple Pie. Most American citizens have suckled the Rule of Law since they were weaned from their mothers' breasts. It is high time to tap directly into this powerful psychic reservoir of respect for the Rule of Law that is so uniquely and most obsessively characteristic of the American people.

When properly and vigorously presented to the American people, a legal argument will always beat a Machiavellian argument on any issue I have ever dealt with. This is due to the fact that Machiavellian power politics violently contradicts several of the most fundamental normative principles upon which the United States of America is supposed to be founded: the inalienable rights of the individual, the self-determination of peoples, the sovereign equality and independence of states, noninterventionism, respect for the Rule of Law, and the peaceful settlement of international disputes. By contrast, according to *The Prince*, the practice of Machiavellianism abroad requires the practice of Machiavellianism at home. The Machiavellian Prince has no friends, only present and potential enemies, both foreign and domestic. Thus, the Prince must wage physical warfare unremittingly against foreign rivals and periodically when necessary against his own people. Furthermore, the Prince is also supposed to continuously engage in psychological warfare against his own subjects in all possible ways and upon all appropriate occasions.

It is for this reason that geopolitical practitioners of Machiavellian power politics such as Kissinger, Brzezinski, Haig, Kirkpatrick, Shultz, Wolfowitz and the other neo-conservatives, etc., demonstrate little appreciation, knowledge, or sensitivity to the requirements of the U.S. constitutional system of government with its basic commitment to the Rule of Law, whether at home or abroad. Despite the Machiavellian predilections held by these self-anointed "realists," it is the inalterable nature of this "legalist" reality so intrinsic to the United States that has been unconsciously understood, internalized, and effectuated by the common people of America. They can almost innately comprehend that Machiavellianism abroad will inevitably destroy Constitutionalism and the Rule of Law at home.

That is precisely why these self-styled realists have attempted to fence-off the domain of foreign affairs and war as some exclusive preserve for their Machiavellian priesthood. Hence the key to victory is to repudiate their claims to expertise over arcane rites, and then proceed to democratize the conduct of American foreign policy down to the grassroots level of this country. I would submit that the more genuinely democratic American foreign policy decision-making becomes, the more peaceful and law-abiding the U.S. government will be.

However, Machiavellian power politics remains a present danger, both domestically and internationally. The only known antidote is the Rule of Law, both domestically and internationally. In a thermonuclear age, humankind's existential choice is that stark, ominous, and compelling. As Americans, we must not hesitate to apply this curative regimen immediately before it becomes too late for all humanity. Towards that end this book has been published.

Chapter One

International Crisis and Neutrality: U.S. Foreign Policy Toward the Iraq-Iran War

Written in 1986 and delivered before the University of New Orleans Symposium on Neutrality, this paper was published with a Postscript in the Winter 1992 issue of the Mercer Law Review, *whose editors noted that it provided an important historical background to the Iraq-Iran War necessary for analyzing the first U.S. war against Iraq. It is reprinted here for the same reason: to facilitate understanding of all succeeding events.*

The Historical Background of U.S. Neutrality Policies

On the domestic level, current U.S. neutrality legislation dates back to the first Neutrality Act of June 5, I794,[1] which expired after two years and was renewed in I797 for two more years[2] before its permanent enactment with amendments by an Act of April 20, I8I8.[3] The I8I8 Act made it a crime: for an American citizen within U.S. territory to accept and exercise a commission in the military forces of a foreign government engaged in a war against another foreign government with which the United States was at peace; for any person within U.S. territory to enlist or to procure the enlistment of another person, or proceed beyond U.S. territory with the intent to be enlisted in the forces of a foreign sovereign, subject to a proviso for transient foreigners; for any person in U.S. territory to fit out and arm a vessel for the purpose of engaging in hostilities on behalf of a foreign sovereign against another foreign sovereign with which the United States was at peace; for any U.S. citizen outside U.S. territory to fit out and arm a vessel of war for the purpose of committing hostilities on U.S. citizens or their property; for any person within U.S. territory to increase or augment the force of foreign armed vessels at war with another foreign government with which the United States was at peace; and, finally, for any person in U.S. territory to set on foot any military expedition or enterprise against the territory of a foreign sovereign with which the United States was at peace.[4] The President was authorized to employ the land or naval forces or the militia for the purpose of carrying the provisions of the I8I8 Act into effect or to compel any foreign ship to depart from the United States when so required by the laws of nations or treaty obligations.[5]

Historically, the United States government played a leading role in the development of the international laws of neutrality by endeavoring to obtain general acceptance of its internal policy pronouncements on such matters from the countries of Europe throughout the late eighteenth, nineteenth, and early twentieth centuries. Such active support for the institution of "neutrality" was due to the fact that during this isolationist period of its history, the United States government anticipated being neutral in the event of another general war in Europe. For example, the aforementioned proscriptions of U.S. domestic neutrality legislation and practice found their way into the three great principles of the seminal 1871 Treaty of Washington concluded between the United States and Great Britain that settled the famous "*Alabama* Claims" arising out of the latter's provision of assistance to Confederate raiders during the American Civil War.[6] The three rules of article 6 provided that:

A neutral Government is bound

First, to use due diligence to prevent the fitting out, arming, or equipping, within its jurisdiction, of any vessel which it has reasonable ground to believe is intended to cruise or to carry on war against a power with which it is at peace; and also to use like diligence to prevent the departure from its jurisdiction of any vessel intended to cruise or carry on war as above, such vessel having been specially adapted, in whole or in part, within such jurisdiction to war-like use.

Secondly, not to permit or suffer either belligerent to make use of its ports or waters as the base of naval operations against the other, or for the purpose of the renewal or augmentation of military supplies or arms, or the recruitment of men.

Thirdly, to exercise due diligence in its own ports and waters, and, as to all persons within its jurisdiction, to prevent any violation of the foregoing obligations and duties.[7]

Although formulated with reference to a non-international armed conflict (*i.e.,* the U.S. Civil War), these three principles were eventually considered to enunciate requirements of customary international law concerning neutrality that were applicable to an international armed conflict as well.

On the international level, the next major development in the institution of "neutrality" occurred when the First Hague Peace Conference of 1899 adopted a *voeu* to the effect that the second conference should consider the question of the rights and duties of neutrals in warfare.[8] Pursuant to that wish, the Second Hague Peace Conference of 1907 adopted the Convention Respecting the Rights and Duties of Neutral Powers and Persons in Case of War on Land[9] and the Convention Respecting the Rights and Duties of Neutral Powers in Naval War.[10] In addition, the 1907 Convention Relative to the Laying of Submarine Contact Mines was primarily designed to protect neutral shipping,[11] and the 1907 Convention Relative to Certain Restrictions on the Exercise of the Right of Capture in Maritime War contained protections for neutral postal correspondence.[12] When the Great War in Europe erupted in the summer of 1914, the United States was a party to these four Hague Conventions.[13] Since the time of that conflagration, these two major 1907 Hague neutrality conventions governing land and sea warfare, respectively, have been universally considered to enunciate the rules of customary international law on this subject that bind parties and non-parties alike even today.

Taken as a whole, the laws of neutrality were designed to operate in a system of international relations where war was considered to be an inescapable fact of international life and yet where the outbreak of war, even between major actors, did not automatically precipitate a total systemic war among all global powers. According to the laws of neutrality, the conduct of hostilities by a belligerent was supposed to disrupt the ordinary routine of international intercourse between neutral nationals and the belligerent's enemy to the minimal extent required by the dictates of military necessity.[14] Such arrangements were intended to permit the neutral power to stay out of the conflict; at the same time, they allowed its nationals to take advantage of international commerce and intercourse with all belligerents.

The political and strategic dimensions of the international laws of neutrality were complicated by the fact that they operated upon the basis of a legal fiction concerning the neutral government's reputed non-responsibility for what were intrinsically non-neutral acts committed by its citizenry against a belligerent during wartime. Generally, a belligerent state could not hold a neutral government accountable for the private activities undertaken by the neutral's citizens—even if they worked directly to the detriment of the belligerent's wartime security interests. The laws of neutrality were essentially predicated upon Lockeian assumptions concerning the nature of government and its proper relationship to the citizen: namely, that the political functions of government must impinge upon the private affairs of the citizen to the least extent possible, especially in the economic realm where the right to private property and its pursuit were deemed fundamental.[15] Typical of this Lockean attitude was the prohibition on the confiscation of private property found in article 46 of the Regulations annexed to both the 1899 and 1907 Hague Conventions with Respect to the Laws and Customs of War on Land.[16] In the same category fell the futile attempts by the United States government at both the First and the Second Hague Peace Conferences to secure international agreement upon the principle of immunity from capture and confiscation of noncontraband private property during maritime warfare.[17]

Hence, the primary duty of a neutral government was to maintain strict impartiality in its governmental relations with all belligerents. Yet the laws of neutrality specifically denied that the neutral government had any obligation to guarantee that its nationals conduct their affairs with belligerents in a similar fashion or, indeed, in accordance with any but the most rudimentary set of rules. For example, according to the 1907 Hague Convention Respecting the Rights and Duties of Neutral Powers and Persons in Case of War on Land, the territory of neutral powers was "inviolable" (art. 1), and belligerents were forbidden to move troops or convoys of either munitions of war or supplies across the territory of a neutral power (art. 2). Yet a neutral power was not required to prevent the exportation or passage through its territory, on account of either belligerent, of arms, ammunition or anything useful to an army or navy (art. 7); or to forbid or restrict the use, in behalf of belligerents, of telegraph or telephone cables or wireless telegraph apparatus belonging to it or to companies or private individuals (art. 8); provided that all restrictive or prohibitive measures taken by a neutral power in regard to these matters be applied uniformly to both belligerents, and this rule must be respected by companies or individuals owning such telecommunication facilities (art. 9). The national of a neutral power would not compromise his neutrality by furnishing supplies or loans to one of the belligerents, provided he did not reside in the territory of the other belligerent or territory occupied by it and that the supplies did not come from these territories (art. 18). Finally, article 10 made it clear that it would not be considered a hostile act for a neutral power to take measures, even forcible, to prevent violations of its neutrality.

In a similar vein, according to the 1907 Hague Convention Respecting the Rights and Duties of Neutral Powers in Naval War, belligerents were bound to respect the sovereign rights of neutral powers and to abstain, in neutral territory or neutral waters, from any act which would, if knowingly permitted by any power, constitute a violation of neutrality (art. 1); and any act of hostility committed by belligerent warships in the territorial waters of a neutral power was deemed to constitute a violation of neutrality and was strictly forbidden (art. 2). In return, a neutral government could not supply warships, ammunition, or war materials of any kind to a belligerent under any circumstances (art. 6). Yet the neutral government was under no obligation to prevent the export or transit for the use of either belligerent of arms, ammunitions, or, in general, of anything which could be of use to any army or fleet (art. 7). Nevertheless, the neutral power must apply equally to the two belligerents any conditions, restrictions, or prohibitions made by it in regard to the admission into its ports, roadsteads, or territorial waters of belligerent warships or of their prizes. Finally, article 26 made it clear that a neutral government's exercise of its rights under the convention could never be considered an "unfriendly act" by any belligerent that was a contracting power.

Historically, the United States government had vigorously opposed the international recognition of any requirement for neutral powers to impose a mandatory embargo upon trade in contraband of war between neutral nationals and belligerents for the express purpose of ensuring the economic well-being of American citizens during a European war in which the United States expected to remain neutral.[18] Yet contraband of war shipped by neutral nationals to a belligerent was properly subject to capture and confiscation by the offended belligerent. Nevertheless, the belligerent had to undertake these actions in accordance with the laws of war at sea and the international law of prize. For this reason, then, these latter two interrelated bodies of customary international law can also be said to have contained important protections for the rights of neutrals during an international armed conflict.

As a result of the failure by the Second Hague Peace Conference to codify this international law of maritime warfare and prize, Great Britain summoned a conference of representatives of the major maritime powers of the world (Germany, the United States, Austria-Hungary, Spain, France, Great Britain, Italy, Japan, the Netherlands, and Russia) to meet in London at the end of 1908. The goal of this conference was to determine the generally recognized principles of international law applicable to maritime warfare and national prize adjudications. This meeting resulted in the 1909 Declaration of London Concerning the Laws of Naval War.[19] The Declaration of London built upon the foundations established by an informal compromise on the codification of maritime warfare that had been worked out, but not adopted, at the Second Hague Peace Conference. At the beginning of the First World War, the Declaration of London was generally considered to be the most authoritative enunciation of the customary international laws of maritime warfare applicable to belligerents in their conduct of hostilities as well as by the belligerents' respective national prize courts.[20] Its provisions set forth substantial protections for the rights of neutral nationals that were generally honored by both sets of belligerents during the first two years of the Great War.

Without the recognition of a status such as "neutrality" by international law, non-belligerents would be virtually compelled by circumstances to choose up sides in a war so as to maintain political and economic relations with at least one set of belligerents. In theory, the neutral state had an economic disincentive to participate in the war because its citizens could greatly prosper from an increasing degree of only moderately restricted international trade with all belligerents in desperate need for more goods purchased from nationals of the neutral state. Conversely, a belligerent would supposedly not act to violate the neutral's rights and those of its nationals in order to keep the neutral from entering the war on the side of its enemy. Another theory prevalent at the time held that since the number and strength of neutral states in a future war would be proportionately greater than those of belligerents, the community of neutral states could impose obedience to the laws of neutrality upon the belligerents.[21]

In practice, however, these theories were undercut by the fact that each neutral's normal international trading patterns invariably worked to the greater advantage of one set of belligerents during the war.[22] So the disadvantaged belligerent had to engage in a complicated cost-benefit analysis over whether the greater harm was the continued sufferance of this strategic disadvantage in trade or its termination through outright destruction of the neutral commerce with the consequent risk that the neutral power would eventually enter the war against it. Also, instead of acting as part of some international community of neutrals, each neutral state constantly assessed the relative advantages and disadvantages of maintaining its own neutrality as opposed to belligerency on one side of the war or the other in accordance with quite selfish calculations of its own vital national security interests. Unless guaranteed by treaty, the violation of one neutral's rights did not obligate another neutral to declare war or even to undertake measures of retorsion against the violator.

For example, the United States did not enter the First World War in order to defend the international laws of neutrality in the abstract. This was evidenced by its failure to consider the German invasions of either neutral Belgium or neutral Luxemburg as a casus belli. It was only when Germany's gross and repeated violations of American citizens' neutral rights of trade and intercourse with Great Britain seriously interfered with their ability to engage in international commerce which resulted in the large-scale destruction of American lives and property that the United States government invoked the sacred cause of neutrality as one of the primary justifications for its intervention into the war. It was generally believed within the United States that the quality and quantity of violations against its neutral rights by the Allied Powers were of a nature and purpose materially different from, and far less heinous than, those perpetrated by the Central Powers—*i.e.*, destruction of property as opposed to destruction of life and property.

As the intensity of the war heightened and the Allies imposed their stranglehold over commerce shipped by nationals from the neutral United States to the continent of Europe, the Central Powers took the position that the American government was under an obligation to take affirmative measures to rectify the developing imbalance of trade in arms, munitions, and supplies that U.S. nationals were successfully transporting to the Allies but not to them. Yet the United States government was quite emphatic in its rejection of their complaint. If one belligerent was militarily unable to secure the safe passage of neutral commerce to its shores because of the misfortunes of war, that was its problem and not that of the neutral government, which possessed the perfect right under international law to permit its citizens to continue trading with the militarily more powerful belligerent. For a neutral government to discriminate in favor of the weaker belligerent in order to compensate for the military imbalance would constitute an unneutral act that could ultimately precipitate a declaration of war upon it by the stronger belligerent. Moreover, it was argued that even if the neutral government were to embargo all trade in contraband of war by its citizens with both sets of belligerents, this affirmative departure from the normal rules of neutral practice during the course of an ongoing war could compromise its neutrality.[23]

The U.S. government's insistence upon the international legal right of its citizens to trade with the Allies no matter how unequal the military situation appeared would play a significant part in the decision by the Central Powers to pursue their policy of waging "unrestricted submarine warfare" in order to destroy this vital neutral commerce irrespective of the international laws of neutrality and of the laws of war at sea. The United States government would eventually respond by entering the war in order to secure those rights of its nationals and thus uphold the international laws of neutrality and armed conflict. Indeed, that was exactly how the European system of public international law was supposed to operate before the foundation of the League of Nations.

Resort to warfare by one state against another was universally considered to constitute the ultimate sanction for the transgressor's gross and repeated violations of the victim's international legal rights. The United States ultimately fought in the Great War precisely in order to vindicate the international laws of neutrality. America's decision to abandon its neutrality and enter the war on the side of the Allied Powers ineluctably spelled defeat for the Central Powers. This proved to be the definitive and most effective "sanction" for Germany's violation of the international laws of neutrality.

Nevertheless, the incongruous suppositions underlying the international laws of neutrality could not withstand the rigors of twentieth century "total warfare" with its all-encompassing political, military, economic, and propagandistic dimensions. The First World War demonstrated the abject failure of the laws of neutrality to perform their intended purpose of constricting the radius of the war. This tragic experience led many American international lawyers, diplomats, and statesmen to the unavoidable conclusion that in the postwar world the international community had to abandon neutrality as a viable concept of international law and politics and instead create a system of international relations in which some organization would be charged with the task of enforcing international law against recalcitrant nations.[24] Henceforth, the international legal rights of one state must be treated as rights pertaining to all states. National security could no longer be a matter of just individual concern, but rather it must be a collective responsibility shared by the entire international community organized together. This line of reasoning induced many powerful American international lawyers both in and out of government to support the creation of the League to Enforce Peace and later to champion the foundation of the League of Nations.[25]

In their opinion, the United States government must at last definitively repudiate its traditional policies of isolationism in peace and neutrality in war in order to become a formal participant in the new European and worldwide balance of power system. Admittedly, this balance had been wrought by brute military force. Yet its continued existence could nevertheless be legitimized, if not sanctified, by the adoption and effective enforcement of the principles of international law set forth in the Covenant of the League of Nations. In this manner, America's vital national security interests on the one hand, and its professed philosophical and moral ideals on the other, could most successfully be reconciled and indeed would coincide and reinforce each other by means of U.S. membership in the League.

According to the prevailing viewpoint at that time, the creation of the League of Nations was supposed to have sounded the deathknell for the institution of "neutrality" and thus for the international laws of neutrality. This supposed watershed in international legal and political relations was made quite clear by articles 10 and 11(1) of the League Covenant:

> ARTICLE 10. The Members of the League undertake to respect and preserve as against external aggression the territorial integrity and existing political independence of all Members of the League. In case of any such aggression or in case of any threat or danger of such aggression the Council shall advise upon the means by which this obligation shall be fulfilled.

> ARTICLE 11.--1. Any war or threat of war, whether immediately affecting any of the Members of the League or not, is hereby

declared a matter of concern to the whole League, and the League shall take any action that may be deemed wise and effectual to safeguard the peace of nations. In case any such emergency should arise, the Secretary-General shall on the request of any Member of the League forthwith summon a meeting of the Council.[26]

Nevertheless, contemporaneous prognostications concerning the imminent demise of "neutrality" proved to be quite premature. This was because the United States government never joined the League of Nations and never became a party to the Statute of the Permanent Court of International Justice (PCIJ) due to strident opposition to both international organizations consistently mounted by isolationist members of the United States Senate and their supporters. Even the technical separation of the Court from the League by the device of adopting a Protocol of Signature for the PCIJ Statute, which permitted non-League members to ratify the latter without joining the League, was insufficient to induce the Senate into giving its advice and consent to the Protocol on terms acceptable to the latter's contracting parties. Shorn of United States participation, the League of Nations arrived into the world stillborn. So it came as no surprise that in the absence of the United States, the League ultimately proved to be congenitally incapable of preserving world peace against the onslaughts of fascist dictatorships.

During the period between the First and Second World Wars, it was America's innate isolationist tendencies, dating all the way back to President George Washington's Farewell Address of 1796, that reasserted themselves and triumphed over America's relatively more recent internationalist foreign policies promoting multilateral organizational solutions to the problems of maintaining international peace and security. U.S. membership in the World Court and some "league to enforce the peace" would occur only after and as a direct result of the tragic experience of World War II. The shocked reaction of the U.S. government and people to this second worldwide conflagration produced a profound realization of the extreme dangers of a continued American foreign policy premised upon the interrelated principles of isolationism in peace and neutrality in war.

Whether accurate or not, the thesis developed that if the habitually obstructionist United States Senate had ratified the Treaty of Versailles, which contained the League of Nations Covenant, there was a strong possibility that the Second World War might never have occurred. Hence, in order to avoid a suicidal Third World War, the United States must not repeat the same near fatal mistake it had made after the termination of the First World War by retreating into "isolationism in peace and neutrality in war." These perceptions convinced the U.S. government of the compelling need for it to sponsor and join the United Nations Organization in 1945.

Thus under the regime of the United Nations Charter, neither the Organization itself nor any of its members were supposed to remain "neutral" in the face of an unjustified threat or use of force (article 2(4)), nor when confronted by the existence of a threat to the peace, breach of the peace or act of aggression (article 39), nor in the event of an actual armed attack or armed aggression by one state against another state (article 51). According to article 2(5), all U.N. members were to give the Organization every assistance in any action it took in accordance with the Charter, and they must refrain from giving any assistance to any state against which the Organization took preventive or enforcement action. Article 2(6) even empowered the Organization to act against non-members "so far as may be necessary for the maintenance of international peace and security."

Article 24 determined that the Security Council shall have "primary responsibility" for the maintenance of international peace and security, and article 25 required all members of the U.N. "to accept and carry out" the decisions of the Security Council. This injunction included their mandatory adoption of Security Council "enforcement measures" under articles 41, 42, and 43, though the special agreements needed to bring this last article into effect were never concluded. Finally, Charter article 51 also permitted, but did not obligate, U.N. members to come to the assistance of any state that was the victim of an armed attack or armed aggression by another state pursuant to what was therein denominated the international legal right of "collective self-defense."

Clearly, the continued existence of the institution and laws of "neutrality" did not fall within the contemplation of the drafters of the United Nations Charter. Nevertheless, once again, reports of the death of the international laws of neutrality proved to be greatly overexaggerated. At the time of the founding of the United Nations Organization, the most that could have been reasonably expected was that the Security Council would somehow preserve and extend the uneasy wartime alliance among the five great powers into the postwar world upon the basis of its fundamental underlying condition—unanimity. To the degree that the five permanent members of the Security Council (*viz.*, the U.S., U.K., U.S.S.R., France, and China) could maintain, or at least selectively reinstitute, their World War II coalition in order to handle postwar international crises, the U.N. Security Council would provide a mechanism to enforce the peace of the world in a manner basically accepted as legitimate by the remainder of the international community.

The atomic bombings of Hiroshima and Nagasaki, however, occurred shortly after the U.N. Charter had been signed in San Francisco on June 26, 1945 and even before the Organization itself came into existence on October 24, 1945. The ensuing "Cold War" between the United States and the Soviet Union, each supported by its respective allies, led to a breakdown of their World War II coalition and thus to a stalemate at the U.N. Security Council because of the veto power over substantive matters accorded to its five permanent members by Charter article 27(3). Hence, if the Security Council should fail to act in the event of a threat to the peace, breach of the peace or act of aggression, and the state members of the United Nations choose not to exercise their right of collective self-defense to come to the assistance of the victim of an armed attack or armed aggression as permitted by article 51, presumably the customary international laws of neutrality would come into effect to govern the relations between the neutral states on the one hand, and each set of belligerents on the other. Thus, even under the reign of the intrinsically non-neutral United Nations Charter, in default of the Security Council taking measures "necessary to maintain international peace and security," the customary international laws of neutrality still have an important role to play in the preservation of international peace and security by constricting the radius and intensity of an ongoing war.

U.S. "Neutrality" Toward the Iraq-Iran War

In the modern world of international relations, the only legitimate justifications and procedures for the perpetration of violence and coercion by one state against another are those set forth in the United Nations Charter. The Charter alone contains those rules which have been consented to by the virtual unanimity of the international community that has voluntarily joined the United Nations Organization. These include and are limited to the right of individual and collective self-defense in the event of an "armed attack" as defined by article 51, chapter 7 "enforcement action" by the U.N. Security Council, chapter 8 "enforcement action" by the appropriate regional organizations acting with the authorization of the Security Council as required by article 53, and the so-called "peacekeeping operations" organized under the jurisdiction of the Security Council pursuant to chapter 6 or under the auspices of the U.N. General Assembly in accordance with the Uniting for Peace Resolution,[27] or by the relevant regional organizations acting in conformity with their proper constitutional procedures and subject to the overall supervision of the U.N. Security Council as specified in chapter 8 and articles 24 and 25. All other threats or uses of force are deemed to be presumptively illegal and are supposed to be opposed in one fashion or another by the members of the Organization acting individually or collectively or both.

In light of the aforementioned historical background, it will now be possible to critically analyze and evaluate the U.S. policy of so-called "neutrality" toward the Iraq-Iran War from an international law perspective. There were several indications from the public record that the Carter Administration tacitly condoned, if not actively encouraged, the Iraqi invasion of Iran in September of 1980 because of its shortsighted belief that the pressures of belligerency might expedite release of the U.S. diplomatic hostages held by Teheran since November of 1979.[28] Presumably the Iraqi army could render Iranian oil fields inoperable and, unlike American marines, do so without provoking the Soviet Union to exercise its alleged right of counter-intervention under articles 5 and 6 of the 1921 Russo-Persian Treaty of Friendship.[29] These articles were unilaterally abrogated by Iran on November 5, 1979,[30] the day after the American diplomats were seized in Teheran.

The report by columnist Jack Anderson that the Carter Administration was seriously considering an invasion of Iran to seize its oil fields in the Fall of 1980 as a last minute fillip to bolster his prospects for reelection was credible.[31] It coincided with a substantial increase of U.S. military forces stationed in the Indian Ocean and Arabian Gulf. In the aftermath of the

Anderson exposé, the Soviet government raised the specter of their counter-intervention in order to ward off any contemplated American invasion of Iran.

In any event, American efforts to punish, isolate, and weaken the Khomeini regime because of the hostages crisis simply prepared the way for Iraq to invade Iran in September l980.[32] The American policy of "neutrality" toward the Iraq-Iran war, first adopted by the Carter Administration and supposedly continued by its successor, misrepresented fact if not the law. A substantial body of diplomatic opinion believed that the American government consistently "tilted" in favor of Iraq throughout the war despite its public proclamation of "neutrality."[33]

For example, from the very outset of the conflict, U.S. Airborne Warning and Control Aircraft (AWACS) that had been stationed in Saudi Arabia for the alleged purpose of legitimate self-defense of that country proceeded to supply Iraq with intelligence information they had collected on Iranian military movements.[34] Clearly, this activity constituted a non-neutral, hostile act directed against Iran which, under pre-U.N. Charter international law, would have been tantamount to an "act of war" in accordance with the traditional and formal definition of that term. Under the regime of the United Nations Charter, such provision of outright military assistance by the U.S. government to Iraq against Iran rendered America an accomplice to the former's egregiously lawless aggression upon the latter.

This illegal U.S. policy toward Iran progressively worsened after the simultaneous termination of the hostages crisis and the installation of the Reagan Administration in January of 1981. At the outset of the Reagan Administration, Secretary of State Alexander Haig and his mentor, Henry Kissinger, devoted a good deal of time to publicly lamenting the dire need for a "geopolitical" approach to American foreign policy decision-making, one premised on a "grand theory" or "strategic design" of international relations. Their conceptual framework toward international relations consisted essentially of nothing more sophisticated than a somewhat refined and superficially rationalized theory of Machiavellian power politics. Consequently, Haig quite myopically viewed the myriad of problems in the Persian Gulf, Middle East, and Southwest Asia primarily within the context of a supposed struggle for control over the entire world between the United States and the Soviet Union. Haig erroneously concluded that this global confrontation required the United States to forge a strategic consensus with Israel, Egypt, Jordan, Saudi Arabia, the Gulf Sheikhdoms and Pakistan in order to resist anticipated Soviet aggression in the region.

Haig's vision of founding a U.S. centered strategic consensus in Southwest Asia was simply a reincarnated version of Kissinger's "Nixon Doctrine" whereby regional surrogates were intended to assist the United States in its efforts to "police" its spheres of influence throughout the world by virtue of massive American military assistance. According to the Reagan Administration's scenario, Israel would become America's new policeman for stability in the Middle East, filling the position recently vacated by the deposed Shah of Iran whom the Nixon/Kissinger Administration had deputized to serve as America's policeman for the region. Hence, according to Haig's strategic consensus rationale, the United States had to more fully support the Israeli government of former Prime Minister Menachem Begin, even during the pursuit of its blatantly illegal policies in Lebanon and in the territories occupied as a result of the 1967 and 1973 wars, primarily because of Israel's overwhelming military superiority (courtesy of the United States) over any Arab state or combination thereof except Egypt, which had been effectively neutralized by its 1979 peace treaty with Israel.

Whereas the Shah fell over internal domestic conditions that were only exacerbated by the large-scale U.S. military presence in Iran, Haig's scheme was tragically flawed from the very moment of its conception. Haig totally disregarded the fundamental realities of Middle Eastern international politics where traditionally all regional actors have been far more exclusively concerned about relationships with their surrounding neighbors than about some evanescent threat of Soviet aggression. The more immediate danger to stability in the Middle East and Persian Gulf was not the distant prospect of Soviet intervention but rather a continuation of the ongoing Iraq-Iran War and the interminable Arab-Israeli dispute. Nevertheless, the Begin government shrewdly manipulated Haig's Machiavellian delusions in order to generate American support for Israel's plan to invade Lebanon in the summer of 1982 for the express purpose of destroying the PLO and, as a result of the process, further consolidating its military occupation of the West Bank. The Israeli invasion of Lebanon was intended to serve as a prelude to the gradual de facto annexation of the West Bank in explicit violation of the most basic principles of international law.

With particular respect to the Persian Gulf, the Reagan Administration's persistent characterization of the Iranian hostage-taking as an act of international terrorism impeded the formulation of a rational U.S. foreign policy toward Iran that could protect America's legitimate national security interests in a manner fully consistent with the requirements of international law. The Reagan Administration readily succumbed to the seductive temptation of exploiting the American public's paranoid fear over the spread of Islamic fundamentalism from Khomeini's Iran throughout the Persian Gulf oil fields in order to justify covert assistance and overt alignment by the United States and its European allies and Middle Eastern friends with the Iraqi aggressor. Apparently, this perception blindly led the Reagan Administration to foment a comprehensive campaign to destabilize the Khomeini government by means of C.I.A. sponsorship for paramilitary raids launched from Egypt, Turkey, and Iraq into Iran by various Iranian opposition groups and for an internal military countercoup, among other nefarious projects.[35]

These developments represented a serious retrograde step for both American national security interests in the Persian Gulf and the overall integrity of the international legal order. Undaunted, the Reagan Administration could not content itself with the mere sponsorship of such covert measures that were specifically designed to topple the Islamic government in Teheran. More ominously, it proceeded to forge an overt diplomatic and military alignment with Iraq against Iran throughout the subsequent course of the Iraq-Iran War.

Presumably, this was because the Reagan Administration intended Iraq to play a key role in the implementation of its strategic consensus approach toward the region by preventing revolutionary Iran from subverting its conservative, wealthy, pro-Western and strategically important neighbors. Hence the Reagan Administration accelerated the policy of its predecessor to encourage the reestablishment of normal diplomatic relations between the United States and Iraq, which had been severed by the latter in reaction to the 1967 Arab-Israel war. Somewhat paradoxically, seventeen years later the pressures of another Middle Eastern war would propel Iraq into re-instituting normal diplomatic relations with the United States in November of 1984.[36] In point of fact, Iraq's governing Baathist Party had originally come to power in a 1963 coup with the assistance of the C.I.A.

As part of this progressive development in their anti-Iranian rapprochement, in March of 1982 the Reagan Administration removed Iraq from the official list of states that allegedly provided support to so-called acts of international terrorism despite the fact that there was little evidence that Iraq had fundamentally altered whatever its policies were in this regard.[37] Such de-listing rendered Iraq eligible to purchase "dual-use" equipment and technology in the United States that could readily be employed for either civilian or military purposes and would most probably be used for the latter.[38] This administrative act prepared the way for the Reagan Administration to issue a license permitting the export of six Lockheed L-100 civilian transport aircraft to Iraq.[39] Although the sale of the aircraft was licensed to Iraqi Airways, the L-100 is the civilian version of the Lockheed C-130 Hercules military transport and troop carrier.[40] In a similar vein, four months later the Commerce Department licensed the sale of six small jets to Iraq, four of which admittedly possessed military applications.[41]

Nevertheless, despite the Reagan Administration's best efforts, the provision of political, military, and economic assistance by the United States, its NATO allies and Middle Eastern friends to Iraq proved insufficient to stem the tide of Iranian military advances. Hence, near the start of 1984, it was publicly announced that the United States government had informed various friendly nations in the Persian Gulf that Iran's defeat of Iraq would be "contrary to U.S. interests" and that steps would be taken to prevent this result.[42] Accordingly, in April of 1984 it was revealed that President Reagan had signed two National Security Decision Directives to set the stage for the United States government to take a more confrontational stance against Iran.[43] One of the options under consideration was the further U.S. provision of so-called dual-use equipment such as helicopters to Iraq.[44] In addition, the Reagan Administration let it be known that it would look "more favorably" upon the sale of weapons to Iraq by friends and allies of the United States government.[45] The very next month, it was publicly revealed that the Reagan Administration was prepared to intervene militarily in the Iraq-Iran War in order to prevent an Iranian victory that would install what was anticipated to be a radical Shi'ite government in Baghdad.[46]

Pursuant to this set of decisions, in February of 1985, Textron's Bell helicopter division agreed to sell 45 large helicopters to Iraq, and Iraqi defense officials were involved in negotiating this transaction.[47] Six months later it was reported that these 45 American-made helicopters being sold to Iraq were initially developed as Iranian troop carriers. One official of the United States government monitoring the transaction said the helicopter model involved was "clearly a dual-use item" with "a potential for military use."[48]

Given these facts, it can be concluded that since the Reagan Administration's ascent to power in 1981, the United States government abandoned all pretense of American neutrality toward the Iraq-Iran War in order to come down decisively on the side of Iraqi aggression against Iran. Under the traditional customary international laws of neutrality, these activities clearly constituted hostile acts that Iran would have been entitled to oppose with a formal declaration of war against the United States. Of course prudence dictated that Iran avoided being provoked by the United States and Iraq into making a formal declaration of war against the United States.

Acute danger arose from Iraq's calculated policy of escalating the severity of its attacks against Iranian oil installations and supplies for the express purpose of precipitating direct U.S. military intervention to keep the Straits of Hormuz free from retaliatory interference by Iran. Baghdad hoped that such outright U.S. military involvement in the Iraq-Iran War would ultimately rescue Iraq from capitulation or defeat at the hands of Iran. The boarding of a U.S. merchant ship by Iranian sailors near the Straits of Hormuz proved how difficult it was for Iran and the United States to avoid some form of outright military conflict in the region.[49]

Restoring International Peace and Security to the Persian Gulf

Even if the United States had been factually as well as legally neutral in the Iraq-Iran War, such a position would itself be shocking and indefensible under the most rudimentary principles of international law. When in the post-U.N. Charter world has the United States been "neutral" in the face of outright aggression? As the United States government should have learned from the tragic history of American neutrality toward widespread acts of aggression committed by fascist dictatorships during the 1930s, peace is indeed indivisible. In a thermonuclear age, aggression per se is the most dangerous threat to world peace. The United States could not possibly have been consistent, believable, or effective in condemning the Soviet invasion of Afghanistan without likewise condemning the Iraqi invasion of Iran. America's rank hypocrisy in this matter fooled no one but itself.

The United States, its NATO allies, and Japan possessed vital national security interests in preventing the disintegration of Iran due to factional strife, regionally based autonomous breakaway movements, or external aggression or subversion originating from Iraq or the Soviet Union. Continued destabilization of Iran only generated further opportunities for Soviet penetration and exploitation. The United States should not have permitted the development of a permanent threat to Saudi Arabia and to the free flow of Gulf oil through the Straits of Hormuz by encouraging conditions that might have led to the installation of an Iranian regime acting at the behest of the

Soviet Union. Nevertheless, it is crucial to reiterate that the Iranian people possess the exclusive right to determine their own form of government without overt or covert U.S. intervention, even if this means the continuation of an Islamic fundamentalist regime in Teheran.

In order to forestall any potential for a Soviet invasion of Iran under the pretext of the 1921 Russo-Persian Treaty, the most prudent course for the Reagan Administration to have taken would have been to work toward the establishment of a strong, stable, and secure government in Teheran that was able to undertake the military measures necessary to offset Russian divisions massed on Iran's borders with the Soviet Union and Afghanistan. With the hostages crisis far behind it, the Reagan Administration should have moved to restore normal diplomatic relations with Iran as soon as possible and without any prior conditions. Most importantly, the Reagan Administration should have completely reversed and publicly repudiated the Carter Administration's policy of alleged "neutrality" toward the Iraq-Iran War.

The American government should have officially labeled Iraq as the aggressor in the Iraq-Iran War and publicly called for an immediate ceasefire. The Reagan Administration should have attempted to convince its NATO allies, Egypt, Jordan, and the Sudan, to terminate their provision of military weapons, equipment, supplies, and soldiers to Iraq. Operating in conjunction with its allies and Iran, the United States could have worked at the United Nations Security Council for the formal adoption of this program and its implementation by the deployment of a U.N. peacekeeping force along the Iraq-Iran border designated to replace withdrawing Iraqi and Iranian troops on a transitional basis.

The dispute between Iraq and Iran over the Shatt al-Arab estuary could have been submitted to the procedures for compulsory arbitration set forth in article 6 of the 1975 Iran-Iraq Treaty on International Borders and Good Neighborly Relations.[50] Although insufficient to justify a counter-invasion of Iraq, Iranian demands for the payment of reparations and for the deposition of President Saddam Hussein because of Iraq's war of aggression were quite reasonable and fully supportable under fundamental principles of international law. The United States government should have recognized these Iranian concerns as valid and should have accommodated them to some extent within the framework that was ultimately adopted for the peaceful settlement of this dispute by the U.N. Security Council.

Of course the improvement and normalization of American diplomatic relations with Iraq was a desirable objective as well. But it should not have been purchased by derogation from the fundamental principle of international law requiring the condemnation of aggression and by writing off Iran to its own fate or to the account of the Soviet Union. Indeed, if the Reagan Administration truly believed that the major U.S. strategic objective in the Persian Gulf was to counteract a threatened Soviet thrust through Iran toward Saudi Arabia, the best American defense could have been mounted, not from the borders of Iraq, but from the eastern and northern frontiers of Iran, at the request of the Iranian government and with the assistance of the Iranian army. Within this context a creditable American Rapid Deployment Force

(RDF) could have played an effective role consistent with the requirements of international law. Such action would have been in furtherance of the right of collective self-defense recognized by article 51 of the U.N. Charter.

As for the Iranian threat to close the Straits of Hormuz, in the event Iraq had launched attacks against Iranian oil installations, world public opinion should have held the U.S. government's illegal pro-Iraqi policies fully accountable for whatever political, military, and economic catastrophes might have resulted therefrom. As long as the conflict continued, the Iranian government had the perfect right under international law to board and search merchant ships transiting the Straits of Hormuz for the purpose of confiscating any contraband of war en route to Iraq. In the future, to the extent Persian Gulf oil can be transported via pipelines terminating on the Red Sea, the strategic importance of controlling the Straits of Hormuz will diminish.

The criticism that such a dramatic reversal of American policy in the Gulf would alienate friendly regimes in Egypt, Saudi Arabia, Kuwait, and Jordan, inter alia, overlooked the fact that American "neutrality" in this war simply encouraged these Arab countries temporarily to put aside their deep-seated animosities for the purpose of aligning themselves with an aggressive Iraq against non-Arab Iran. Furthermore, the direct contribution of massive war loans to Iraq by Saudi Arabia, Kuwait, and the Gulf Sheikhdoms fatally compromised their alleged neutrality toward the Iraq-Iran War as well.[51] Under the pre-U.N. Charter customary international law of neutrality, Iran would have been entitled to treat the provision of such military and economic assistance by these countries to Iraq as an act of hostility directed against it, thus warranting a declaration of war. Iran wisely refrained from so acting. Nevertheless, the United States government did not discourage, and indeed in many instances encouraged and assisted, such non-neutral practices by numerous Middle Eastern countries against Iran. The failure to reverse this misguided American policy served to further destabilize international peace and security in the Persian Gulf and Middle East.

Restoring peace to the Persian Gulf demanded vigorous American leadership acting in strict accordance with the rules of international law and in full cooperation with the relevant international institutions. Unfortunately, despite its continued protestations of "neutrality" toward the Iraq-Iran War, the Reagan Administration still tilted quite strenuously in favor of Iraq against Iran. Continued and demonstrable U.S. partiality for Iraq only prolonged this tragic conflict by discouraging Iran from working with the U.N. Security Council to end the war precisely because one of the latter's permanent and most important members was viscerally and implacably prejudiced against it. For this very reason, those inexcusably few U.N. Security Council resolutions that were adopted on the Iraq-Iran War were all clearly and admittedly biased in favor of Iraq.[52]

From a long-term perspective on Persian Gulf security, the Reagan Administration should have abandoned Haig's Machiavellian objective of creating a formal anti-Soviet strategic consensus in the region under American leadership and substituted for it a policy that promoted the foundation of an effective regional collective self-defense and policing arrangement. Therefore, the Reagan Administration should have encouraged the efforts of six regional states (*i.e.*, Saudi Arabia, Kuwait, Bahrain, United Arab Emirates, Oman, Qatar) to form a viable Gulf Cooperation Council. Such an organization could someday have metamorphosized into an effective Gulf Security Organization, affiliated with the United Nations Organization under chapter 8 of the Charter, and possess a standing peacekeeping force or the ability to field one on short notice. Though at the time, the Council aimed to keep both superpowers out of the region, a Gulf Security Organization could only advance the interests of the U.S., its NATO allies, and Japan by the establishment of some degree of peace, order, and stability in this volatile area.

Geography gave the Soviet Union advantages the West could not have matched without supporting the creation of such an effective regional collective self-defense and policing system. A Gulf Security Organization would be far more successful at the pacific settlement of local disputes, opposing intra-regional aggression, and the suppression of externally fomented disturbances than the American Rapid Deployment Force (now renamed the U.S. Central Command) ever could.[53] The United States must not become a member of or play any formal role within such a Gulf Security Organization so as not to undermine the organization's claims to regional legitimacy and to formal non-alignment. But America should make clear its intention to provide military assistance to such an organization in the event of an armed attack upon one of its members by an extra-regional power. Such assistance would be in furtherance of the right of collective self-defense recognized by article 51 of the United Nations Charter.

In regard to U.S. measures designed to promote individual self-defense by the states of this region, the purveyance of sophisticated American weapons systems and technology to Israel, Saudi Arabia, Jordan and Pakistan was and remains a most disturbing factor. As events in Iran demonstrated, arms sales can easily become counterproductive. Any U.S. arms transfer policy must be required by the legitimate defensive needs of these countries as defined by international law and interpreted in good faith by the American government. Unilateral policy determinations by these foreign governments do not provide adequate criteria. Thus the Reagan Administration should not have provided weapons to Saudi Arabia simply to curry favor and thus secure a stable flow of expensive oil to the West; to China in the expectation of utilizing that country as a geopolitical "card" to be played in some Machiavellian balancing game of power politics with the Soviet Union over Afghanistan; or to Jordan for the purpose of creating a surrogate force for illegal military intervention throughout the Persian Gulf.

Nor must such weapons be given to any state in this or other regions of the world that manifests a tendency to employ them in a manner either the U.S. government or the U.N. Security Council deems violative of international law. Hence, the Israeli air strikes with American-made planes against the Iraqi nuclear reactor and the PLO headquarters in Beirut combined with Israel's threat to bomb Syrian anti-aircraft missiles in Lebanon during the summer of 1981, followed by its patently illegal invasion of that country one year later, should have been grounds for additional concern and reevaluation by the

Reagan Administration. The same could have been said for Pakistan's three wars with India and its frantic pursuit of a nuclear weapons capability.

All of these states bore heavy burdens of proof in regard to pending American arms transfers that were not discharged in a manner satisfactory to the requirements of both international law and U.S. domestic law.[54] Unfortunately, the Reagan Administration apparently chose to rely upon the wholesale provision of American military equipment to various governments in this region and around the globe, which served as an ineffectual and ultimately self-defeating substitute for the hard task of formulating a set of coherent principles for the conduct of American foreign policy on some basis other than Haig's Machiavellian predilections. Most regrettably, his successor, George Shultz, proceeded to heedlessly and quite enthusiastically embrace Haig's "strategic consensus" approach to this region of the world.

Finally, as current events in the Middle East continue to demonstrate, the success of any American foreign policy in the Persian Gulf cannot be divorced from the compelling need to achieve an overall peace settlement between Israel and its Arab neighbors. Active American support for progress toward implementing the international legal right of the Palestinian people to self-determination in accordance with the rules of international law and in full cooperation with the relevant international institutions is an absolute prerequisite to the security of the Persian Gulf oil lifeline. Otherwise the primary political objective of Gulf states will continue to be to organize their efforts and substantial resources in opposition to both Israel and the United States. The Reagan Administration's decision to assign troops from the 82nd and 101st Airborne Divisions, already designated as parts of the Rapid Deployment Force, to serve as component units within the multinational peacekeeping force policing the easternmost section of the Sinai desert in the aftermath of Israel's withdrawal on April 25, 1982, was egregiously shortsighted. The monumental peace between Egypt and Israel should not have been linked in any way to the prospect of illegal American military intervention in the Persian Gulf.

Conclusion

If a Third World War should occur, it will probably result from a direct confrontation over the Middle East/Persian Gulf region. Southwest Asia could readily become the Balkans of the 1980s. For example, the promulgation of the so-called Carter Doctrine—in which this American president committed the U.S. government to use military force to prevent "any outside force to gain control of the Persian Gulf region"—constituted a dangerous bluff whose potential for nuclear confrontation and escalation was immeasurable. A Pentagon report had already concluded that even with a creditable RDF the United States could not by itself successfully defend Iranian oil fields from a Soviet conventional invasion unless, perhaps, America resorted to the first-use of tactical nuclear weapons.[55] But their deployment in a conventional conflict with the Soviet Union would probably have degenerated into strategic nuclear warfare between the two superpowers and their allies.

Likewise, as publicly admitted, the RDF could not have succeeded at its two other appointed tasks of seizing and operating Persian Gulf oil fields against the wishes of the local governments in the event of another cutoff along the lines of 1973 or of protecting petroleum facilities from destruction by opposition movements indigenous to the region or by externally supported saboteurs.[56] Such disruptions are beyond the substantial capacity of the RDF to counteract. Consequently, since the Carter Doctrine could neither deter a Soviet invasion nor stem the tide of revolutionary change in the Gulf, the Reagan Administration should have abandoned it.

Nevertheless, somewhat paradoxically, the Reagan Administration eagerly embraced this ill-conceived, rhetorical flourish by a former opponent, hastily uttered during the heat of an unsuccessful election campaign, as the cornerstone of its foreign policy toward the Persian Gulf. Worse yet, the Reagan Corollary improvidently extended the Carter Doctrine to ordain U.S. opposition to internally-based interference with the free flow of Saudi Arabian oil. The U.S. government should not have been tempted to enter into de facto alliances with feudal or reactionary regimes in order to guarantee their continued survival against internal adversaries in return for stable supplies of expensive oil, especially at the calculated risk of precipitating a theoretically "limited" tactical nuclear war with the former Soviet Union. As demonstrated by the Iranian revolution, even a perceptibly radical successor regime will recognize the need to sell oil to Western Europe, Japan, and the United States for the hard currency necessary to finance imports essential to fulfilling the basic human needs of its citizenry (*e.g.*, U.S. food supplies), let alone to pay for an economic development program.

Because of the Rapid Deployment Force's demonstrative susceptibility to abuse and to its impermissible use under international law, the American Congress should amend the War Powers Act of 1973 to provide that the President of the United States cannot order the introduction of RDF troops into hostilities or into situations where imminent involvement in hostilities is clearly indicated by the circumstances without prior authorization by a joint resolution of Congress.[57] A narrowly drawn exception to this amendment could permit the President to use RDF troops solely for the purpose of rescuing a substantial number of American citizens from situations where they face imminent danger of death without the need for prior Congressional authorization, though subject to the other requirements of the Act. Without such an amendment, any American President will be constantly tempted to order the RDF into combat for all sorts of reasons and under a variety of pretexts simply because a seemingly effective U.S. interventionary force might be in existence and would be subject to his unfettered discretion. Otherwise, direct U.S. military intervention in the Persian Gulf/Middle East could readily serve as the harbinger for nuclear Armageddon.

Postscript

At the 1986 Neutrality Symposium, this author stated: "As events in Iran have demonstrated, arms sales can easily become counterproductive. Any U.S. arms transfer policy must be required by the legitimate defensive needs of these countries as defined by international law and interpreted in good faith by the American government." These words were not written in reference to or with knowledge of the Iran-Contra scandal, but they nevertheless seem to have constituted the major lesson to be learned from it. This author saw nothing wrong with the Reagan Administration attempting to negotiate and compromise for the release of American hostages being held in Lebanon by an Islamic fundamentalist group acting in sympathy with Iran over U.S. support for Iraqi aggression throughout the Iraq-Iran War. But arms transfers should not have been the currency employed by the Reagan Administration to purchase liberty for the hostages.

These hostages were seized by an Islamic fundamentalist group in order to obtain the release of their comrades imprisoned in Kuwait—some of whom were subject to execution—for bombing attacks they had perpetrated against Kuwaiti, French, and American political targets in that country out of opposition to the latters' joint support for Iraq against Iran. A negotiated exchange of American hostages in Lebanon for the release of Lebanese prisoners in Kuwait would have been a proper policy for the Reagan Administration to have pursued with the Iranian government, inter alia.

The Reagan Administration's provision of sophisticated weapons to some of the most radical elements in Iran was never part of a self-styled "strategic opening" to that country, but simply constituted a straight out arms-for-hostages swap that could not be justified under basic norms of international law and U.S. domestic law. These weapons were not required by Iran for the legitimate defense of that country, which was then no longer in jeopardy. Rather, Iran used the arms to continue the prosecution of its war against Iraq deep into the territory of that country despite repeated calls by the international community for a peaceful settlement. According to articles 2(3) and 33 of the United Nations Charter, Iran was under an obligation to pursue a peaceful termination of its war with Iraq despite the undeniable fact that Iran was the original victim of Iraqi aggression. The sale of sophisticated weapons by the United States government to Iran at this penultimate stage in the Iraq-Iran War only exacerbated and compounded the already daunting political complexities of the situation.

In any event, the exposé of the U.S. arms transfers to Iran revealed to the entire international community that the basis of the Reagan Administration's alleged "neutrality" policy toward the Iraq-Iran war had been thoroughly unprincipled, duplicitous and hypocritical from the outset. The same can be said for the Reagan Administration's congenitally defective "war against international terrorism" that had been intended to be the keystone of its bankrupt foreign policy toward the Middle East since 1981. Such unscrupulous policies violated the basic principles of international law set forth above, as well as several well-established prohibitions of United States constitutional, civil, and criminal law that would be too numerous to list here but were invoked by the Independent Counsel/Special Prosecutor Lawrence Walsh when he indicted the principals in the Iran-Contra scandal.

In the aftermath of the Iran-Contra revelations starting in October of 1986, the Reagan Administration sought to undo this self-inflicted damage to its credibility with the American people and with Arab states in the Middle East by adopting an even more intransigent and overtly hostile stance against Iran. The Reagan Administration abandoned even the pretense of neutrality toward the war and actively and directly intervened by means of U.S. military forces on the side of Iraq against Iran. This decision produced the so-called "reflagging" of Kuwaiti oil tankers under the American flag in order to provide a thin veneer of legal respectability to purportedly justify to the American people and Congress the introduction of U.S. military forces directly into the war in overall support of Iraq's strategic objectives.

But after the destruction of the *Stark* by an Iraqi (not Iranian) jet fighter, both the American people and Congress should have made it quite clear to the Reagan Administration that they would not tolerate U.S. sailors and airmen being put "in-harm's-way" to support the bloodthirsty dictatorship of Saddam Hussein for any reason. Nevertheless, after expressing some lukewarm reservations, Congress caved in by refusing to insist that the Reagan Administration obey the terms of the War Powers Act when introducing U.S. naval and air forces to escort the "reflagged" Kuwaiti tankers into the Iraq-Iran War. How many more U.S. servicemen might have died in the Iraq-Iran War? How likely was it that the U.S. government would have refrained from further escalating its direct involvement into the war in the event of more American casualties or Iranian victories (*e.g.,* at Basra)? This was precisely the type of outcome the War Powers Act was designed to prevent—at least without formal Congressional authorization for direct U.S. military intervention into a situation of armed combat.

Despite this, several otherwise sensible political leaders and public pundits disingenuously argued that since the Reagan Administration apparently successfully got away with refusing to obey the War Powers Act in the Persian Gulf, the Act itself demonstrated its impracticability and therefore should either be repealed or eviscerated. To the contrary, the Reagan Administration's creeping military intervention into the Iraq-Iran War on the side of Iraq during seven years demonstrated precisely the need for the more (not less) restrictive amendment to the Act that this author called for in 1986:

> Because of the Rapid Deployment Force's demonstrative suscepti-
> bility to abuse and to its impermissible use under international
> law, the American Congress should amend the War Powers Act
> of 1973 to provide that the President of the United States cannot
> order the introduction of RDF troops into hostilities or into situations
> where imminent involvement in hostilities is clearly indicated by
> the circumstances without prior authorization by a joint resolution
> of Congress.

The RDF was renamed the U.S. Central Command, and it was under this rubric that direct U.S. military intervention in the Iraq-Iran War took place.

No international legal significance was given to the Reagan Administration's so-called reflagging of Kuwaiti oil tankers. First, the reflagged Kuwaiti oil tankers lacked the "genuine link" between the United States and the tankers that is required by article 5 of the 1958 Geneva Convention on the High Seas in order to establish U.S. nationality for the tankers.[58] Furthermore, pursuant to the ruling of the International Court of Justice in the *Nottebohm Case*[59], concerning the meaning of a "genuine link" as it related to the contrived alteration of nationality by a person in contemplation of war, Iran would have the perfect right to disregard this obviously sham transaction and continue to treat the tankers as possessing Kuwaiti nationality. Moreover, even if the change of nationality for the tankers were considered to be effective under international law and "opposable" by the United States against Iran, for the Reagan Administration to have undertaken this admittedly partial type of activity in favor of one belligerent during the course of an ongoing war fatally compromised its alleged neutrality and constituted a hostile act directed against Iran.

Finally, as discussed above, Iran had a perfect right under international law to exercise its belligerent rights by stopping, searching for contraband, and if necessary confiscating or, in certain circumstances, destroying merchant ships that proceeded through the Straits of Hormuz into and out of the Persian Gulf on their way to and from Kuwait and the other Gulf states that were acting as de facto allies of Iraq throughout the war. Despite the Reagan Administration's disingenuous protestations to the contrary, Kuwait, inter alia, had never been neutral in the war against Iran. Rather, Kuwait consistently sided with Iraq throughout the course of the war, though perhaps against its better judgment. Kuwait's acts of co-belligerence included the provision of billions of dollars of loans to Iraq; the trans-shipment of munitions, equipment, and supplies through Kuwait to and from Iraq; the allocation of a fixed percentage of Kuwaiti oil exports to the account of Iraq in order to finance the war; the provision of reconnaissance information and intelligence to Iraq; some degree of military cooperation with and logistical support for Iraq, etc.

Recall that it was Kuwait—Iraq's de facto ally—that had originally requested Soviet and American protection for its non-neutral merchant shipping. Perhaps somewhat foolishly, the Reagan Administration readily acquiesced to an Iraqi-Kuwaiti plan specifically designed to acquire direct U.S. military intervention on the side of Iraq against Iran under the flimsy pretext of protecting the passage of allegedly neutral ships through international straits and on the high seas. However, this author is of the opinion that the Reagan Administration most probably orchestrated the Kuwaiti/Iraqi request to both superpowers in the full knowledge and expectation that the White House could then successfully manipulate the evanescent threat of a picayune Soviet naval presence in the Gulf for the purpose of convincing a reluctant American people and Congress to acquiesce in an already planned direct intervention by U.S. military forces into the war. This would be needed, it felt, in order to prevent a feared Iraqi defeat following Iran's anticipated renewal of its annual offensive near Basra in the winter of 1988.

For all of the above reasons, therefore, the Kuwaiti tankers had never been "neutral shipping" that would be entitled to the benefits of such a designation under the international laws of neutrality. And this held true irrespective of their so-called reflagging by the United States government. The United States Navy was escorting non-neutral shipping in violation of U.S. obligations as a neutral under international law, in direct contradiction to Iran's belligerent rights under the laws of war, and at the risk of precipitating an Iranian declaration of war or at least acts of hostility directed against the United States in the Gulf or elsewhere for such belligerent behavior.

In other words, the Reagan Administration proceeded to provide military assistance to Kuwait which was an ally of Iraq against Iran, and thus rendered the United States a de facto ally of Iraq against Iran in the Iraq-Iran War. In no sense of the traditional meaning of that term, therefore, can it even be arguably said that the United States government was any longer "neutral" in the Iraq-Iran war. Hence, the claim by the Reagan Administration that U.S. naval forces were directly introduced into the Iraq-Iran War for the twin purposes of (1) permitting "neutral" shipping to transit the Straits of Hormuz and the Persian Gulf and (2) ensuring the free flow of Gulf oil through the Straits became legal, factual and political nonsense.

The State Department publicly admitted that it was Iraq which started the so-called tanker war in 1984. It has also been generally agreed that the vast majority of destruction that has been inflicted against any type of shipping in the Gulf has been perpetrated by Iraq, not by Iran. According to the supposed logic of the Reagan Administration's legal rationale (whose very premises this author completely rejects), if the purpose of direct U.S. military intervention was either in fact or in law designed to prevent the destruction of genuinely neutral shipping in the Gulf, then protective U.S. military activities should have been directed primarily against Iraq, not Iran. To be sure, this author did not advocate that course of conduct either.

Well before direct U.S. military intervention into the Iraq-Iran War, the Pentagon had publicly stated that Iran was essentially respecting the international laws relating to the exercise of its belligerent rights when it came to the search and seizure of merchant ships and contraband in the Persian Gulf and Straits of Hormuz. With respect to the Iranian destruction of merchant tankers destined to or from Iraq/Kuwait, Iran engaged in this activity primarily in reprisal for Iraqi attacks against merchant shipping destined to and from Iran. Under the customary international law doctrine known as reprisal, in time of war what otherwise would be a violation of international law can nevertheless be excused if it is undertaken for the express purpose of bringing an original violator of the laws of war (i.e., Iraq) into compliance therewith; provided that the reprisal is essentially proportionate to the original violation and that people and property who are afforded special protections by international law are respected. Under the circumstances of the Iraq-Iran War, that latter restriction would not have applied to protect such non-neutral merchant ships in the Gulf, especially when they voluntarily decided to enter proclaimed exclusion zones by either side, oftentimes carrying contraband of war anyway, and were fully aware of the Iranian reprisal policy.

Moreover, Iran had publicly taken the position that the primary reason it attacked merchant tankers destined to or from Iraq/Kuwait was in reaction to and for the express purpose of discouraging Iraqi attacks on merchant shipping sailing to or from Iran. It was in the national interest of Iran to maintain the free flow of oil through the Straits of Hormuz in order to continue financing its war effort. By contrast, with the closure of Iraqi ports on the Shatt al-Arab estuary and the diversion of its oil exports by pipelines running through Syria and Turkey to the Mediterranean and through Saudi Arabia to the Red Sea, it was in Iraq's interest to close the Straits of Hormuz and the Persian Gulf to oil tanker shipping destined from Iran.

In light of this fact, Iraq did far more damage to the free flow of oil from the Gulf than did Iran. Once again, if the Reagan Administration had really intended to intervene in order to maintain the flow of oil from the Gulf through the Straits, it should have intervened against Iraq, not Iran. Just like the neutrality argument, therefore, this oil rationale was totally spurious to begin with and quite cynically manipulated by the Reagan Administration as another pretext in order to justify to the American people and Congress an overt and direct U.S. military intervention in favor of Iraq against Iran. As a direct result of the Iraqi attack upon Iran in 1980 as well as the institution of the tanker war by Iraq in 1984, only a miniscule percentage of annual world oil supplies actually transited the Straits of Hormuz by tanker, and a good deal of that was Iranian oil anyway.

Ironically, but not surprisingly, it was Iran, not Iraq, that demonstrated the greater degree of respect for the rules of international law concerning neutrality and belligerency in the Gulf and the Straits. Furthermore, it was the United States that engaged in hostile and provocative military maneuvers and actions against Iran—not vice versa—and was illegally preventing Iran from exercising its belligerent rights under well-recognized principles of international law. Thus, when United States naval forces attacked Iranian ships and Iranian oil drilling platforms in the Gulf, this was not a legitimate act of self-defense as recognized by article 51 of the United Nations Charter.

Indeed, these actions were specifically designated to be measures of "retaliation" by President Reagan. Yet until the advent of the Reagan Administration, it had never been the case that the United States government took the position that retaliation is a legitimate act of self-defense under article 51 of the United Nations Charter. To the contrary, even during the darkest days of the Vietnam War, the United States government had always argued that retaliation was not self-defense and therefore was prohibited by the terms of article 51.

The Reagan Administration's interpretation of the right of self-defense to include retaliation in the Gulf (as well as in Lebanon, Libya, and its so-called war against international terrorism) represented a truly perverse innovation in the universally accepted corpus of both customary and conventional international law on self-defense going all the way back to the famous 1837 case of the good ship *Caroline*. There, U.S. Secretary of State Daniel Webster took the official position on behalf of the United States government that alleged measures of self-defense can only be justified when the "necessity of that self-defence is instant, overwhelming, and leaving no choice of means, and no moment for deliberation." The *Caroline* test for the validity of any act of alleged self-defense was later adopted and approved by the International Military Tribunal convened at Nuremberg in 1945 for the purpose of trying the major Nazi war criminals.

More recently came the World Court's seminal *Corfu Channel Case*[60] that, interestingly enough, involved a state's use of force to remove mines from an international strait by entering another state's territorial waters. In that case a squadron of British warships traversing the North Corfu Strait struck some mines with the loss of lives and ships. Three weeks later, British minesweepers swept the North Corfu Channel under the protection of a British armada and entered Albanian territorial waters for the purpose of removing and later examining moored mines. All fifteen members of the International Court of Justice, together with a judge ad hoc appointed by Albania, were unanimous in holding, 16 to 0, that by reason of the acts of the British Navy in Albanian territorial waters in the course of the minesweeping operation, the United Kingdom had violated the sovereignty of Albania. In this regard, the World Court emphatically rejected all grounds of alleged defense under customary international law that were proffered by the British government:

> The Court cannot accept such a line of defense. The Court can only regard the alleged right of intervention as the manifestation of a policy of force, such as has, in the past, given rise to most serious abuses and such as cannot, whatever be the present defects in international organization, find a place in international law. Intervention is perhaps still less admissible in the particular form it would take here; for, from the nature of things, it would be reserved for the most powerful States, and might easily lead to perverting the administration of international justice itself.
>
> ....
>
> The United Kingdom Agent, in his speech in reply, has further classified [the minesweeping operation] among methods of self-protection or self-help. The Court cannot accept this defence either. Between independent States, respect for territorial sovereignty is an essential foundation of international relations. The Court recognizes that the Albanian Government's complete failure to carry out its duties after the explosions, and the dilatory nature of its diplomatic notes, are extenuating circumstances for the action of the United Kingdom Government. But to ensure respect for international law, of which it is the organ, the Court must declare that the action of the British Navy constituted a violation of Albanian sovereignty.[61]

Even more significantly, the World Court repudiated these vagarious doctrines without explicitly relying upon the U.N. Charter because Albania was not yet a party while Great Britain was. Hence, the Court's holding on this point can be construed to constitute an authoritative declaration of the requirements of customary international law on the use of force that is binding upon all members of the international community irrespective of the Charter. *A fortiori*, therefore, when both parties to an international conflict are U.N. members, such as the United States and Iran, articles 2(3), 2(4), and 33 absolutely prohibit any threat or use of force that is not specifically justified by the article 51 right of individual or collective self-defense. Furthermore, pursuant to article 38(1)(c) of the Statute of the International Court of Justice, under "the general principles of law recognized by civilized nations," retaliation is not self-defense but murder and aggression.

The *Corfu Channel Case* invokes the memory of one of history's great conflagrations that started as a simple dispute over the colonial status of Epidamnus between ancient Corinth and Corcyra, then a city-state on the island of Corfu. The Reagan Administration's demented interpretation of self-defense to include retaliation is a throwback to the Athenian position taken at the Melian Conference in Book 5 of Thucydides' *The Peloponnesian War*. The strong do what they will, and the weak suffer what they must! Not coincidentally, the Athenians had rejected a Melian offer of neutrality in their war against Sparta as incompatible with their imperial destiny:

> *Melians.*—"So that you would not consent to our being neutral, friends instead of enemies, but allies of neither side."
> *Athenians.*—"No; for your hostility cannot so much hurt us as your friendship will be an argument to our subjects of our weakness, and your enmity of our power."
> *Melians.*—"Is that your subjects' idea of equity, to put those who have nothing to do with you in the same category with peoples that are most of them your own colonists, and some conquered rebels?"
> *Athenians.*—"As far as right goes they think one has as much of it as the other, and that if any maintain their independence it is because they are strong, and that if we do not molest them it is because we are afraid; so that besides extending our empire we should gain in security by your subjection; the fact that you are islanders and weaker than others rendering it all the more important that you should not succeed in baffling the masters of the sea."[62]

Twenty-five hundred years later—even at this writing—today's "masters of the sea" is another self-styled democracy with a belligerent populace and truculent leaders who imperiously threaten to engulf the civilized world in a cataclysm of unpredictable dimensions if a small power does not capitulate to its diktat.

There was an alternative solution, however, to the Reagan Administration's fictitious dilemma of choosing between either further escalation of direct U.S. military intervention in support of Iraq, or acquiescing to the installation of a what it regarded as likely to be a puppet regime in Baghdad acting at the behest of Iran. This third option could have been constructed on the basis of international law and organizations if the Reagan Administration or its successor really desired to do so in good faith. Pursuing this third alternative would essentially have required that the United States government indicate a willingness to satisfy those reasonable Iranian conditions for terminating the war that could be fully justified by the principles of international law.

The basic components of and reasons for a practicable peace plan that merited support by the United States government and endorsement by the U.N. Security Council included: (1) the condemnation of Iraq as the original aggressor in the war; (2) the removal of Saddam Hussein from power; (3) the payment of war reparations to Iran; (4) the interposition of a U.N. peacekeeping force along the Iraq-Iran border to facilitate a withdrawal of forces; and (5) the restoration of the 1975 border between the two countries. Iran gave every indication that it would be prepared to terminate the Iraq-Iran War on essentially these terms.

Instead of working along these lines, however, the Reagan Administration sponsored and obtained the passage of U.N. Security Council Resolution 598 (1987)[63] which did not meet any of the minimal Iranian demands for the termination of the war but rather seemed to incorporate the maximalist Iraqi position. In particular, Resolution 598 required that Iran must *first* withdraw from *all* Iraqi territory *before* steps are taken by the Security Council to satisfy *any* of the legitimate Iranian conditions under international law. The U.S. government's stubborn insistence that the terms of Resolution 598 be implemented in this precise sequence of events was an obvious non-starter in the first place and was thus probably designed to produce Iranian non-compliance precisely in order to serve as a pretext for imposing U.N. Security Council sanctions against Iran to stave off an Iraqi defeat.

This author seriously doubted that after seven years of being on the receiving end of incredible bloodshed and devastation, Iran would have withdrawn from Iraq upon the mere promise by the Security Council that the inequities of the situation might be redressed somewhat afterwards. Recall that due to the influence of the U.S. government, the U.N. Security Council had not even passed a resolution condemning Iraq for its initiation of aggression against Iran in 1980, with all its incalculable consequences for the Iranian and Iraqi peoples. Under the pernicious influence of the Reagan Administration, Resolution 598 did not either. The purported reason was that the Security Council must be "balanced" and "even-handed" between both belligerents when passing resolutions on the Iraq-Iran War. Nothing could be further from what is appropriately called for under international law. The Security Council was never designed to be neutral in the face of outright aggression. If it purports to be so for any reason, then the Security Council and its membership—especially the five permanent members possessing the veto power—have simply betrayed their partiality in favor of an aggressor against its victim and thus seriously undermined, if not permanently abnegated, their "primary responsibility for the maintenance of international peace and security" under U.N. Charter article 24(1). So long as the Security Council continued to act at the behest of the U.S. government and Iraq in this matter, it probably would have had little positive effect upon the ultimate outcome of the Iraq-Iran war.

Despite these inherent defects, Iran nevertheless demonstrated a considerable amount of flexibility on the terms and the timing for the implementation of Resolution 598. The Iranians indicated that they would be prepared to declare and observe an informal ceasefire that should be followed by the establishment of an international commission to examine responsibility for the outbreak of the war. Once that commission had reported—presumably determining that Iraq was responsible for committing aggression—and the logical consequences from that determination were implemented (i.e., the departure of Saddam Hussein and at least a promise by Iraq and/or the Gulf states to pay war reparations to Iran), then Iran indicated that it would be prepared to engage in a complete withdrawal from Iraqi territory. The United States government should have taken the Iranians at their word and immediately proceeded to implement this promising procedure for ending the war. Instead, the Reagan Administration continued to work at the Security Council to obtain the latter's full support for the maximalist Iraqi position that Iran must first withdraw completely from Iraqi territory before meeting any Iranian terms for ending the war. Later, the Reagan Administration demonstrated its own gross disrespect for and rank hypocrisy toward Resolution 598 by specifically violating the terms of paragraph 5 thereof when it decided to use the U.S. Navy to escort the Kuwaiti tankers and to engage in acts of hostility against Iranian ships and oil drilling platforms in the Gulf: "The Security Council .... 5. Calls upon all other States to exercise the utmost restraint and to refrain from any act which may lead to further escalation and widening of the conflict, and thus to facilitate the implementation of the present resolution . . ." Direct U.S. military intervention in support of the Kuwaiti tankers and retaliatory acts against Iranian ships and oil drilling platforms did the exact opposite from what the Security Council had ordered. Then the Reagan Administration sanctimoniously demanded that the Security Council impose an arms embargo against Iran because it had failed to comply with Resolution 598!

Even if the Reagan Administration had been ultimately successful in its quest for Security Council sanctions against Iran, the latter would probably have a limited impact upon Iranian calculations because the Security Council had no credibility in their eyes. Furthermore, any additional forms of unilateral direct U.S. military intervention into the Iraq-Iran War would probably have been doomed to failure as well. The same can be said for the American-orchestrated multilateral naval force consisting of warships drawn from NATO countries but operating without any type of imprimatur by the U.N. Security Council in the Persian Gulf.

In any event, the Reagan Administration surrendered the initiative for war and further acts of hostility to Iran as part of some cosmic game of "chicken," wherein the U.S. government publicly admitted that its military calculations were based upon the assumption that Iran will not do something "foolish" or "irrational" as the Reagan Administration defined those terms. In other words, the American people and Congress had to depend upon the good sense of Iran to keep us out of further involvement in the Iraq-Iran War. The Reagan Administration's apparent resurrection of Thomas Schelling's discredited and dangerous theory propounding "the rationality of irrationality" as the basis for its interventionary policy in the Iraq-Iran War could readily have producd an incredible disaster for everyone concerned. Fortunately it did not materialize—assuming that one is prepared to write off the 37 dead crewmen of the *Stark* as an "accident," which this author is not willing to do. One would hope that the American people had seen quite enough of President Reagan on national television shedding crocodile tears over the bodies of American servicemen whom he had needlessly ordered to their deaths because of his penchant to send in the Marines, Navy, Army, or Air Force, whenever his illegal and bankrupt foreign policies have finally demonstrated their genetic futility. By contrast, President Bush Jr. does not even bother to mourn U.S. war casualties.[64] Out of sight, out of mind—and vice versa.

Chapter Two

United States War Crimes During the First Persian Gulf War

On February 27, 1992, Albany Law School in Albany, N.Y., convened a Symposium on the subject of "International War Crimes: The Search for Justice." The Symposium organizers invited the author to come in for the express purpose of arguing the case against the Bush Sr. administration for committing international crimes during their Gulf War I against Iraq, and then to debate this position with the other Symposium speakers, who were law professors or lawyers. The Symposium proceedings were taped for later broadcast by C-SPAN.

Introduction

1. For the past year I have been working with the International Commission of Inquiry into United States war crimes that were committed during the Persian Gulf War. This Commission has conducted the largest independent worldwide investigation of war crimes in history. Since last May, the Commission has held thirty hearings across the United States and in twenty countries across five continents to expose the war crimes that the United States government inflicted upon the people and State of Iraq.

2. On Saturday, February 29, 1992, in New York City, at the Martin Luther King, Jr. Auditorium, the Commission will publicly present its evidence before an International War Crimes Tribunal consisting of distinguished jurists and human rights activists drawn from around the world. In the brief space that has been allotted to me, I would like to present the basic gist of the charges that will be brought before the Tribunal against President George Bush, Vice President Dan Quayle, Secretary of State Jim Baker, Secretary of Defense Dick Cheney, National Security Assistant Brent Scowcroft, CIA Director William Webster, Chairman of the Joint Chiefs of Staff General Colin Powell, General Norman Schwarzkopf, and other members of the High Command of the United States military establishment who launched and waged this brutal, inhumane, and criminal war. Hereinafter, these individuals will be collectively referred to as the Defendants.

The Charges

3. The international crimes that have been charged and will be proved

against these Defendants consist principally of the three Nuremberg Offenses: the Nuremberg Crime Against Peace, that is, waging an aggressive war and a war in violation of international treaties and agreements; Nuremberg Crimes Against Humanity; and Nuremberg War Crimes. In addition, these Defendants also committed grievous war crimes by wantonly violating the Hague Regulations on Land Warfare of 1907; the Declaration of London on Sea Warfare of 1909; the Hague Draft Rules of Aerial Warfare of 1923; the Four Geneva Conventions of 1949 and their two Additional Protocols of 1977; and the international crime of genocide against the people of Iraq as defined by the International Convention on the Prevention and Punishment of the Crime of Genocide of 1948 as well as by the United States' own Genocide Convention Implementation Act of 1987, 18 U.S.C. §1901. Finally, and most heinously of all, these Defendants actually perpetrated a Nuremberg Crime against their own troops when they forced them to take experimental biological weapons vaccines without their informed consent, in gross violation of the Nuremberg Code on Medical Experimentation that has been fully subscribed to by the United States government.

Universal Jurisdiction

4. These international crimes create personal criminal responsibility on the part of all these Defendants that warrant their prosecution under basic norms of customary international law, treaties, and statutes in any state of the world community that obtains jurisdiction over them for the rest of their lives. We believe that the International War Crimes Tribunal will produce a Judgment that can be put into the hands of every government in the world with the injunction that should any of these Defendants ever appear within their territorial jurisdiction, they must be apprehended and prosecuted for the commission of the specified international crimes. Like unto pirates, these Defendants are *hostes humani generis*—the enemies of all humankind!

The Historical Origins of the War

5. I do not have the time in this brief presentation to analyze the entire history of illegal U.S. military interventionism into the Middle East— especially the Persian Gulf region—and in particular its divide-and-conquer (*divide et impera*) policies. Suffice it to say here that the "immediate cause" of the United States war to destroy Iraq and take over the Arab oil fields in the Persian Gulf goes back to the 1973 Arab oil boycott of Europe. The Arab oil states imposed the boycott in solidarity with those Arab states that were then attempting to reclaim their lands that had been illegally stolen from them by Israel in 1967. The Arab oil boycott brought Europe to its knees. Subsequently, Arab oil states were able to increase the price of oil to a point of economic fairness that would enable them to provide for the basic human needs of their own Peoples.

6. But the success of the Arab oil boycott led several prominent

U.S. government officials in the Nixon administration, and especially Henry Kissinger, to publicly threaten that the United States government would prepare itself to seize the Arab oil fields in order to prevent something like the boycott from ever happening again. This illegal governmental threat was stated openly, publicly, and repeatedly during the course of the Nixon administration, the Ford administration, the Carter administration, and the Reagan administration. The Bush administration would finally be the one to carry this threat out—but only after a decade of active preparations.

The Rapid Deployment Force

7. During the course of the Carter administration, the United States government obtained authorization from Congress to set up, arm, equip, and supply the so-called Rapid Deployment Force (RDF), whose primary mission was to seize and steal the Arab oil fields of the Persian Gulf region. So the planning and preparations for the U.S. war against Iraq go all the way back to the so-called "liberal" Carter administration—at the very least. The United States foreign policy establishment consists of liberal imperialists, reactionary imperialists, and middle-of-the-road imperialists. But they all share in common a firm belief in America's "Manifest Destiny" to rule the world.

8. For the next decade, the Pentagon obtained a new generation of high-technology conventional weapons possessing massive destructive power and lethality; the logistical support network necessary to convey a force of 500,000 soldiers over to the Persian Gulf region within six months; and base access rights and facilities for that purpose throughout Africa, the Middle East, and Southeast Asia. Working in conjunction with its de facto allies in the region such as Egypt and Israel, the Pentagon stockpiled enormous quantities of weapons, equipment, and supplies in the immediate vicinity of the Persian Gulf as a prelude to military intervention. Hence, the United States government had been planning, preparing, and conspiring to seize and steal the Persian Gulf oil fields for over a decade.

United States War Plans Against Iraq[1]

9. Sometime after the termination of the Iraq-Iran War in the summer of 1988, the Pentagon proceeded to revise its outstanding war plans for U.S. military intervention into the Persian Gulf region in order to destroy Iraq. Defendant Schwarzkopf was put in charge of this revision. In early 1990, Defendant Schwarzkopf informed the Senate Armed Services Committee of this new military strategy in the Gulf allegedly designed to protect U.S. access to and control over Gulf oil in the event of regional conflicts. In October 1990, Defendant Powell referred to the new military plan developed in 1989. After the war, Defendant Schwarzkopf referred to eighteen months of planning for the campaign—a campaign whose public rationale was based on the illegal invasion of Kuwait by Iraq, which occurred on August 2, 1990.

10. Sometime in late 1989 or early 1990, the Pentagon's war plan for destroying Iraq and stealing Persian Gulf oil fields was put into motion. At that time, Defendant Schwarzkopf was named the Commander of the so-called U.S. Central Command—which was the re-named version of the Rapid Deployment Force—for the purpose of carrying out the war plan that he had personally developed and supervised. During January of 1990, massive quantities of United States weapons, equipment, and supplies were sent to Saudi Arabia in order to prepare for the war against Iraq, again prior to Iraq's invasion of Kuwait.

11. Pursuant to this war plan, Defendant Webster and the CIA assisted and directed Kuwait in its actions of violating OPEC oil production agreements to undercut the price of oil for the purpose of debilitating Iraq's economy; in extracting excessive and illegal amounts of oil from pools it shared with Iraq; in demanding immediate repayment of loans Kuwait had made to Iraq during the Iraq-Iran War; and in breaking off negotiations with Iraq over these disputes. The Defendants intended to provoke Iraq into aggressive military actions against Kuwait that they knew could be used to justify U.S. military intervention into the Persian Gulf for the purpose of destroying Iraq and taking over Arab oil fields. To be sure, the recitation of these facts is not intended to justify the Iraqi invasion of Kuwait.

The U.S. "Green Light" to Invade Kuwait[2]

12. The Defendants showed absolutely no opposition to Iraq's increasing threats against Kuwait. Indeed, when Saddam Hussein requested U.S. Ambassador April Glaspie to explain State Department testimony in Congress about Iraq's threats against Kuwait, she assured him that the United States considered the dispute to be a regional concern, and that it would not intervene militarily. In other words, the United States government gave Saddam Hussein what amounted to a "green light" to invade Kuwait.

13. This reprehensible behavior was similar to that of the Carter administration during September of 1980, when United States government officials gave Saddam Hussein the "green light" to invade Iran and thus commence the tragic Iraq-Iran War. A decade later, Saddam Hussein simply surmised that he had been given yet another "green light" by the United States government to commit overt aggression against surrounding states. Only this time, the Defendants knowingly intended to lead Iraq into a provocation that could be used to justify intervention and warfare by United States military forces for the real purpose of destroying Iraq as a military power and seizing Arab oil fields in the Persian Gulf.

Bush Is the Bigger War Criminal

14. On August 2, 1990, Iraq invaded and occupied Kuwait without significant resistance. The Kuwaiti government itself estimated that

approximately 300 people were killed as a result of Iraq's invasion of Kuwait, and a few hundred more as a result of the military occupation. By comparison, Defendant Bush's invasion of Panama in December of 1989 took between 2,000 and 4,000 Panamanian lives, and the United States government is still covering up the actual death toll. Defendant Bush killed more innocent people in Panama than Saddam Hussein did in Kuwait.

15. Defendant Bush's invasion of Panama was even more illegal, reprehensible, and criminal than Saddam Hussein's invasion of Kuwait. The world must never forget that the first step in the construction of Bush's "New World Order" was his illegal invasion of Panama and the murder of thousands of completely innocent Panamanian civilians. America's self-anointed policeman in the Persian Gulf had the blood of the Panamanian People on his hands.[3]

Bush's Perversion of the Constitution

16. Pursuant to the Pentagon's war plan for destroying Iraq and stealing Persian Gulf oil fields—and without consultation or communication with Congress—Defendant Bush initially ordered 40,000 U.S. military personnel into the Persian Gulf region during the first week of August 1990. He lied to the American people and Congress when he stated that his acts were purely defensive. Right from the very outset of this crisis—and even beforehand— Defendant Bush fully intended to go to war against Iraq and to seize the Arab oil fields in the Persian Gulf. Defendant Bush deliberately misled, deceived, concealed and made false representations to the Congress to prevent its free deliberation and informed exercise of legislative power.

17. Defendant Bush intentionally usurped Congressional power, ignored its authority, and failed and refused to consult with the Congress. He individually ordered a naval blockade against Iraq—itself an act of war—without approval by Congress or the U.N. Security Council. Defendant Bush waited until after the November 1990 elections to publicly announce his earlier order sending more than 200,000 additional military personnel to the Persian Gulf for offensive purposes without seeking the approval of Congress. Pursuant to the Pentagon's war plan, Defendant Bush switched U.S. forces from a defensive position and capability to an offensive capacity for aggression against Iraq without consultation with, and contrary to assurances given to, Congress and the American people.

18. On the very eve of the war, Defendant Bush then strong-armed legislation through Congress that approved enforcement of U.N. resolutions vesting absolute discretion in any nation, providing no guidelines, and requiring no reporting to the United Nations. Defendant Bush demonstrated, through the prior planning above indicated, the intention to destroy the armed forces and civilian infrastructure of Iraq. Those acts were undertaken to provide an international legal cover, under the pretext of responding to an act of aggression,

for the commission of a Nuremberg Crime Against Peace and war crimes. This conduct violated the Constitution and Laws of the United States and especially the War Powers Clause found in Article 1, Section 8 of the Constitution, the U.S. War Powers Act of 1973, 87 Stat. 555, and the United Nations Charter, which is the "Supreme Law of the Land" under Article 6 of the Constitution. For this reason alone, Defendant Bush and his co-conspirators committed "High Crimes and Misdemeanors" that warrant their impeachment, conviction, removal from office, and criminal prosecution.

Bush's Mad Rush to War

19. While concealing his true intentions, Bush continued the military buildup of U.S. forces from August into January 1991 for the purpose of attacking and destroying Iraq. Bush pressed the military to expedite preparations and to commence the war against Iraq before military conditions were optimum for domestic political purposes so that the war would not interfere with his presidential reelection campaign. Indeed, the entire timing, conduct, and duration of the war were planned so as to promote Defendant Bush's reelection prospects. But as a direct result of Defendant Bush's mad rush to war, United States military personnel suffered needless casualties. Defendant Bush has continued to lie and cover up to the American people and Congress the true nature and extent of U.S. casualties during the Persian Gulf War.

Bush Corrupted the United Nations

20. Defendant Bush repeatedly coerced the members of the United Nations Security Council into adopting an unprecedented series of resolutions that culminated in his securing authority for any nation to use "all necessary means" to enforce these resolutions. To secure these votes in the Security Council, Defendant Bush paid multi-billion-dollar bribes; offered arms for regional wars; threatened and carried out economic retaliation; illegally forgave multi-billion-dollar loans; offered diplomatic relations despite human rights violations; and in other ways corruptly exacted votes. This illegal activity subverted and perverted the very purposes and principles of the United Nations Charter itself found in articles 1 and 2 thereof.

Bush Circumvented and Violated Chapter VI of the United Nations Charter

21. In his mad rush to war, Defendant Bush caused the United Nations to completely bypass Chapter VI of the U.N. Charter that mandates the pacific settlement of international disputes. Defendant Bush consistently rejected and ridiculed all of Iraq's efforts to negotiate a peaceful resolution of the dispute. Defendant Bush proudly boasted that there would be no negotiation, no compromise, no face-saving, etc.

22. Defendant Bush's successful attempt to subvert every effort for negotiating a peaceful resolution of this dispute violated the solemn obligation mandating the peaceful resolution of international disputes found in article 2, paragraph 3 of the United Nations Charter; in article 33, paragraph 1 of the United Nations Charter; and in article 2 of the Kellogg-Briand Pact of 1928. Just like the Nazi war criminals before him, Defendant Bush pursued recourse to war as an instrument of his national policy and for the solution of international controversies in violation of article 1 of the Kellogg-Briand Pact. Just as the Nazi war criminals had done by invading Poland in September of 1939, these Defendants perpetrated a Nuremberg Crime Against Peace in their decision to go to war against Iraq with the intent to seize and steal the oil resources of the Persian Gulf.

The Conduct of the War Itself

23. Obviously, in the brief space that has been allotted to me, there is no way that I could adequately describe all of the atrocities and war crimes that were committed by these Defendants and their Agents during the course of their actual conduct of military hostilities against the People and State of Iraq. These matters have been covered in great detail during the course of the public investigations and hearings conducted around the world by the Commission during the past year. The results of this work will be presented to the members of the International War Crimes Tribunal for their consideration and adjudication. Nonetheless, I will provide you here with a succinct account of the major categories of war crimes committed by these Defendants during the course of their criminal war against Iraq.

Bush Ordered the Destruction of Facilities Essential to Civilian Life and Economic Productivity Throughout Iraq.

24. Systematic aerial and missile bombardment of Iraq was ordered to begin at 6:30 p.m. E.S.T., January 16, 1991, in order to be reported on prime time TV. The bombing continued for 42 days. It met no resistance from Iraqi aircraft and no effective anti-aircraft or anti-missile ground fire. Iraq was basically defenseless.

25. Most of the targets were civilian facilities. The United States intentionally bombed and destroyed centers for civilian life, commercial and business districts, schools, hospitals, mosques, churches, shelters, residential areas, historical sites, private vehicles, and civilian government offices. In aerial attacks, including strafing, over cities, towns, the countryside and highways, United States aircraft bombed and strafed indiscriminately. The purpose of these attacks was to destroy life and property, and generally to terrorize the civilian population of Iraq. The net effect was the summary execution and indiscriminate corporal punishment of men, women, and children, young and old, rich and poor, of all nationalities and religions.

26. As a direct result of this bombing campaign against civilian life, at least 25,000 men, women, and children were killed. The Red Crescent Society of Jordan estimated 113,000 civilian dead, 60% of them children, the week before the end of the war. According to the Nuremberg Charter, this "wanton destruction of cities, towns, or villages" is a Nuremberg War Crime.

27. The intention and effort of this bombing campaign against civilian life and facilities was to systematically destroy Iraq's infrastructure leaving it in a pre-industrial condition. The U.S. assault left Iraq in near apocalyptic conditions as reported by the first United Nations observers after the war. As a direct, intentional, and foreseeable result of this anti-civilian destruction, over one hundred thousand people have died after the war from dehydration, dysentery, diseases, and malnutrition caused by impure water, inability to obtain effective medical assistance, and debilitation from hunger, shock, cold, and stress. More will die until potable water, sanitary living conditions, adequate food supplies, and other necessities are provided. Yet Defendant Bush continues to impose punitive economic sanctions against the people of Iraq in order to prevent this from happening.

The United States Intentionally Bombed and Destroyed Defenseless Iraqi Military Personnel; Used Excessive Force; Killed Soldiers Seeking to Surrender and in Disorganized Individual Flight, Often Unarmed and Far from Any Combat Zones; Randomly and Wantonly Killed Iraqi Soldiers; and Destroyed Material After the Cease-Fire.

28. In the first hours of the aerial and missile bombardment, the United States destroyed most military communications and began the systematic killing of Iraqi soldiers who were incapable of defense or escape, and the destruction of military equipment. The U.S. bombing campaign killed tens of thousands of defenseless soldiers, cut off from most of their food, water and other supplies, and left them in desperate and helpless disarray. Defendant Schwarzkopf placed Iraqi military casualties at over 100,000. Large numbers of these soldiers were "out of combat" and therefore not legitimate targets for military attack.

29. When it was determined that the civilian economy and the military were sufficiently destroyed, the U.S. ground forces moved into Kuwait and Iraq attacking disoriented, disorganized, fleeing Iraqi forces wherever they could be found, killing thousands more and destroying any equipment found. In one particularly shocking maneuver, thousands of Iraqi soldiers were needlessly and illegally buried alive. This wholesale slaughter of Iraqi soldiers continued even after and in violation of the so-called cease-fire.

30. The Defendants' intention was not to remove Iraq's presence from Kuwait. Rather, their intention was to destroy Iraq. The disproportion in death and destruction inflicted on a defenseless enemy exceeded 1000 to one. The Defendants conducted this genocidal war against the male

population of Iraq for the express purpose of making sure that Iraq could not raise a substantial military force for at least another generation.

The United States Used Prohibited Weapons Capable of Mass Destruction and Inflicting Indiscriminate Death and Unnecessary Suffering Against Both Military and Civilian Targets.

31. Fuel air explosives were used against troops in place, civilian areas, oil fields, and fleeing civilians and soldiers on two stretches of highway between Kuwait and Iraq. One seven mile stretch called the "Highway of Death" was littered with hundreds of vehicles and thousands of dead. All were fleeing to Iraq for their lives. Thousands were civilians of all ages, including Kuwaitis, Iraqis, Palestinians, Jordanians, and other nationalities.

32. Napalm was used against civilians and military personnel, as well as to start fires. Oil well fires in both Iraq and Kuwait were intentionally started by U.S. aircraft dropping napalm and other heat intensive devices.

33. Cluster bombs and anti-personnel fragmentation bombs were used in Basra, and other cities and towns, against the civilian convoys of fleeing vehicles and against military units.

34. "Superbombs" were dropped on hardened shelters with the intention of assassinating Iraqi President Saddam Hussein—a war crime in its own right.

The United States Intentionally Attacked Installations in Iraq Containing Dangerous Substances and Forces in Violation of Article 56 of Geneva Protocol I of 1977.

35. The U.S. intentionally bombed alleged nuclear sites, chemical plants, dams, and other "dangerous forces." The U.S. knew such attacks could cause the release of dangerous forces from such installations and consequently severe losses among the civilian population. While some civilians were killed in such attacks, there are no reported cases of consequent severe losses. Presumably, lethal nuclear materials, and dangerous chemical and biological warfare substances, were not present at the sites bombed.

The United States Waged War on the Environment.

36. Before the war started, the Pentagon had developed computer models that accurately predicted the environmental catastrophe that would occur should the United States go to war against Iraq. These Defendants went to war anyway, knowing full well what the consequences of such an environmental disaster would be. Attacks by U.S. aircraft caused much if not all of the worst oil spills in the Gulf. Aircraft and helicopters dropped napalm and fuel-air explosives on oil wells, storage tanks, and refineries,

causing oil fires throughout Iraq and many, if not most, of the oil well fires in Iraq and Kuwait.

Defendant Bush Encouraged and Aided Shiite Muslims and Kurds to Rebel Against the Government of Iraq Causing Fratricidal Violence, Emigration, Exposure, Hunger and Sickness, and Thousands of Deaths. After the Rebellion Failed, the U.S. Invaded and Occupied Parts of Iraq Without Lawful Authority in Order to Increase Division and Hostilities Within Iraq.

37. Without authority from the U.S. Congress or the United Nations, Defendant Bush encouraged and aided rebellion against Iraq, failed to protect the warring parties, and encouraged mass migration of whole populations, placing them in jeopardy from the elements, hunger, and disease. After much suffering and many deaths, Defendant Bush then without authority used U.S. military forces to distribute aid at and near the Turkish border, ignoring the often greater suffering among refugees in Iran. He then arbitrarily set up bantustan-like settlements for Kurds in Iraq and demanded that Iraq pay for U.S. costs. When Kurds chose to return to their homes in Iraq, he moved U.S. troops further into northern Iraq against the will of the government and without any legal authority to do so. As Defendant Baker correctly put it when he visited the area, these atrocities constituted a Nuremberg "crime against humanity." Although he was referring to the culpability of Saddam Hussein, Baker effectively condemned the relevant members of the Bush Sr. administration under international criminal law as complicit to a Nuremberg crime against humanity.

Defendant Bush Intentionally Deprived the Iraqi People of Essential Medicines, Potable Water, Food, and Other Necessities.

38. A major component of the assault on Iraq was the systematic deprivation of essential human needs and services, to terrorize and break the will of the Iraqi people, to destroy their economic capability, and to reduce their numbers and weaken their health. Towards those ends, the Defendants:

• imposed and enforced embargoes preventing the shipment of needed medicines, water purifiers, infant milk formula, food, and other supplies;

• froze funds of Iraq and forced other nations to do so, depriving Iraq of the ability to purchase needed medicines, food, and other supplies;

• prevented international organizations, governments, and relief agencies from providing needed supplies and obtaining information concerning such needs;

- failed to assist or meet urgent needs of huge refugee populations and interfered with efforts of others to do so, etc;

- intentionally bombed water treatment plants, despite their awareness of the likely resultant spread of diseases from drinking non-potable water.

As a direct result of these cruel and inhuman acts, thousands of people died, many more suffered illnesses and permanent injury. For these actions, the Defendants are guilty of Nuremberg Crimes Against Humanity and the Crime of Genocide as recognized by international law and U.S. domestic law.

Defendant Bush, Having Destroyed Iraq's Economic Base, Demands Reparations Which Will Permanently Impoverish Iraq and Threaten Its People with Famine and Epidemic.

39. Defendant Bush seeks to force Iraq to pay for damages to Kuwait largely caused by the U.S. and even to pay U.S. costs for its violation of Iraqi sovereignty in occupying northern Iraq to further manipulate the Kurdish population there. Such reparations are neo-colonial means of expropriating Iraq's oil, natural resources, and human labor. Meanwhile, the United States government dominates and controls the respective governments and oil resources of Kuwait, Saudi Arabia, Bahrain, Oman, the United Arab Emirates, and Qatar.

40. The United States government has successfully carried out its longstanding threat and war plan to seize and steal the oil resources of the Persian Gulf for its own benefit. The United States now either directly or indirectly controls the natural energy resources that fuel the economies of Europe and Japan. Acting with their de facto allies in Israel and Great Britain, the Defendants are today seeking to consolidate their control over the entire Middle East in a blatant bid to establish worldwide hegemony.

Bush's "New World Order"

41. Today, the government in the United States of America constitutes an international criminal conspiracy under the Nuremberg Charter, Judgment, and Principles that is legally identical to the Nazi government in World War II Germany. The Defendants' wanton extermination of approximately 250,000 people in Iraq provides definitive proof of the validity of this Nuremberg Proposition for the entire world to see. Indeed, Defendant Bush's so-called New World Order sounds and looks strikingly similar to the New Order proclaimed by Adolf Hitler over fifty years ago. You do not build a *real* New World Order with stealth bombers, Abrams tanks, and Tomahawk cruise missiles. For their own good and the good of all humanity, the American people must condemn and repudiate Defendant Bush and his grotesque vision

of a New World Order that is constructed upon warfare, bloodshed, violence, and criminality.

Impeachment

42. All of these aforementioned international crimes constitute "High Crimes and Misdemeanors" as defined by the Article 2, Section 4 of the United States Constitution and therefore warrant the impeachment, conviction, and removal from office of Defendants Bush, Quayle, Baker, Cheney, Powell, and Scowcroft. In regard to this matter, Congressman Henry Gonzalez of Texas has already introduced an Impeachment Resolution into the House of Representatives, that is numbered House Resolution 86, calling for the impeachment and removal from office of these Defendants because they have committed these international crimes and also because they have subverted and perverted constitutional government in America "to the manifest injury of the people of the United States."

A Special Prosecutor

43. These Defendants must be impeached by the House, tried and convicted by the Senate, and removed from office. Thereafter, we believe that the Commission of Inquiry and the International War Crimes Tribunal will have produced sufficient evidence to trigger the application of the Ethics in Government Act, 28 U.S.C. §591 et seq., that would lead to the appointment of an Independent Counsel (i.e., Special Prosecutor) to investigate and prosecute these high-ranking officials for the wholesale violation of federal criminal laws in their decision to launch and wage this criminal war against the people and State of Iraq. We fully intend to see Bush, Baker, Cheney, Quayle, Scowcroft, Webster, Powell, Schwarzkopf, and the rest of the U.S. High Command sitting in jail for the rest of their natural lives.

Conclusion

44. Make no mistake about it: the very nature, future, and existence of the American Republic depend upon the success of these endeavors. Today, the battle begins for the hearts and minds of the American People between the Warmongers and the Peacemakers. We ask all of you to join us in this legal campaign and moral crusade to reclaim for the United States of America a democratic government with a commitment to the Rule of Law and the Constitution both at home and abroad.

Chapter Three

The Court Martial of Captain Dr. Yolanda Huet-Vaughn for Desertion

Dr. Yolanda Huet-Vaughn, M.D., was sworn as a commissioned officer in the U.S. Army Reserves in Kansas City, MO, on June 18, 1990. A few weeks after her military service began, Kuwait was invaded by Iraq. Dr. Huet-Vaughn had previously served as an officer in the Tennessee National Guard. She had been excused from serving her full service obligation because she entered the U.S. Public Health Service.

Dr. Huet-Vaughn has stated that she joined the Army Reserves because she believed that officers who were critical of current military policy regarding the use of nuclear weapons could play an important role. She also felt a "moral obligation" to complete the tour which she had originally committed to in the Tennessee reserve unit.

She received mobilization orders placing her on active-duty in support of Operation Desert Shield on December 18, 1990. She was ordered to report, along with other members of her unit, the 325th General Hospital unit, to Ft. Leonard Wood, MO, on December 23, 1990.

After Dr. Huet-Vaughn reported, as ordered, to Ft. Leonard Wood, she consulted an Army Judge Advocate General lawyer, Captain Deborah Hooper, concerning the possible filing of a Conscientious Objector (C.O.) application. Hooper advised her that under a new Army directive, all C.O. applicants were to be sent to their ultimate duty station while their claim was reviewed, even if that was Saudi Arabia or another part of the Persian Gulf.

On December 29, 1990, Dr. Huet-Vaughn traveled with other members of her hospital unit from Ft. Leonard Wood to Ft. Riley, KS, arriving in the evening. It quickly became apparent to Dr. Huet-Vaughn that her activation orders were directly related to providing support for impending military operations against Iraq in the Persian Gulf.

She then sought counseling from Tod Ensign, attorney and director of Citizen Soldier, a New York City based GI and veterans' rights advocacy organization, and from other attorneys. Dr. Huet-Vaughn told Ensign and other attorneys that she was opposed, on moral and political grounds, to assisting or participating in any way in Operation Desert Shield (later to be named Desert Storm).

On December 30, 1990, the night after she had arrived at Ft. Riley, KS, Dr. Huet-Vaughn left the base with permission. She was scheduled to report for duty the following morning at 8:00 a.m. Instead, Dr. Huet-Vaughn traveled by airplane to New York City so that she could consult with Tod Ensign. Mr. Louis Font, a civilian attorney who specializes in military defense work, was brought into the case at this point.

During the next month, Dr. Huet-Vaughn was actively engaged in expressing her concerns about impending war in the Persian Gulf and her opposition, on moral and political grounds, to participating in such a war. In addition to traveling to Washington, D.C. and meeting with a number of Congressional staff members and Members of Congress, she spoke out to numerous newspaper, radio, and television reporters.

On January 9, 1992, Citizen Soldier organized a press conference at the National Press Club in Washington, D.C. at which Dr. Huet-Vaughn presented a detailed account of her reasons for refusing further service in the U.S. Army.

During this period, accounts of her resistance appeared in: Kansas City Star, Knight-Ridder newspapers, Associated Press, Cable Network News, USA Today, French radio, Canadian Radio Network, LINK magazine, the Guardian newspaper, the Nation, New Directions for Women, MS Magazine, Avvenimenti (Italian), American Medical News, the Army Times newspaper, New York Newsday, and the New York Times. She also appeared on "Sally Jesse Raphael Show," "CBS Morning Show", Pacifica Network, and was scheduled to appear on "the Joan Rivers Show."

On February 2, 1991, Dr. Huet-Vaughn publicly surrendered to the military authorities at Kansas City, KS, following a well-attended support rally at a church in Kansas City, MO. As soon as military police personnel took Dr. Huet-Vaughn into custody, she was driven directly to Ft. Leonard Wood.

Upon arriving at Ft. Leonard Wood in the evening, Dr. Huet-Vaughn was taken to the Military Police barracks and locked up. The following afternoon, about 1:00 p.m., she was released from confinement.

Dr. Huet-Vaughn was assigned to administrative duties at the base hospital, and for the next month her movement was not restricted in any fashion. For the next three weekends, she traveled home to Kansas City (a five hour journey by car) to visit with her three small children, ages 8, 5, and 3, and her husband, David.

The day after Dr. Huet-Vaughn returned to Ft. Leonard Wood, her commander, Lt. Colonel Keith Copeland, issued a written order requiring her to contact the hospital duty officer by telephone at 6:00 a.m. and 10:00 p.m. on work days and at 8:00 a.m., noon, 5:00 p.m., and 10:00 p.m. on non-work days. The order also required her to sign out with the hospital duty officer giving her destination and expected time of return whenever she wished to leave the post and to sign in upon her return.

On March 6, 1991, Captain Huet-Vaughn was formally charged with desertion with intent to shirk hazardous or important duty. On the same day, LTC Copeland revised his restriction order so that Dr. Huet-Vaughn was no longer allowed to leave the base at any time without written permission to do so. Over the next three months, Dr. Huet-Vaughn submitted over fifty such written requests, but only three were granted: two to conduct off-post *interviews with reporters, and the other to purchase computer equipment that was not available at the post commissary.*

Subsequently, Lt. Colonel Copeland attempted to justify his decision to restrict Dr. Huet-Vaughn to the base by noting the criminal charge against her. However, the facts that she had voluntarily surrendered to authorities in the first place and that she had always returned to the base when previously allowed to leave suggested that these restrictions were punitive in nature.

On February 21, 1991, Captain Yolanda Huet-Vaughn filed a formal application (DA Form 4187) for "release from the military as a conscientious objector under the provisions of Army Regulation 600-43, or as a selective or partial objector under the principles enunciated by the United Nations and other international and domestic laws and customs."

The military's procedure for submitting a C.O. application requires, among other things, that the applicant answer, in essay form, seven questions. In addition, the applicant must submit to interviews by both a military psychologist or psychiatrist and a military chaplain of the applicant's faith.

Army chaplain Colonel Robert F. Berger submitted a report on his interviews with Dr. Huet-Vaughn on March 26, 1991 in which he concluded: "I find her attitude and behavior consistent with her beliefs." He continued, "She adequately convinces me that she does indeed object to participation in war in any form." He then concluded: "I find her opposition to war arising from a central conviction based on her religious training and belief [and] I don't doubt her sincerity."

An Article 32 Investigation was begun at Ft. Leonard Wood on April 1, 1991. This proceeding, which is similar to a grand jury in civilian judicial systems, is charged with reviewing relevant evidence from both the prosecution and the defense and determining what criminal charge, if any, should be brought. On the first day of this hearing, attorney Louis Font demonstrated that Army prosecutor Captain Bradley Page had unduly influenced the selection of the Investigating Officer. Embarrassed by these disclosures, the command decided to abort the hearing and ordered the appointment of a new officer.

On May 6 and 7, 1991, a second Article 32 investigation was conducted, this time under the auspices of Lt. Colonel Miles Franklin, who had been brought in from Ft. Knox, KY. Because this proceeding is considered an investigation, the rules of admissibility are relaxed and broad latitude is allowed in the kind of evidence that is permitted.

Captain Huet-Vaughn's attorneys moved aggressively to bring forth expert testimony concerning the nature of the warfare conducted by the U.S.-led coalition in the Persian Gulf. They offered three principal witnesses: former U.S. Attorney General Ramsey Clark; international legal expert Professor Francis Boyle; and Dr. Victor Sidel, an expert on medical ethics. Their testimony is summarized below.

Ramsey Clark. *He reported on the findings of a recent (February 1991) fact-finding trip to Iraq. He described the U.S. air campaign as "random and indiscriminate bombing to terrorize" the civilian population. In Basra, he witnessed at least six residential areas which had suffered heavy damage* *from intensive bombardment. He described the attacks on electric, sewage, water, and communications systems as "war crimes." He expressed the opinion that Captain Huet-Vaughn had a right and a duty to refuse to participate, even indirectly, in such military operations.*

Clark also narrated a video entitled "No Place to Hide" which documented his seven-day trip into Iraq while it was being subjected to the heaviest aerial bombardment in world history.

Professor Francis Boyle. *He testified that Dr. Huet-Vaughn was not absent without authority since the laws of war gave her authority for her actions. He cited numerous international treaties, the Nuremberg Principles, and the Army's own Field Manual, 27-10, as authority. Boyle stated that the wanton destruction of cities is specifically mentioned as a Nuremberg war crime. He noted that months before the war actually began, U.S. Air Force Commander Dugan was fired because he had told reporters that the U.S. planned to devastate central Baghdad if war began.*

Dr. Victor Sidel. *He testified that military doctors must follow a unique set of rules for medical triage, whereby slightly injured GIs are treated ahead of more seriously wounded civilian casualties. This, he argued, would force Dr. Huet-Vaughn to violate her Hippocratic oath as a physician. He also discussed the military's compulsory inoculation program in which thousands of GIs assigned to the Persian Gulf were injected with experimental botulism and anthrax vaccines which had not been approved for human use by the FDA. Sidel noted that if Dr. Huet-Vaughn were required to give these shots that she could become liable under the Nuremberg Code which punished Nazi doctors for conducting medical experiments without first obtaining their patients' consent.*

The defendant's attorneys also requested that a number of other witnesses be made available, including President George Bush, Secretary of State James Baker, Secretary of Defense Richard Cheney, Generals Colin Powell and Norman Schwarzkopf, as well as Kansas City police chief Steven Bishop and unnamed undercover police officers who surveilled the surrender rally in Kansas City, MO, on February 2, 1991. After considerable discussion and debate, Lt. Col. Franklin, the hearing officer, refused to allow any of the above witnesses to be called as per the defense's request.

Approximately two weeks later, Lt. Col. Franklin submitted his recommendation to the convening authority. He proposed that Dr. Huet-Vaughn be tried for desertion with intent to shirk hazardous or important duty by a general court-martial.

A formal hearing on Dr. Huet-Vaughn's application for discharge as a conscientious objector (C.O.) was held at Ft. Leonard Wood on May 8, 1991. Major Frank Horna was designated as the hearing officer and his first act was to deny Dr. Huet-Vaughn's attorney's request that the hearing be open to the public and media and that a verbatim transcript be prepared.

Captain Huet-Vaughn presented a number of witnesses who testified to her sincerity and integrity. Among these witnesses were: Dr. John Swomley, a theologian with many years' experience working with C.O.s; Dr. Lydia Moore, MD, who had worked with Dr. Huet-Vaughn in a low-income medical clinic;

Sister Mary McNellis, a Catholic nun who had known the claimant for many years; and Major Mark Borserine, of the Kansas National Guard who stated that while he disagreed with her position, he believed Dr. Huet-Vaughn to be sincere in her beliefs.

In a memo dated May 28, 1991, Major Horna recommended denial of Dr. Huet-Vaughn's application. He based this on his conclusion that "there was not clear and convincing evidence that her beliefs evolved, are sincerely held and govern her word and deed such (as to) qualify her under the regulation...."

Staff Judge Advocate Colonel James Rosenblatt endorsed Horna's recommendation in a July 9, 1991 memo, and acting base commander Colonel Donald Wolff adopted this endorsement in a memo dated the next day.

The General Court Martial convening authority referred Dr. Huet-Vaughn's case to a general court martial on June 6, 1991. She was arraigned on a charge of desertion (Article 85 of the UCMJ) on June 11, 1991, to which she entered no plea.

On a related front, the Kansas Board of Healing Arts notified Dr. Huet-Vaughn in April 1991 that it had received formal complaints from several Kansas doctors in which they sought action against her license because of her refusal to deploy to the Persian Gulf as an Army doctor. After much procedural maneuvering, the board's Executive Director, Lawrence Buening, announced on November 19, 1991 that the board had voted to begin license revocation action against Dr. Huet-Vaughn. He predicted that a petition to commence proceedings would be filed "within the next month or two."

Once a petition has been filed, a presiding officer, who is usually a retired judge or lawyer, is appointed to hear the facts, take evidence from all parties and make a ruling on whether a medical license shall be suspended or not. The Healing Arts Board then reviews this decision and makes the final decision.

On July 12, 1991, the requirement that Dr. Huet-Vaughn remain on base and phone in at regular intervals was lifted.

Pre-trial motions were argued at a hearing on July 15 and 16, 1991 at Ft. Leonard Wood. Prosecutor Captain Bradley Page submitted a Motion In Limine which asked the judge to exclude the following testimony at court-martial: "Any documentary or testimonial evidence during the case on the merits concerning the accused's alleged status as a conscientious objector, her beliefs about the Persian Gulf conflict or war generally, the dictates of her conscience, religion, personal philosophies, or her world views."

In response, the defense submitted a brief to oppose the motion. It argued that the testimony which the prosecution attempted to exclude would: 1) establish a legitimate defense, and 2) negate or reasonably tend to negate the requisite mens rea of the offense charged (i.e., the intent to avoid hazardous duty and important service). In addition, the defense argued that the extensive documents which it had requested from the government should be produced, as should the witnesses which it had requested.

Military Judge Richard Russell granted the prosecution's motion in limine and denied the defense's request for numerous documents and most of the forty-five witnesses requested. Essentially, he ruled that a defense based on the Nuremberg Principles and international law was irrelevant and he disallowed any evidence relating to the conduct of U.S. military forces in the Persian Gulf as it relates to laws of warfare.

After a jury of seven high-ranking career military officers was impaneled, Judge Russell instructed them that "[Dr. Huet-Vaughn's] matters of conscience are not relevant" to this case. Further, he told them that they could only consider whether Dr. Huet-Vaughn purposely quit her unit in order to avoid deployment—nothing else.

After deliberating for only an hour, the jury returned with a verdict of guilty. During the "extenuation and mitigation" phase of the court martial, when the jury is weighing the appropriate sentence to impose, Dr. Huet-Vaughn was able to offer a number of witnesses, including: Rev. John Swomley; actress Margot Kidder; Bill Monning, Executive Director of the International Physicians for Prevention of Nuclear War; Dr. Victor Sidel, past president and co-founder of the Physicians for Social Responsibility (PSR); Dr. Megan Passey, who led the Harvard Public Health School team that surveyed post-war damage to Iraq and its citizens; Dr. Gordon Livingston, a former anti-war Army doctor; Thomas Fox, editor of the National Catholic Reporter; *and Army Chaplain Col. Robert Burger, who endorsed Dr. Huet-Vaughn's application for discharge as a conscientious objector.*

Following this phase of the court-martial, the jury returned with a sentence of thirty months' imprisonment, dishonorable dismissal from the military, and the loss of all pay and benefits. Only one other Persian Gulf resister, Enrique Gonsalez (a Marine sentenced at Camp LeJuene, N.C.), received such a severe sentence.

As is the military practice (since there is no appellate bail), Captain Huet-Vaughn was immediately transferred the same day to the military prison at Ft. Leavenworth, KS. The convening authority does have the authority to order that a convicted GI not be confined pending appeal, but this is seldom done.

Upon arriving at Ft. Leavenworth's Disciplinary Barracks, Dr. Huet-Vaughn was confined in a maximum security cell for three weeks. During this period, she was virtually incommunicado, except for limited contact with her attorneys and family.

After three weeks, a hearing was held before the Initial Assignment Board. After reviewing her Initial Custody Classification Worksheet, which assigns points for various factors (such as prior criminal records, parole violations, etc.) Dr. Huet-Vaughn was placed on medium custody status.

According to the rating forms used by the Board, Dr. Huet-Vaughn was given two points for a "military offense," two points for having a sentence of 1-2 years, and one point for having a "prior criminal record" to wit, two minor traffic violations. Although five points is supposed to qualify an inmate for minimum custody "within the walls" of the prison, Dr. Huet-Vaughn was assigned instead, to medium custody.

Later, when she filed a complaint regarding the treatment of a traffic violation as a "prior criminal record" the prison re-evaluated her on December 20, 1991, using a new point system. This time, they came up with ten points, which is the cut-off point for "medium" custody.

On September 9, 1991, Amnesty International's International Secretariat in London, U.K., officially designated Yolanda Huet-Vaughn as a "prisoner of conscience" and called upon Amnesty International members throughout the world to petition General Daniel Christman, commander of Ft. Leonard Wood, to exercise clemency by reducing or ending her sentence.

Following the receipt of literally hundreds of letters, FAXs, and telephone calls from around the world, General Christman exercised his clemency authority on December 3, 1991 by reducing Dr. Huet-Vaughn's sentence from thirty to fifteen months. – Kate O. McLellan, '93

ARTICLE 32 HEARING
CAPTAIN DR. YOLANDA HUET-VAUGHN
MAY 6, 1991
TESTIMONY OF PROFESSOR FRANCIS A. BOYLE
FT. LEONARD WOOD, MO.

Mr. Font: The defense calls Professor Francis A. Boyle.

...

Captain Page: Mr. Boyle . . . to the investigating officer, he will swear you in.

Col. Franklin: Do you have a preference for an oath or an affirmation?

Prof. Boyle: Oath is fine.

. . . .

[Qualification as an Expert deleted.][1]

. . . .

LF: Can you tell us who Professor Baxter is?

PB: Professor Baxter was my teacher of the laws of war at Harvard Law School. At the end of the Second World War he was a military officer in the United States Army and was in charge of the Pentagon's division on international law. After he did that work he then went to the Harvard Law School where he taught courses on international law and the laws of war. He remained in the U.S. Army Reserves rising to the rank of Colonel; and the United States Army did request Professor Baxter to draft U.S. Army Field Manual 27-10 of 1956, the Laws of Armed Conflict, which is still the document in the field today that is binding on all U.S. military personnel in the United States Army.

LF: Did you study that field manual under Professor Baxter?

PB: He was my teacher of the laws of war, that's correct, and I was his top student when I was at Harvard Law School and later Professor Baxter became judge at the International Court of Justice, and unfortunately he died an early death.

. . . .

LF: . . . Professor Boyle, in your field of study do you do research, writing or thinking about the applicability of international law to international events?

PB: Well, that's what I've devoted my whole professional career to since oh, at least, the past 23 or 24 years, yes, is how do you apply international law to particularly situations of armed conflict where force is used or threatened to be used.

LF: I'm handing you what I would like to have marked as exhibit 2, which is the charge sheet, the cover to the charge sheet pertaining to Captain Yolanda Huet-Vaughn. Will you take a look at that?

. . . .

PB: Yes.

LF: Alright. Do you see the . . . offense that designates the word desertion?

PB: Yes, I do.

. . . .

LF: Can you tell us, Professor Boyle, whether or not there is a defense pertaining to this charge which is applicable to international law?

PB: Definitely. For sure. And it will take a bit to explain it but I'll do the best I can. I think the Captain here described it himself when he said did Dr. Huet-Vaughn absent herself without authority? And ...if you look at the law in court martial which I have done briefly it is what we criminal law professors call a specific intent crime. That means that beyond general *mens rea* the government must prove beyond a reasonable doubt a specific intent. And in the case of desertion, it would be that the defendant absented herself without authority, knew that she was doing that. And the government would have to prove that beyond a reasonable doubt. That's decided by the United States Supreme Court in *In re Winship* and *Mullaney vs. Wilbur*. In my opinion, then the issue is did the defendant have authority to absent herself under international law as incorporated into United States domestic law and also military law, Field Manual 27-10.

LF: Can you tell us Professor Boyle whether or not the Nuremberg Charter or the Nuremberg Principles apply to situations such as this?

PB: Definitely they do. The Nuremberg Charter and then the Judgment rendered under the Charter, and then followed up by . . . the Nuremberg Principles, that were approved by the International Law Commission of the United Nations, established very clearly that military personnel, an officer, enlisted personnel, have an obligation not to obey illegal orders, or orders to commit war crimes. And later on this was specified to mean that did they know to a moral certainty that orders given to them might be illegal, under the Nuremberg Principles, if they do, they are under an obligation not to obey those orders. You can find the same principle of law in Field Manual 27-10; you can also find the same principle of law in the Uniform Code of Military Justice. And I'll point out that goes back to the Nuremberg proceedings themselves, that is why that principle of law is both in Field Manual and the UCMJ.

LF: Professor Boyle, to this offense of desertion there is a lesser included offense of unauthorized absence, is that the case?

PB: That's correct, yes.

LF: Alright. And are you saying Professor Boyle in your opinion rather than being without authority the accused in this case had authority in taking the action she did?

PB: Yes, if you read through the court martial manual where they explain the elements of that charge as well, they point out that that is not a specific intent offense, however, it also makes it very clear that the defendant must have absented herself without authority. And that was the exact language used. So then that opens up the entire question of what authority did the defendant have to absent herself under the laws of war, which are binding on the United States Army, they're binding on all military personnel in this courtroom, they are even binding upon all civilians sitting in this courtroom. They are binding on the President of the United States of America himself; he's in the chain of command. They are binding on everyone. And so these charges directly open up that issue. What was her authority under the laws of war to absent herself from this particular military operation?

LF: Can you tell us Professor Boyle some of the laws that generate such authority pertaining to the Gulf Crisis?

PB: Well, of course, there are large numbers of laws that apply here. The first would be the United Nations Charter of 1945; the Hague Regulations of 1907, that are still binding on the United States military, that's a treaty, the supreme law of the land; the Kellogg-Briand Pact of 1928 that the United States and Iraq are both parties to, mandating a peaceful resolution of disputes; the Geneva Conventions of 1949 are directly on point; the Hague Air Rules of 1923 dealing with the conduct of aerial warfare that the United States government has accepted as binding, are directly relevant to this situation;

the Declaration of London of 1909 is relevant to the conduct of warfare by naval forces. Those are just the leading treaties and principles of law. Then second, all of these principles that I have discussed with you are also part of United States domestic law. This is not some abstraction off there in the sky. All this law has been fully incorporated into United States domestic law by Article VI of the United States Constitution, the so-called Supremacy Clause, saying that treaties are the supreme law of the land. And likewise, the U.S. Supreme Court has held in the *Belmont* and *Pink* cases that executive agreements, that is international agreements such as the Nuremberg Charter, that are not formally treaties within the meaning of the Constitution, are nevertheless the supreme law of the land, and that they are binding on all courts, whether civilian or military, sitting anywhere in the United States of America, or anywhere else subject to the jurisdiction of the United States of America. Likewise, the United States Supreme Court has held in the very famous *Paquet Habana* case, 1899, that customary international law, that is, law not necessarily expressed in treaties or formal agreements, is binding on all United States courts, whether civilian or military. These principles then, are not just principles of international law, they are also principles of United States constitutional law. And it is for that reason then, that when Judge Baxter drafted U.S. Army Field Manual 27-10, he incorporated all of this law and put it into U.S. Army Field Manual 27-10 and you can read it right there. And when that Field Manual was promulgated, it was made binding on all members of the United States Army, and indeed if you read it, arguably, it also makes it clear that it could be binding . . . on civilians and that under certain circumstances, civilians could be tried for war crimes, for violations of laws and customs of war. Though generally, the U.S. Army does not do that.

LF: I want you to assume, Professor Boyle, for the sake of this discussion, that Captain Yolanda Huet-Vaughn committed each of the acts that are reflected in the charge sheet in front of you. Are you saying that nonetheless she was authorized by international law to engage in those activities that give rise to this charge?

PB: Let me say first that the government must prove beyond a reasonable doubt the absence of authorization here. She doesn't have to prove anything. It is the government that must prove that she acted without authorization. The burden is upon the government, and that has been decided by the U.S. Supreme Court. Second, however, that being said, yes, that is I believe from what I've read here, that the defendant had a good faith belief that the war, the operation that she was going to be called upon to engage in, would result in the commission of war crimes and other violations of the international law, crimes against peace, crimes against humanity, war crimes, violations of the Geneva Conventions, the Hague Regulations, the Hague Rules of Air Warfare. And that under those circumstances, from what I've read of her public statements, she believed that she had an obligation not to participate in this operation. And again, from all my studies of international law going back to the Nuremberg Principles, it is made very clear that a soldier has a right to refuse to participate in a military operation if that soldier has a reasonable good faith belief that the soldier is going to be called upon to commit war crimes or other types of international crimes.

LF: Professor Boyle, I want you to assume that on January 9 of 1991, Captain Yolanda Huet-Vaughn stated publicly as follows, "A bombing raid over Baghdad, a city of over four million will not target only Saddam Hussein, but also the civilian population of whom two million are children. Are we as Americans, knowing this in advance, knowing that this is not fate but choice, willing to live with the moral burden of these deaths?" Professor Boyle, the question that I have for you based upon that hypothetical is, is that such a statement consistent with your testimony using your defenses in this case under international law?

PB: Definitely, yes. As a matter of fact, her statement directly raises a Nuremberg defense, namely, if you read the Nuremberg Charter, it says quite clearly that the wanton devastation of a city is a Nuremberg war crime. Nothing could be clearer; it is stated right in there. And what the defendant was doing here was saying I want no part of a military operation that is going to be resulting in a Nuremberg war crime. And indeed in my opinion she had good grounds to take this position. Earlier that fall General Dugan gave an interview to the press in which he stated quite openly and quite clearly that the bombing campaign for Iraq would consist of bombing downtown Baghdad. He said that. He also said it would consist of attempting to kill Saddam Hussein, his wife, and his mistress, o.k.? I remember noting to my students at the time when General Dugan said this, that if this were true, it is clearly a Nuremberg war crime. You cannot blow up downtown Baghdad. It is prohibited by the Nuremberg Principles. You cannot knowingly attempt to assassinate a head of state or head of government. That is prohibited by the Hague Regulations and an international convention to that effect. Let alone attempting to assassinate someone's wife and someone's mistress. In the aftermath of the war and the bombing campaign, the general consensus, at least in the public record, seems to be that the bombing campaign was conducted precisely as General Dugan said it was going to be conducted. So again, it would seem to me, that the defendant knew full well what was going to happen, and decided with full authority under international law, especially the Nuremberg Principles, to have nothing to do with it. And in my opinion that was her right.

LF: Professor Boyle, I am going to read to you the following, and I want you to assume pertaining to this discussion that Captain Yolanda Huet-Vaughn on February 2 of 1991 at a surrender rally and press conference stated as follows: "As a mother I am keenly aware of the long term medical and environmental consequences that may occur in the Middle East region and which may indeed have a global impact if war breaks out. A Jordanian physicist estimates that burning of the oil fields could last six months with over one million barrels of oil burning per day. This burning could generate pyrotoxins that could accelerate global warming by two decades." Is that statement, Professor Boyle, consistent with the defenses that you have raised pertaining to international law?

PB: Yes, it is now well recognized too, that the infliction of severe damage on the environment is an international crime in its own right. There has been expansion in the scope of international criminal law, the laws of war, to include that type of activity. You could see that, for example, in Geneva Protocol 1 of 1977. There is also the Environmental Modification Convention too. And again, as I interpret that statement which I had read, the doctor was saying that she wanted no part in a war that was going to result in severe devastation to the environment. And I should point out that based upon my research into documents that are available in the public record, it does appear 1) a severe amount of environmental damage was caused by the U.S. bombing campaign itself, that is a certain amount of the pollution that was put into the Persian Gulf was done because of U.S. bombing of tankers sitting in port and then 2) a certain amount, and again we don't know what amount, but a certain amount, perhaps a significant amount, of the environmental catastrophe in Kuwait from the destruction of the oil fields likewise came as a direct result of the U.S. bombing campaign. Number three, we also know as a matter of public record that the United States government had planned this, in the sense that they had studied what would be the environmental impact of a bombing campaign of Kuwait and Iraq. And they had run computer models, they had run computer models, to try to predict what would be the environmental impact of a bombing campaign, and its impact on things such as nuclear winter, global warming, and things of this nature. So all this, to the best of my knowledge, studying what is available in the public record, had been planned for, prepared, and despite whatever conclusions they reached, and the conclusions seem to be that there would be severe environmental damage, they went ahead with the bombing campaign anyway. And as I understand it here, the defendant is saying that she wanted no role to play in this.

LF: Professor Boyle, pertaining to the use of nuclear weapons, I want you to assume that Captain Yolanda Huet-Vaughn on February 2, 1991, at her surrender rally and press conference in Kansas City, stated as follows: "Perhaps the greatest medical catastrophe awaiting civilian and military personnel is the possible use of chemical, biological, or nuclear weapons. Never before have such vast arsenals of weapons of mass destruction been assembled." Can you tell us Professor Boyle the relevance, if any, of the deployment of nuclear weapons in the Gulf to any violations of international law?

PB: Clearly there were deployed to the Gulf several hundred nuclear weapons. They were there on the scene to be used if necessary. And this goes back to the so-called Carter Doctrine; when the Soviets invaded Afghanistan, President Carter stated that the U.S. government would use military force, and if necessary the implication was nuclear weapons, to prevent any outside power, as he put it, he was referring to the Soviet Union, from seizing Persian Gulf oil fields. So to the best of my knowledge, it is the official position of the United States government, that we are fully prepared to use nuclear weapons with respect to defending, as we put it, Persian Gulf oil fields. And those weapons were there on place, ready to be used if necessary as part of this war. And indeed, in several press statements if I remember correctly, the highest level officials of our land, including Secretary of Defense Cheney, refused to rule out the use of nuclear weapons during the course of this war. So it directly raised the Nuremberg issues of planning and preparation. Were we planning and preparing to use nuclear weapons here? From everything I've seen the answer is yes; we did not use them. As for the use of chemical weapons, the doctor pointed out, I have read as a matter of public record, that there was some use of chemical weapons by Iraq. We do not know precisely what were the casualties of U.S. military personnel in the Gulf. Indeed in my opinion I think the extent of casualties have been significantly underestimated on purpose here. I have very serious problems with the casualty figures as given out by the Pentagon. But, there were reports that chemical weapons were used on some scale by Iraqi forces, but again we have been so far looking into this and been unable to break down precisely what if any extent of U.S. casualties are attributable to chemical weapons. I do not have an answer to that question.

LF: Professor Boyle, does it make any difference that the charge sheet reflects that Captain Yolanda Huet-Vaughn according to the allegations quit her unit prior to the actual start of hostilities. In other words, was she still authorized under international law to take the action that she did?

PB: Well clearly she had every right not to participate in a war that she reasonably believed would result in numerous violations of the laws and customs of warfare, the Nuremberg Principles, the Hague Regulations, the Hague Rules of Aerial Warfare, etc., etc., certainly.

LF: Is it fair to say that international law can be broken down into two separate areas? One is the planning and preparation for war and the other is the actual conduct of the war itself.

PB: Yes, before Nuremberg the laws of war did not directly have incorporated within them what we criminal law professors call inchoate crimes. That is planning, preparation, conspiracy, solicitation, aiding and abetting, and things of that nature. What happened was this, that in the negotiation of the Nuremberg Charter that was undertaken by the United States government, we took our concept, the Anglo-American concept of inchoate crimes, and put it into the Nuremberg Charter. And here Justice Robert Jackson made it quite clear in his opening statement at Nuremberg that there is no point in, it makes little sense not to deal with inchoate planning, preparing, and conspiring to because if you wait until there is a war it is too late. It is very hard during the course of a war for military personnel to make decisions when they are in the heat of combat. So what you want to do is establish a body of law that applies before a war starts to try to prevent a war from starting. And so for that reason we, the U.S. government, put into international law, the laws of war, the notion of inchoate crimes. And indeed you can read that in U.S. Army Field Manual. Judge Baxter put it right in there. Aiding and abetting, planning, preparing, conspiring, incitement, these inchoate crimes are criminal activities in their own right. So as I understand from, you know, what the doctor was seeing here, and I think that this was a correct assessment, that at the time she decided not to report for duty, she believed that the U.S. government was planning and preparing to commit crimes under international law. And certainly under the Nuremberg Principles, if that was her reasonable good faith belief, she had a right if not a duty to absent herself from participation in such conduct.

CF: May I, I'm sorry, may I interrupt sir? You asked a question a few back and I didn't quite understand. I think it was something to the effect she quit her unit prior to authorization of hostilities?

LF: No, initiation of hostilities. In other words, the charge sheet reflects 30 or 31 December 1990, whereas the actual air war began January 16 or 17.

....

LF: The charge sheet reflects, according to the charge sheet, the allegations are that Captain Huet-Vaughn absented her unit at the end of December of 1990, alright? Actual hostilities, in terms of a shooting war had not started until January 17 of 1991. Do you follow me?

....

PB: Colonel, that was later. Congress authorized the use of military force, as it were, later. It was about two weeks or so after that. Yes, it was after the relevant time frame here when she absented herself. And indeed that raises the other issue which we have not yet had a chance to get to, namely, the lack of any type of Congressional authorization for what the President had done up until he got this resolution out of both Houses of Congress. The Constitution is quite clear that only Congress has the power to declare war. The War Powers Act made it very clear that the President was obliged to withdraw all U.S. military forces from the Persian Gulf within sixty days after their deployment, unless expressly authorized to keep them there by Congress. And the President refused to comply with the terms of the War Powers Act. So between arguably the expiration of that sixty day period and the authorization given by Congress, which is when the defendant acted here, the President had no authority to be doing what he was doing and indeed the law clearly said he had to pull those troops out. He simply paid no attention to it.

CF: One more and then I won't interrupt your basis here. When did, the

United Nations did something, they authorized the use of force. When did that happen? Can you, can you . . .

. . . .

PB: It was late November. First, the United Nations never authorized the use of force. In the negotiations leading up to the passage of Resolution 678 the United States government wanted to get a resolution that expressly authorized the use of force by that name. And both the Soviet government and the Chinese government said no, that they would veto any resolution that expressly authorized the United States government to use force. So for those reasons, what you ended up with was a resolution that basically referred to the preceding resolutions and said the United States government or other members of the U.N. could try to carry out, they had permission to carry out those earlier resolutions by all means necessary, but it never expressly authorized the use of force. And that you can see in the negotiating history of the resolution; the word use of force is not there. Just as when the President unilaterally imposed a blockade in August, the United Nations never authorized the imposition of a blockade. A blockade technically is an act of war under naval law. And it was never authorized by the United Nations. The President just did it.

LF: Professor Boyle, the defense in this case has requested that the Chairman of the Joint Chiefs of Staff, General Colin Powell, be brought forward to testify. Would his testimony be relevant in this case?

PB: Definitely, on two grounds. First, the issue of this war and the President, what appears to me certainly from the public record and indeed I think many people would agree, the President's rush to war raises the issue of a violation of the Kellogg-Briand Pact of 1928, the United Nations Charter of 1945 and the Nuremberg Charter, the concept of crime against peace. And all of this you can find in Army Field Manual 27-10 . . . This is binding law on U.S. military personnel. Now the latest reports indicate that General Powell strongly advised the President against going to war. He believed that economic sanctions would work and that they were the preferable alternative here for him to be followed. The President ignored that advice. Now it is true, of course, that under our Constitution civilian officials give the orders and the military carry them out unless they are illegal. Again, when you are indoctrinated into the military you are trained that you are under an obligation not to carry out any illegal order. But the key point for General Powell's testimony here would be did the President go to war against the advice of his top military advisor as mandated by law, and the opinion that this dispute with Iraq could have been resolved without resort to warfare? If General Powell can say, yes that is what I advised him, it then directly raises the question, did the President violate the Kellogg-Briand Pact, did he violate the United Nations Charter, did he commit a Nuremberg crime against peace as recognized by U.S. Army Field Manual 27-10? And if the answer to any of those questions is yes then certainly the defendant had every right in the world to have nothing at all to do with this operation. Second, according to the public record, again from what I have read, General Powell personally approved the target list for bombing sites in Baghdad itself, within the city of Baghdad. Now again, all this information are things that you read about in the papers, the *New York Times*, the *Washington Post*, the *Wall Street Journal*, the *Washington Times*. We don't know exactly for sure if it is true or if it isn't or whatever, but the information that has so far surfaced into the public record tends to indicate that he personally approved the target list. Well, if he did, all the accounts I have read of the bombing of Baghdad were that large amounts of civilian targets, civilian buildings were hit and were destroyed. And it raises the questions, what did General Powell think was going to be blown up in Baghdad when they were bombing Baghdad? Did he know that they were going to be blowing up civilian houses? What did he think he was ordering to be blown up? What was the target list that he was given? I should point out that under a Department of Defense directive, all plans for the use of U.S. military forces must be approved by a legal affairs officer. That is a DOD directive, I don't have the number here in the top of my head but it is there on the books. Well, did General Powell discuss this target list with his lawyers? Did he discuss the propriety of hitting any of these targets under the Hague Rules of aerial warfare or the Hague Regulations of 1907? I don't know. If you look at the results and read the reports of the bombing of Baghdad itself, it does not appear to me that this happened... but certainly in my opinion, all these issues are directly relevant to the defense here by Dr. Huet-Vaughn; that she did not want to participate in a war that would result in the bombing of Baghdad, as General Dugan said they were going to do. That clearly would violate the Nuremberg Principles, the Hague Regulations, constitute international crimes. In my opinion, General Powell has evidence that would be directly relevant to that question.

LF: Pertaining to Secretary of Defense Dick Cheney, the defense has also requested that he be brought forth to testify. Can you tell us what the expected testimony of Secretary Cheney would be?

PB: Well, again, he is directly in the chain of command. As you know it goes from the President to the Secretary of Defense and then from there to the Chairman of the Joint Chiefs of Staff, General Powell. It would get into questions, again, of what Secretary of Defense Cheney thought he was approving when he authorized war, when he transmitted these orders, apparently when he approved bombing lists, targeting lists, the deployment of nuclear weapons to the Gulf I'm sure could only take place with the approval of both the President and the Secretary of Defense. Again, I am simply here speculating as an expert, I don't have access to secret government information. All I have access to is what emerges in the public record. But certainly, Secretary Cheney would have large amounts of information as to what he approved, what he authorized with respect to this war, the actual conduct of the war itself, what advice he gave to the President as to preferring economic sanctions over warfare itself, also the state of readiness of U.S. forces to engage in warfare. As you know, General Waller, who was over in the Persian Gulf, and he was the Deputy Commander to Schwarzkopf, openly and publicly stated, on the public record, that U.S. military forces were not prepared to go to war early, when the President had decided to go to war. Again, this raises questions of why did the President so quickly go to war without exhausting the peaceful means for the resolution of this dispute as required by the United Nations Charter and general principles of international law. And did this decision to go to war result in needless casualties among U.S. military forces as well as horrendous casualties against Iraq, innocent Iraqi civilians, and I must point out, under the laws of war Iraqi civilians are completely innocent. There is no justification or excuse at all for what I have read are the massive casualties that did occur to Iraqi civilians as a result of the bombing campaign. As you know the Republican guards and the Iraqi army was martialed in Southern Iraq and Kuwait. If the United States government had bombed them exclusively to kingdom come, that probably would not have raised any questions, perhaps, with respect to laws of war violations. But blowing up Iraqi cities is a very different issue. And tomorrow, as I understand it, you will be having Ramsey Clark, former Attorney General of the United States, coming here to testify. He visited these Iraqi cities after the bombing campaign, all of them, or most of them. He took video tapes of the destruction, and from my speaking with Mr. Clark, although I have not been to Iraq myself, this was a campaign that as he saw it, and others who have been to Iraq too whose accounts I have read, seem to be directly targeting civilian centers, civilian population centers, civilian infrastructure. And if so, that would clearly be prohibited under the laws of war, U.S. Army Field Manual 27-10, and I believe Secretary Cheney would be able to shed some light as to what they really thought they were doing over there.

LF: Professor Boyle, pertaining to this matter of legal officers putting there [*sic*] sign-off or approval on bombing targets, can you tell us whether or not you had occasion to research the bombings in Libya, and whether or not there were irregularities pertaining to lawyers signing-off on bombing targets?

PB: Yes, yes, and again, I'm, I'm not, you know you have to understand here, I'm not standing accusing any officer one way or the other of anything. The issue here is the good faith belief of the defendant that crimes might be committed here. Mr. Clark and I were involved in the lawsuit relating to the bombing of Libya, of Tripoli and Bengazi [*sic*]. Mr. Clark was the attorney of record, he represented the victims of the bombing, he did not represent the government of Libya. And I was the international law advisor and consultant on that case. We turned up evidence, actually some reporters turned up evidence, which I believe is good evidence, that when the pilots were originally briefed on the bombings of Tripoli and Bengazi [*sic*], they were told that they were going to be striking military targets. At the last minute a new target list was substituted for the targeting list they had originally been given, and the pilots apparently realized that the targets on the new targeting list were civilian and not military targets. And several of them were quite upset over the fact that they were being ordered to go off on a bombing raid and hit what some of them knew to be civilian targets. I visited Tripoli. I saw what was blown up, and I can tell you they were not military targets. They blew up a part of Tripoli itself, a civilian area where hundreds of people live, was just blown up. They blew up the civilian airport that services Tripoli that I flew in. They did not blow up the military airport. The military airport is the old Wheelus Air Force Base, or the Wheelus Base that we used to have there. The Libyans used that as a military airport; they could have blown that up. They did not. They blew up the civilian airport. And then third, they blew up the Khaddafi residence, the man's home where he lived with his wife and his children. And I saw that too, I toured it and I visited. So, certainly, again, I am not casting blame here on anyone except to say based on prior performance the selection of bombing targets leaves much to be desired. And who authorized these targets? And was the Department of Defense directive followed with respect to all of the, any plans to the point of U.S. nuclear weapons being vetted by legal affairs officers? I don't know, but I think that all those questions are directly relevant to the defense of this defendant, whether or not she absented herself with authority under international law and the laws of war.

LF: So to summarize, pertaining to Secretary of Defense Dick Cheney, it is your testimony, is it not that this investigation would be relevant to this case?

PB: Definitely. And I should also point out U.S. Army Field Manual makes it very clear that someone such as Secretary of Defense Cheney, even though he does not wear a uniform, is nevertheless subject to the laws and customs of warfare. That is a civilian such as Cheney who is in the chain of command is himself obliged to obey the laws and customs of warfare. And in theory, he could be court-martialed, despite the fact that he is a civilian, since he is in the chain of command, he could be court-martialed in a military court for his conduct should such proceedings be brought.

LF: The defense has requested Secretary of the Army Michael Stone. Would he have testimony that would be relevant to this case?

PB: Well, again, to the conduct of hostilities, again, to the extent that he is within the chain of command, yes. I think that as I understand it you have, you know, the chain of command does go down, and as I understand it you have requested from the listings of the individuals, the people who are in the chain of command who would have knowledge.

LF: The defense has also requested Secretary of State James Baker. Would his testimony be relevant?

PB: . . . it goes back to the type of advice Powell was giving the President and Baker was giving the President. Again, the public record tends to indicate that General Powell and Secretary Baker were strongly encouraging the President not to resort to warfare. But to resort to the economic sanctions.

And for some reason the President discounted the advice that was given by both of them. Again, if that can be established, it raises the question of violation of the Kellogg-Briand Pact, that requires the exhaustion of all means for the peaceful resolution of disputes before force can be used; the United Nations Charter that requires the exhaustion of all means for the peaceful resolution of disputes before force can be used; and the Nuremberg Charter, that is a Nuremberg crime against peace, planning, preparation, or conspiracy to wage an aggressive war or a war in violation of other international treaties and agreements. And here I am not saying necessarily it would be a closer question whether or not this was an aggressive war but clearly, it seems to me, this would be a war in violation of international treaties and agreements, that President Bush decided to go off and to wage. And Secretary Baker certainly would have testimony that is relevant to establishing some of those issues, at least the bearing on the reasonability of the defendant's good faith here. And again I'll point out these principles are in the U.S. Army Field Manual 27-10. You can read them right there. It recognizes the existence of a Nuremberg crime against peace and the definition is right there in the Field Manual, you can read it.

LF: By the way, Professor Boyle, these are mixed issues of law and fact.

PB: Oh yes, definitely. Of course, I am just stating my opinion here based on what facts are available in the public record. To the extent that there are more facts that can be obtained through other witnesses, or subpoenas, or other documents, I think that that would have a substantial bearing on the defendant's case. What evidence has surfaced in the public record so far is severely disturbing to me as an expert on international law as to what the President ordered here.

LF: The defense has also requested that General H. Norman Schwarzkopf be brought forward on this investigation. Would his testimony be relevant?

PB. Yes, for two reasons. First, of course, he is in the chain command and he, again, would have direct evidence and knowledge as to what were the battle plans that were formulated and developed for the conduct of hostilities in this war. Some of which at least to me, specifically the bombing campaign, appeared to be a direct violation of international law, the Nuremberg Principles, the Hague Rules of Aerial Warfare, the Hague Regulations, again incorporated into the U.S. Army Field Manual. Secondly, however, is another reason. It is a matter of public record, to the best of my knowledge that I have been able to determine relying on documents that experts in my field rely upon, that shortly after the termination of the Iraq-Iran war, then General Schwarzkopf was put in charge of revising U.S. war plans for military intervention into the Persian Gulf. And he was in charge of revising these plans roughly from perhaps 1989, sometime in early 1989, until the spring of 1990. In the spring of 1990 General Schwarzkopf was appointed to head U.S. Central Command. And at that point in time then the crisis between Iraq and Kuwait and the United States began in the spring of 1990. It is my opinion that General

Schwarzkopf would have definite knowledge as to whatever plans the highest officials in the United States government at that time, including both the Reagan administration and the Bush administration, had for waging war in the Persian Gulf. Shortly after Schwarzkopf arrived then, the crisis occurred and you saw the activation, the activation of the war plans that General Schwarzkopf had spent a year and a half to two years developing. And clearly, it would ... definitely be relevant to the defense of Dr. Huet-Vaughn what those war plans said. What did they contemplate? How, when, where did they contemplate using force? Were these war plans approved in accordance with the DOD directive requiring that they be signed off by legal affairs officers? I don't have answers to those questions, but I take it that General Schwarzkopf would.

LF: The defense has requested former President Ronald Reagan. Would his testimony be relevant to this investigation?

PB: Well, again, yes, for the reason that I've indicated. After the defeat, well after the end of the Iran-Iraq war, as you know it ended by means of U.S. military intervention, naval intervention. And I should point out that that naval intervention was opposed by the Pentagon. The Armed Forces opposed this intervention, and indeed at the time Secretary of the Navy James Webb, whom you have also requested here, was against sending U.S. military forces over to the Persian Gulf. This advice was overruled by President Reagan; he decided to send the naval flotilla over there. As you know the *Stark* was blown up and then in turn the *Vincennes* blew up the Iran airbus. And shortly thereafter the war terminated. As best as can be determined from the public record, somewhere in there a decision was made to then start revising U.S. war plans for military intervention in the Middle East and perhaps including Iraq itself. Again, I don't know. But certainly President Reagan would know; Secretary Webb would probably know. Again, I can't say. These are simply questions I have or what I, you know, as a professor and expert call working hypotheses. But certainly plans were being made at somewhere around that time for military operation in the Gulf. I mean look, you don't move a half million man army starting in August. You have to have a plan. And that plan was there, it had been developed. Indeed technically it goes back all the way to the Carter administration with the so-called rapid deployment force, which later became renamed U.S. Central Command. So, what we see here in the war in the Persian Gulf is the unfolding of planning that goes back at least to the Carter administration. Now the capability to do what we saw done in the Persian Gulf was developed throughout the 1980s during the course of the Reagan administration. But the decision to develop that capability goes at least back to the Carter administration.

LF: The defense in this case has requested, I might as well finish with President Bush pertaining to this subject area. The defense has requested that President Bush be brought forward. Would his testimony be relevant pertaining to international law defenses, and if so, how?

PB: Well, again, he is the Commander in Chief of the Armed Forces under the U.S. Constitution, as he is proud of saying, but as Commander in Chief he is also subject to the laws and customs of warfare including U.S. Army Field Manual 27-10 and also the Nuremberg Principles. And then the key question here is when the President made the various decisions that he did do, did he pay any attention at all to Field Manual 27-10, to the Nuremberg Principles, in the decision to go to war, in the decision to use the types of forces that were used, particularly with respect to the bombing campaign that in my opinion raise serious questions of violations of fundamental Nuremberg Principles. So yes, his testimony is relevant, and indeed it has since come out in the public record in the last week now that the President apparently made a decision to go to war quite early on, and didn't tell the American people. And pushed on against the advice given to him by his top military personnel, General Powell, Secretary of State, arguably others, I don't know. But clearly, certainly the President himself would be able to clarify these matters. And they all relate definitely back to the defense here, well not the defense but the position of the defendant, that she did not want to participate in this war because of the numerous problems that it would raise and clearly was going to raise at the time she decided to act here, under international law, under international criminal law.

LF: Professor Boyle, the defense has requested various documents be provided by the investigating officer or by trial counsel, the prosecution in this case, and I just want to read you a couple to find out whether or not they are relevant in this case. Number 12 on my request (. . .) requesting any and all staff studies, after action reports or other writings by whatever name or label relative to the number of civilian hospitals destroyed in Baghdad and the number of Iraqi (citizens) killed in Operation Desert Shield/Storm. Now, would the defense obtaining a report pertaining to the destruction of civilian hospitals in Baghdad be relevant in this case?

PB: Yes, definitely. Hospitals are specially protected under the laws of war and special steps must be taken to avoid any damage to hospitals up to and including staying away from relatively insignificant military targets anywhere near the hospital. And again, if I remember the doctor's statement correctly, she did not want to be involved in any of this type of activity. And clearly, if this type of activity was engaged in, if there was planning to hit targets in the general vicinity of hospitals, it raises the question, you know, did they run this, the planners who drew up the target list, did they run this by their lawyers? What information did the lawyers have? Did they know that when they were trying to blow up X that there was a hospital right across the street that could be blown up too in the process. Under the laws of war, they had to weight [*sic*] that and arguably avoid blowing up whatever targets they were hitting. But again, I can't say here, you know, what people knew, when they knew it, how they knew it. But as I understand it, all of this was documented in great detail. There were tasking orders given on all the targeting, arguably as I understand it, lawyers did look apparently at some of this stuff. . . . I take it these documents would shed some light on all these issues.

LF: The defense has also requested any and all staff studies, before action or after action reports or other writings by whatever name or label relative to the deployment and/or potential use of nuclear weapons by the United States or coalition countries in the Persian Gulf. Is that information relevant to this case?

PB: Well, sure. And again you'll note the doctor stated that she was afraid that nuclear weapons would be used during the course of these hostilities. And I should point out that she had a reasonable belief for that basis. It's standing U.S. policy going back to the Carter administration that the United States government would be prepared to use nuclear weapons in the Persian Gulf. And indeed, at the time when the rapid deployment force was first being put up, put together, and it only consisted of twenty-five, thirty thousand men, it was openly acknowledged that the only way those men could be defended, if they were put in place, was by the use of nuclear weapons. So again, I think those documents would go to the reasonable good faith belief of Doctor Huet-Vaughn as to why she did not wish to participate in this operation.

LF: Furthermore, the defense has requested all staff studies, before action reports, assessments or other writings by whatever name concerning plans to destroy electricity, water, and other basic services in Baghdad, and/or other cities in Iraq and/or Kuwait. Is this information relevant?

PB: Again, definitely yes. The, all the reports I have read indicate that most of the electrical generating centers, water filtration plants, and a good deal of the economic infrastructure that served primarily the civilian population of Iraq, not the military, most of the military was down at the border, but the civilians, were specifically targeted for destruction. And as I understand it, Mr. Clark will be presenting direct, first-hand evidence of this destruction in his testimony tomorrow. If those targets were specifically selected and stated as such in whatever the tasking orders were here, that would raise serious violations of the laws and customs of warfare that prohibit specifically targeting civilian populations as such or things that they are dependent upon, such as dams, dikes, electrical generating stations, water purification plants, and things of that nature. Again, I don't know what are in those documents. I am aware that they do exist. And it seems to me that if you got documents indicating that the Pentagon was specifically targeting civilian population centers, that would go directly to Dr. Huet-Vaughn's position here, that she did not want to participate in that type of war because it would constitute a war crime. She wanted nothing to do with it. And again, in my opinion, if those facts are there, that would certainly have been her right under the Nuremberg Principles and also under the UCMJ.

LF: Professor Boyle, are you aware that inoculation programs took place pertaining to Operation Desert Storm/Desert Shield?

PB: Yes, I am.

LF: I want you to assume for the sake of this discussion, that one of the reasons why physician Huet-Vaughn refused to participate in Operation Desert Shield/Desert Storm was because of her objections as a physician to inoculating persons with secret shots and being part of that program. Could you tell us whether or not there is any basis under international law for an objection along those lines?

PB: Yes, and again the answer is definitely yes. And here let me state I have special expertise there in biological warfare. I was the fellow who drafted the Biological Weapons Anti-Terrorism Act of 1989 that President Bush himself signed into law last year [*sic*], drafted it and I got it through Congress. And I am Counsel with a group called the Council for Responsible Genetics. And so I'm, although not a scientist myself, very actively involved in the question of biological and chemical warfare. To the best of my knowledge, there was absolutely no evidence at all that Iraq had any type of biological weapon. The best evidence I had and everyone else had was that Iraq did have chemical weapons but there was no evidence at all that Iraq had biological weapons. Here, the troops were forcibly inoculated for two types of alleged biological weapons. They were given an anthrax toxin and a botulin toxin. First, there was absolutely no evidence at all, anywhere in the public record or any hearing that I had ever heard of that Iraq had any type of botulin biological weapon. None. As for anthrax, the only evidence that existed was not that Iraq had an anthrax biological weapon, but rather Senator McCain had stated on the floor of the Senate that he had evidence to believe that a German subsidiary of a U.S. multinational had sold a small quantity of anthrax to Iraq. That's all the evidence that is available in the public record. Well, selling a small quantity of anthrax is one thing, for whatever reason who knows why, whether they were studying it, whether they were going ahead and actually develop an anthrax biological weapon, I don't know. But it is a long way from getting a small quantity of anthrax to being in a position to field an anthrax biological weapon that would create a threat to U.S. troops. And indeed the chemical weapons were far more effective, if they wanted to use weapons of mass destruction, the chemical weapons that they had, than anthrax, which would have been very difficult for anyone to control. For example, both our government and the British government had looked into using anthrax as a biological weapon and we've ruled it out. You really can't control it. So, when I read of this inoculation program I simply was astounded, as an expert on biological warfare. All I could conclude was that a high level decision had been made somewhere, and I don't know by whom but we need to find out, to use U.S. troops as guinea pigs to try on them untested vaccines for anthrax and botulin. And I should point out botulin is one of the most virulent poisons known to man; just a small quantity will kill you, a very small quantity. And I was amazed to find out that with almost no evidence at all, large numbers of U.S. troops were forcibly vaccinated without their consent for these two types of biological agents, neither of which materialized in the Persian Gulf war and in the aftermath of the war there is absolutely no evidence at all from anyone that Iraq has or does indeed have or will have either a botulin weapon or an anthrax weapon. Now this gets into another area of international criminal law known as the Nuremberg Code. And the Nuremberg Code was drawn up in reaction to experimentation by Nazi doctors on people during the Second World War to prevent this from ever happening again. And one of the principles there is that you cannot try experimental vaccines on people without their informed consent. And that's exactly what happened here. U.S. troops were used as guinea pigs. They were not given informed consent, indeed they were ordered to be inoculated. And if that is true, and from everything I've seen in the public record it is true, this is a Nuremberg crime, that the President or someone perpetrated on his own troops, *on his own troops.*

LF: Professor Boyle, would it be relevant to the defense in this case to obtain data on the number of persons who were vaccinated. How many persons who were vaccinated died; how many persons had adverse reactions?

PB: Definitely, definitely. Again, as I understand it, you'll be having Dr. Victor Sidel come and testify. Dr. Sidel is a medical doctor, I am not. My knowledge simply comes from my working as a lawyer in these areas, as an international lawyer and advisor to scientists on these questions. But clearly if you have any mass inoculation campaign, if you get the number, people, scientists will be able to estimate and predict how many will suffer an adverse reaction of some type. So that whenever the Pentagon went ahead with these orders to inoculate however many troops they were going to inoculate they probably had a statistical idea that X number of soldiers would have an adverse reaction and that Y number of soldiers would die. And that's what always happens on mass inoculations. A certain number of people, statistically predictable number, will suffer an adverse reaction, and a small number, but still a statistically predictable number when you get up to a large scale, high enough, will die. I have not seen that type of evidence. I don't know if the Pentagon accumulated that type of evidence. I don't know if they even bothered to make a statistical study as to how many adverse reactions and deaths would result from this inoculation campaign. Clearly, they should have. If they didn't I think they were criminally negligent, whoever was in charge of this program. But again, it raises the most serious questions of Nuremberg accountability under the Nuremberg Code on Medical Ethics for what was going on here. And again, as I understand the position of Dr. Huet-Vaughn, she believed that if she went and participated in this operation she would be called upon to engage in activities that violated the code of medical ethics. And certainly under the Nuremberg Code there are good grounds to support that position.

LF: Can you tell us please, Professor Boyle, how the Nuremberg Code differs from the Nuremberg Charter?

PB: Yes. The . . . Nuremberg Charter is a treaty, sorry, it's an international executive agreement that the United States government is a party to. You can find it in U.S. Statutes at Large. It is an executive agreement that is the supreme law of the land under the *Belmont* and *Pink* cases decided by the U.S. Supreme Court. The Nuremberg Code . . . was drawn up after the Second World War by medical doctors to put into the code of medical ethics certain prohibitions to prevent a repetition of what Nazi doctors did to innocent civilians, the type of experimentation that they engaged in with respect to innocent civilians or captured POWs during the Second World War.
. . . .

LF: I would just like to ask a few questions in summation of Professor Boyle. Is it fair to state in your judgment having reviewed the charge sheet in this case, having researched some of the law involved, having investigated as an international law professor the legalities having to do with the Persian Gulf Crisis, that in your judgment Captain Huet-Vaughn was authorized rather than having conducted herself without authorization?

PB: Yes, that's what I'm saying. And in any event I would say that it is clear that the government must prove beyond a reasonable doubt that she absented herself without authority. And there is certainly more than a reasonable doubt here as to her authority. So I would leave it at that, that I believe she had a reasonable good faith belief in her authority not to get involved in what was clearly going to be happening here.

LF: In fact, Professor Boyle, is it a defense under international law that a person followed orders, is that a justification for any crime?

PB: No, as a matter of fact, superior orders is not a defense to the commission of war crimes. That principle of law goes back to the predecessor to Field Manual 27-10 that was issued by the old War Department back in 1941 which I have also written about. And they had a revision, Revision 1, which was added in the fall of 1944, somewhere in there, in contemplation of victory in the Second World War, and in contemplation of trying defeated Nazi and Japanese war criminals. And what this edition one, Rev. 1, stated quite clearly, superior orders is no defense. It can be considered in mitigation of punishment but superior orders is no defense to guilt for the commission of a war crime. That principle of law was then later enshrined in the Nuremberg Charter and the Judgment and the Principles that superior orders is no defense. And then later, Judge Baxter, following this authority put it in U.S. Army Field Manual 27-10 of 1956. You can read it there. Superior orders is no defense. And so, just because someone was ordered to do something illegal that is no defense although again it can be considered in mitigation of punishment.

. . . .

LF: Do you have any questions Colonel Franklin?

CF: Mine is a more general question and I won't attach any specifics. I was just wondering if you could take the United Nations, the work they did prior to the Gulf War Crisis and compare that with the body of international law that you've been taught. I'm not certain if I've understood the direction if you're suggesting that there's a higher law; I mean, I know where you're taking us with the international law, I'm not sure where the United Nations and international law meet, or if one supercedes or what, I'm just unclear on that.

PB: Right. And that is a very valid point. The military law, and again you can read this in U.S. Army Field Manual 27-10, distinguishes between what we law professors call jus ad bellum, the right to go to war or the right to use force, and what is called the jus in bello or the laws of war. And there is an overlapping of the two to be sure. Typically all wars, whether you have a right to use force or not, whether you were justified in the first place in using force, all wars are governed by the laws of war. That generally consists of the Hague Regulations, all the authorities I've discussed today, are the laws of war. And they bind U.S. soldiers whenever they fight in any war; indeed they even bind them in peacetime, as long as they are active duty military personnel. To prohibit even planning, preparation, conspiracy to commit a war crime, and again you can read that in the Field Manual, it's made very clear there. Now, that being said the right to go to war, to use force is governed by a separate body of law, and that is the United Nations Charter as you were correctly groping toward. Alright, now what the Security Council authorized under these circumstances is subject to legitimate debate. As I have pointed out here however, it is very clear they never authorized the use of force. That language was stricken from the Security Council resolution by the Soviets and the Chinese, who said if it was in there they would veto it. O.K. But even if you wish to interpret that Security Council resolution as authorization to use force, the Security Council has no authorization to allow or permit or condone violations of the laws and customs of warfare. They apply anytime, whether it's an offensive war or a defensive war or a U.N. Security Council authorized war. And there is a case directly on point here when the United Nations sent a peacekeeping force to the Congo back in the 1960's of approximately 25,000 men, and at some point these forces no longer were engaged in a peacekeeping mission but were ordered on offensive operations. Now these forces were subject to the direct control of the U.N. as opposed to what happened in the Persian Gulf when these were all U.S. forces, they were not controlled by the U.N. And some of these troops committed atrocities, violations of the laws and customs of warfare. And the U.N. looked into this matter, and the World Court looked into the matter and concluded that they were bound by the laws and customs of warfare. And that therefore the United Nations had to pay damages, reparations for war crimes committed by the United Nations troops. So, no matter how you want to look at the resolutions of the Security Council [they] cannot, for example, authorize violations of the laws of war. And indeed nothing in any of the Security Council resolution did. Nothing in there authorized blowing up Iraqi cities. Nothing in there authorized using U.S. troops for experiment, as guinea pigs for experimental vaccines in violation of the Nuremberg Code. Most of the things I'm talking about here were never authorized by any U.N. Security Council resolution. And the same later on with respect to the Congressional resolution that was passed after Dr. Huet-Vaughn's activities. They did not authorize and indeed they cannot authorize violations of the laws and customs of warfare. No attempt to do so was made. Field Manual 27-10 is still on the books, it is still operative policy today by the Department of the Army. And the Navy has a similar manual, and the Air Force has another manual. So they are all there. This is valid binding law that I have discussed here today. But it's a different body. As I said, there is one body the laws of war, another body the right to go to war. And the intersection comes if you decide to go to war without exhausting all means for the peaceful resolution of disputes, in violation of the Kellogg-Briand Pact, in violation of the United Nations Charter. That arguably could be a war crime too, a separate type of crime. The laws of war typically deal with what law professors and military lawyers will call war crimes. But there are other types of international crimes as well, crimes against peace and crimes against humanity. And again, that category you can find in U.S. Army Field Manual 27-10. Professor Baxter put it in there and he simply tracked the gradations of international crimes found in the Nuremberg Charter. Now the Field Manual says quite clearly after defining these other offenses, crime against peace, crime against humanity, and war crimes, it said normally it is the case that military personnel are only held accountable for war crimes at best. Because a decision to resort to war, to go to war, of course, in our society is not made by the military. It's made by the civilians under the Constitution, the President, Secretary of Defense, his cabinet, whoever. They're the ones who decide. So the Field Manual did not deal extensively or attempt to deal extensively with responsibility by elected officials, but it made it very clear they're accountable too. So the bulk of the Field Manual deals with war crimes. But it also recognizes that the decision to go to war, either wage a war of aggression, and I'm not saying that what happened here was a war of aggression, but a war in violation of other treaties or commitments, such as the Kellogg-Briand Pact, the United Nations Charter could be a crime against peace. Does that try to clarify it?

CF: That helps.

.. . . .

LF: Thank you very much Professor Boyle. We don't have any further questions at this time.

PB: Thank you.

Chapter Four

Petition on Behalf of the Children of Iraq Submitted to the United Nations Charging President Bush and U.S. Authorities with Genocide

Arab Studies Quarterly, Vol. 23, No. 4 (Fall 2001), EDITOR'S NOTE: *In September of 1991 Francis Boyle asked the Coalition to Stop U.S. Intervention in the Middle East to submit an Indictment, Complaint, and Petition for Relief from Genocide by President George Herbert Walker Bush and the United States of America, which he had prepared on behalf of the 4.5 million children of Iraq. Professor Boyle filed the Complaint at the request of several Iraqi mothers whose children were dying as a result of the sanctions. The Petition was submitted to the Secretary General of the U.N., members of the General Assembly, the Economic and Social Council, the Commission on Human Rights, the Sub-Commission on Prevention of Discrimination and Protection of Minorities, UNESCO, and UNICEF.*

Boyle's petition reviewed the factual situation confronting the children of Iraq including malnutrition, starvation, disease, and death, and details the violations of international law upon which this Claim is based. The relief asked for included a lifting of the sanctions against Iraq, massive provision of international humanitarian relief, and compensation to the victims of the policies described.

Boyle has stated, based on the then current—and ongoing—devastating situation for Iraq's children, "Like unto a pirate, the Respondent George Bush is hostis humani generis—*the enemy of all humankind." Boyle asked for an urgent review of this Petition and that the appropriate organs of the United Nations, as well its member states, institute criminal proceedings against President Bush for committing the international crime of genocide against the children of Iraq. The transcript of Boyle's Indictment, Complaint, and Petition for Relief from Genocide follows.*

Despite the best professional efforts by Professor Boyle, who is working pro bono *on this matter, so far the entire United Nations Organization has refused to act upon this Complaint on behalf of the Children of Iraq.*

TO: THE SECRETARY GENERAL OF THE UNITED NATIONS, THE MEMBERS OF THE GENERAL ASSEMBLY, THE ECONOMIC AND SOCIAL COUNCIL, THE COMMISSION ON HUMAN RIGHTS, THE SUB-COMMISSION ON PREVENTION OF DISCRIMINATION AND PROTECTION OF MINORITIES, UNESCO, UNICEF, THE HEADS OF ALL NGO'S, ETC.

RE: INDICTMENT, COMPLAINT AND PETITION BY THE 4.5 MILLION CHILDREN OF IRAQ FOR RELIEF FROM GENOCIDE BY PRESIDENT GEORGE W. BUSH AND THE UNITED STATES OF AMERICA

EXCELLENCY:

On behalf of The 4.5 Million Children of Iraq, I hereby submit to you this Indictment, Complaint, and Petition for Relief from Genocide by President George Bush and the United States of America (hereinafter referred to as the "Respondents"). This Indictment, Complaint, and Petition accuses the Respondents (1) of committing the international crime of genocide against The 4.5 Million Children of Iraq in violation of the International Convention on the Prevention and Punishment of the Crime of Genocide of 1948 and in violation of the municipal legal systems of all civilized nations in the world; (2) of a gross and consistent pattern of violations of the most fundamental human rights of The 4.5 Million Children of Iraq, as recognized and guaranteed to them by the Universal Declaration of Human Rights of 1948; (3) of the complete negation and denial of all the rights guaranteed to The 4.5 Million Children of Iraq by the 1989 Convention on the Rights of the Child; and (4) of the systematic violation of the special protections of international humanitarian law guaranteed to The 4.5 Million Children of Iraq by the Fourth Geneva Convention of 1949 and Additional Protocol I thereto of 1977.

Under the human rights provisions of the United Nations Charter, the Universal Declaration of Human Rights, the Genocide Convention, the Children's Convention, and the Fourth Geneva Convention and Protocol I, The 4.5 Million Children of Iraq are proper parties to invoke the jurisdiction of the United Nations and its various organs in requesting the following Relief in order to be relieved from the inhuman, degrading, cruel, criminal, and genocidal conditions perpetrated upon them by the Respondents. The 4.5 Million Children of Iraq demand (1) the termination of the international economic embargo and all forms of bilateral economic sanctions against Iraq; (2) the massive provision of international humanitarian relief required in order to save themselves from death, disease, malnutrition, starvation, and extermination at the hands of the Respondents; (3) monetary compensation for the harm done to them as well as all other forms of relief deemed necessary and appropriate; and (4) the institution of criminal proceedings against Respondent Bush for committing the international crime of genocide by the appropriate international organs as well as by all States of the World Community under their respective municipal legal systems.

The 4.5 Million Children of Iraq have set forth in the attached Indictment, Complaint, and Petition all of the Facts necessary to constitute a prima facie case against the Respondents for genocide; grave breaches of the Fourth Geneva Convention and Protocol I; and a gross and consistent pattern of violations of the Universal Declaration of Human Rights and the International Convention on the Rights of the Child. Wherefore, The 4.5 Million Children of Iraq demand that the United Nations and its organs immediately undertake a full investigation of the matters presented in this Indictment, Complaint and Petition, and subsequently authorize a complete and public disclosure of all evidence and findings of fact at the conclusion of such investigation. I would appreciate receiving a formal acknowledgment of your receipt of the attached Indictment, Complaint, and Petition by The 4.5 Million Children of Iraq at the address listed above as well as all further communications related to this matter.

THE PEOPLES AND COUNTRIES OF THE WORLD MUST NOT TURN THEIR EYES AWAY IN SHAME FROM IRAQ AS HUMANKIND APPROACHES THE DAWN OF THE NEXT MILLENNIUM OF ITS PARLOUS EXISTENCE. AS IRAQ'S CHILDREN GO, SO GOES THE ENTIRE WORLD!

RESPECTFULLY SUBMITTED
ON BEHALF OF THE 4.5 MILLION CHILDREN OF IRAQ,

FRANCIS A. BOYLE
PROFESSOR OF INTERNATIONAL LAW

MEMBER OF THE BARS OF THE SUPREME JUDICIAL COURT OF THE COMMONWEALTH OF MASSACHUSETTS AND OF THE SUPREME COURT OF THE UNITED STATES OF AMERICA

DATED: SEPTEMBER 18, 1991

. . . .

RE: INDICTMENT, COMPLAINT, AND PETITION BY THE 4.5 MILLION CHILDREN OF IRAQ FOR RELIEF FROM GENOCIDE BY PRESIDENT GEORGE BUSH AND THE UNITED STATES OF AMERICA.

I.

INTRODUCTION

1. The Applicants herein, THE 4.5 MILLION CHILDREN OF IRAQ, invoke the jurisdiction of the United Nations and its organs by virtue of the provisions of the United Nations Charter, the Universal Declaration of Human Rights, and the International Convention on the Prevention and Punishment of

the Crime of Genocide, and file this Indictment, Complaint, and Petition on their own behalf. The Applicants charge the Respondents with committing the international crime of genocide against The 4.5 Million Children of Iraq. Applicants pray for the termination of the international economic embargo and all forms of bilateral economic sanctions against Iraq, and to secure the massive provision of international humanitarian relief required in order to save themselves from death, disease, malnutrition, starvation, and extermination at the hands of the Respondents. Applicants also pray for monetary compensation for the harm done to them and all other forms of relief deemed necessary and appropriate. Finally, Applicants request the institution of criminal proceedings against the Respondent George Bush for committing the international crime of genocide by the appropriate international organs and by all States of the World Community under their respective municipal legal systems.

II.

THE FACTS

2. The Applicants are The 4.5 Million Children of Iraq.

3. The Respondents are (1) George Bush, President of the United States of America, in both his official and personal capacities, and (2) the United States of America, a Permanent Member of the United Nations Security Council.

4. The Respondents are the Person and State primarily responsible for the imposition of the now year-long international economic embargo and bilateral economic sanctions against Iraq.

5. Reports from the United Nations, the Physicians for Human Rights, the International Red Cross, a Harvard Study Team, other independent organizations, and private U.S. citizens have documented the fact that unless the economic sanctions imposed against Iraq are immediately lifted and Iraq is allowed to buy and import food, medicine, and equipment, especially for power generation, hundreds of thousands of innocent Iraqi civilians will die in the upcoming months.

6. A Harvard Study Team estimates that at least 170,000 Iraqi children under the age of five will die within the next year from the delayed effects of the war in the Persian Gulf if the imposition of the sanctions continues.

7. This is a conservative estimate and does not include tens of thousands of Iraqi children above the age of five who are expected to die from similar causes.

8. The Catholic Relief Service estimates that more than 100,000 Iraqi children will die from malnutrition and disease in the upcoming months

due to the economic embargo and destruction of the war, and the United Nations Children's Fund estimates that 80,000 Iraqi children may die from these causes.

9. Malnutrition has become severe and widespread in Iraq since imposition of the embargo and the war due to severe food shortages and the inflation of food prices of up to 1000%, which has effectively priced many Iraqis, especially the poor and disadvantaged, out of the food market.

10. Cholera, typhoid, and gastroenteritis have become epidemic throughout Iraq since the war due to the critical scarcity of medicine and the inability of Iraq to process sewage and purify the water supply.

11. The system of medical care has broken down in Iraq, resulting in the closure of up to 50% of Iraq's medical facilities due to acute shortages of medicines, equipment, and staff.

12. The incapacitation of 18 of Iraq's 20 power plants during the war is a principal cause of the deterioration in public health due to the resultant inability of Iraq to process sewage, purify its water supply, and supply electricity to health facilities.

13. The health care crisis cannot be addressed without the reconstruction of electrical facilities that enable the purification of water and treatment of sewage.

14. Before the economic embargo of Iraq, three quarters of the total caloric intake in Iraq was imported and, moreover, 96% of Iraqi revenue to pay for imports, namely food and medicine, was derived from the exportation of oil now prohibited under the embargo.

15. The summer heat in Iraq has both accelerated the spread of disease and impeded its treatment due to the lack of refrigeration facilities even in hospitals.

16. The acute shortages of food in Iraq, the inflation of up to 1000% in food prices caused by these shortages, the critical scarcity of medicine, and the essential need to reconstruct Iraq's capacity to generate electricity to enable sewage treatment and water purification cannot be addressed or rectified without Iraq's re-entry into global commerce, at present effectively prohibited by the economic sanctions.

17. The immediate lifting of the sanctions would drastically reduce the number of Iraqi children who will die in the upcoming months from malnutrition and disease and would relieve the suffering of the innocent Iraqi population which is now bearing the burden of the embargo.

18. Approximately 500 Iraqi children are dying each day from disease, malnutrition, and lack of proper medical treatment due to the continuation of the international economic embargo and bilateral economic sanctions upon Iraq that have been organized and imposed by the Respondents.

III.

CONTENTIONS

19. The Harvard Study Team Report, *Public Health in Iraq After the Gulf War,* estimated that as of May 1991, 55,000 additional deaths of Iraqi children under five had already occurred because of the Gulf Crisis, and projected that at least 170,000 Iraqi children under five will die in the coming year from the delayed effects of the Gulf Crisis. The Study also emphasized that these projections are conservative: "In all probability, the actual number of deaths of children under five will be much higher."

20. The continuation of multilateral and bilateral economic sanctions against Iraq prevents the massive infusion of international humanitarian assistance necessary to prevent these mortality projections from becoming a reality. The Harvard Report directly raises the question whether Respondents are responsible for the commission of the international crime of genocide against the Applicants, The 4.5 Million Children of Iraq, because of their obstinate insistence that economic sanctions be maintained in order to produce the deposition of the President of Iraq despite the fact that the original purpose for their imposition was achieved with the so-called "liberation" of Kuwait.

21. Respondent United States of America is a Contracting Party to the International Convention on the Prevention and Punishment of the Crime of Genocide of 1948, which will hereinafter be referred to as "the Genocide Convention" for sake of convenience.

22. Article I of the Genocide Convention provides that the Contracting Parties confirm that genocide, whether committed in time of peace or in time of war, is a crime under international law, which they undertake to prevent and to punish.

23. Article II of the Genocide Convention defines the international crime of "genocide" as follows:

Article II. In the present Convention, genocide means any of the following acts committed with intent to destroy, in whole or in part, a national, ethnical, racial or religious group, as such:

(1) Killing members of the group;

(a) Causing serious bodily or mental harm to members of the group;

(b) Deliberately inflicting on the group conditions of life calculated to bring about its physical destruction in whole or in part;

(c) Imposing measures intended to prevent births within the group;

(d) Forcibly transferring children of the group to another group.

24. Article III of the Genocide Convention provides that the following acts shall likewise all be punishable: (a) genocide; (b) conspiracy to commit genocide; (c) direct and public incitement to commit genocide; (d) attempt to commit genocide; (e) complicity in genocide.

25. According to Article IV of the Genocide Convention, persons committing genocide or any of the other acts enumerated in Article III shall be punished, whether they are constitutionally responsible rulers, public officials, or private individuals. This basic requirement of the Genocide Convention is fully applicable to Respondent George Bush.

26. According to Article V of the Genocide Convention, the Contracting Parties undertake to enact, in accordance with their respective Constitutions, the necessary legislation to give effect to the provisions of the Genocide Convention and, in particular, to provide effective penalties for persons guilty of genocide or of any of the other acts enumerated in Article III.

27. Pursuant to Article V, the Congress of the United States of America adopted what is called implementing legislation for the Genocide Convention that makes genocide a crime under U.S. federal criminal law. Basically following the terms of the Genocide Convention, this Genocide Convention Implementation Act of 1987 (found in Title 18 of the United States Code) defines the crime of genocide as follows:

§ 1901. Genocide

(a) BASIC OFFENSE.–Whoever, whether in time of peace or in time of war, in a circumstance described in subsection (d) and with the specific intent to destroy, in whole or in substantial part, a national, ethnic, racial, or religious group as such–

(1)   kills members of that group;

(2)   causes serious bodily injury to members of that group;

(3)   causes the permanent impairment of the mental faculties of members of the group through drugs, torture, or similar techniques;

(4)   subjects the group to conditions of life that are intended to cause the physical destruction of the group in whole or in part;

(5)   imposes measures intended to prevent births within the group; or

(6)   transfers by force children of the group to another group;

or attempts to do so, shall be punished as provided in subsection (b).

28. According to subsection (d), the basic offense must be committed either within the United States, or by a national of the United States. The penalty for violating subsection (a)(1) is a fine of not more than $1 million and imprisonment for life. The penalty for violating subsections (a)(2) to (a)(6) is a fine of not more than $1 million or imprisonment for not more than twenty years, or both.

29. Under the definitional provisions of this Act, 225,000 dead Iraqi children clearly constitute a "substantial part" of "a national, ethnic, racial, or religious group as such." The continuation of economic sanctions against Iraq will (1) kill at least 170,000 more Iraqi children by the end of the year; (2) "cause serious bodily injury to" Applicants, The 4.5 Million Children of Iraq; (3) "cause the permanent impairment of the mental faculties of" Applicants; and (4) subject Applicants "to conditions of life that are intended to cause the physical destruction of the group in whole or in part."

30. Only the "specific intent" of Respondent George Bush to commit genocide against Applicants remains to be proven beyond a reasonable doubt to establish his criminal responsibility under United States municipal law and international criminal law. The open publication and widespread dissemination of the Harvard Report on 22 May 1991 makes that task possible. Any Bush administration official responsible for implementing the economic sanctions policy against Iraq who has knowledge of the conclusions of the Harvard Report would possess the "specific intent" required to serve as the mental element or mens rea of the international and municipal crime of genocide against Applicants, The 4.5 Million Children of Iraq. Applicants assert that Respondent George Bush has full knowledge of the genocidal consequences of the continuation of economic sanctions against Iraq and therefore has the mens rea necessary for committing the crime of genocide as recognized by the Genocide Convention and the Genocide Implementation Act.

31. The same principles of international criminal law have been incorporated into the municipal legal systems of almost all States in the

World Community today. Wherefore, there is universality of jurisdiction for any State to prosecute Respondent George Bush for committing genocide against the Applicants, The 4.5 Million Children of Iraq. Like unto a pirate, the Respondent George Bush is *hostis humani generis*—the enemy of all humankind.

IV.

COMPETENCE

32. Article I of the Genocide Convention makes it quite clear that all 99 states that are Contracting Parties have an international legal obligation "to prevent" the commission of genocide against Applicants, The 4.5 million children of Iraq.

33. Article VIII of the Genocide Convention provides that any Contracting Party "may call upon the competent organs of the United Nations to take such action under the Charter of the United Nations as they consider appropriate for the prevention and suppression of acts of genocide ..."

34. Thus, all 99 states parties to the Genocide Convention have both the right and the duty under international law to bring the genocidal situation in Iraq to the attention of the entire United Nations Organization, as well as its affiliated organizations such as UNESCO, UNICEF, etc.

35. The Genocide Convention expressly confers international legal competence upon all organs of the United Nations—including the Security Council, the Economic and Social Council, the General Assembly, the Secretary General, the International Court of Justice, the U.N. Commission on Human Rights, the Sub-Commission on Prevention of Discrimination and Protection of Minorities, UNESCO, UNICEF, etc.—to do something about the genocidal situation in Iraq. But so far, such individual steps and collective actions by Member States have not been taken for fear of running afoul of the all-powerful Respondents, who represent and constitute the only self-styled "superpower" sitting as one of the five Permanent Members of the Security Council.

36. The Respondents bear ultimate legal responsibility for the imposition of economic sanctions upon Iraq and therefore for the international crime of genocide against Applicants, The 4.5 Million Children of Iraq.

37. Under the current desperate circumstances, responsible officials of Member States permitting the continuation of economic sanctions against Iraq could commit the separate international crime of "complicity" in the crime of genocide that is today being inflicted upon the Applicants by the Respondents, in violation of Article III(e) of the Genocide Convention.

V.

JURISDICTION

38. The the organs and agencies of the United Nations, including the Secretary General, the Economic and Social Council, the General Assembly, the Human Rights Commission, the Sub-Commission on Prevention of Discrimination and Protection of Minorities, UNESCO, and UNICEF, inter alia, have the jurisdiction to receive and hear this Indictment, Complaint, and Petition, and to provide the Relief requested herein.

39. That the organs of the United Nations are endowed with explicit and inherent powers to assume jurisdiction of cases of the kind presented in this Indictment, Complaint, and Petition is reflected in the Charter of the United Nations. Chapter 1, Article I(1) of the Charter obligates the United Nations and its members to "maintain international peace and security." Such peace and security are threatened by many acts short of open interstate warfare. Genocide by the Respondents against the Applicants, The 4.5 Million Children of Iraq, threatens international peace and security.

40. As the situation described above constitutes a constant threat to the maintenance of international peace and security, the Secretary General, under the authority conferred upon him by Article 99 of the Charter, is entitled to bring this matter to the attention of the Security Council. He is also authorized by Rule 13(g) of the Rules of Procedure of the General Assembly to include in the Assembly's agenda any item which he deems it necessary to put before the Assembly. Applicants hereby request the Secretary General to include their Indictment, Complaint, and Petition on the agenda of the 46th General Assembly and to bring it to the attention of the Security Council.

41. The General Assembly is authorized to act under Chapter IV, Article 22 of the United Nations Charter to establish an ad hoc Tribunal empowered to grant the Relief requested herein. For instance, in 1950, the General Assembly established a special tribunal to deal with various claims arising in the former Italian colony of Libya. Given the circumstances detailed in this Indictment, Complaint, and Petition, the creation of such a Tribunal would be justified and necessary to carry out the very Purposes and Principles for which the United Nations was established: to ensure peace and security and to guarantee the protection of fundamental human rights. Applicants request the 46th General Assembly to establish such a Tribunal as a subsidiary organ and to charge it with the responsibility to investigate and adjudicate their Indictment, Complaint, and Petition, as well as to order all forms of Relief requested in Section VI herein.

42. All Members of the United Nations have pledged themselves under U.N. Charter Chapter IX Articles 55 and 56 to take action to ensure respect for human rights. Article 55 states in part:

With a view to the creation of conditions of stability and well being which are necessary for peaceful and friendly relations among nations based on respect for the principle of equal rights and self-determination of peoples, the United Nations shall promote:

(c) universal respect for, and observance of, human rights and fundamental freedoms for all without distinction as to race, sex, language, or religion.

Article 56 states:

All Members pledge themselves to take joint and separate action in co-operation with the Organization for the achievement of the purposes set forth in Article 55.

43. Such a pledge indicates that under the Charter, Member States must be prepared to take action to assist in enforcing and protecting human rights. Should an organ of the United Nations determine that the rights of Applicants were violated by Respondents and recommend action, Member States have pledged themselves to co-operate with the United Nations in taking necessary steps under the Charter to promote "universal respect for, and observance of, human rights."

44. These human rights provisions of the United Nations Charter were further elaborated upon and specified by the Universal Declaration of Human Rights, which was adopted by consensus by the United Nations General Assembly in 1948. The Universal Declaration of Human Rights enunciates the basic standards of international human rights law to which all individuals around the world are entitled. Indeed, it is the official position of the United Nations Organization and of the Respondent United States of America that the Universal Declaration of Human Rights is binding upon all States and for the benefit of all People around the world as a matter of customary international law.

45. Among the plethora of rights guaranteed to the Applicants by the Universal Declaration of Human Rights that are currently being systematically violated by the Respondents, the most sacred and most fundamental right of all is their very right to life itself, as recognized by Article 3 thereof: "Everyone has the right to life, liberty and security of person." Respondents act as if the "everyone" referred to in Article 3 does not include the Applicants, The 4.5 Million Children of Iraq.

46. Applicants also assert that the Respondents have grossly, consistently, and systematically violated the fundamental right that has been guaranteed to them by Article 5 of the Universal Declaration of Human Rights: "No one shall be subjected to torture or to cruel, inhuman or degrading treatment or punishment."

47. Applicants, The 4.5 Million Children of Iraq, also assert that the Respondents have violated all of the rights guaranteed to them by the International Convention on the Rights of the Child of 1989.

48. Applicants also assert that the Respondents have violated the special protections of international humanitarian law guaranteed to children by the Fourth Geneva Convention of 1949 and the Additional Protocol I thereto of 1977.

49. Under the human rights provisions of the United Nations Charter, the Universal Declaration of Human Rights, the Genocide Convention, the Children's Convention, and the Fourth Geneva Convention and Protocol I, Applicants are proper parties to invoke the jurisdiction of the United Nations in requesting Relief on their own behalf in order to be relieved from the inhuman, degrading, cruel, criminal, and genocidal conditions perpetrated upon them by the Respondents.

50. Due to the fact that the Respondents represent and constitute the only self-styled "superpower" sitting as one of the five Permanent Members of the Security Council, the Respondents have repeatedly and abusively used and threatened to use their voting power and their so-called "veto power" to continue the international economic embargo upon Iraq in a manner that is ultra vires the "primary responsibility" for the maintenance of international peace and security that has been conferred upon the Security Council by Article 24(1) and (2) of the United Nations Charter: "2. In discharging these duties the Security Council shall act in accordance with the Purposes and Principles of the United Nations." According to Article 1(3) of the Charter, one of the foremost Purposes of the United Nations is proclaimed to be ". . .pomoting and encouraging respect for human rights and for fundamental freedoms for all . . ."

51. As a direct result of the illegal and ultra vires conduct by the Respondents at the Security Council, the Applicants have nowhere else to turn for Relief except to the General Assembly, the Secretary General, the Economic and Social Council, the Human Rights Commission, the Sub-commission on Prevention of Discrimination and Protection of Minorities, UNESCO, and UNICEF, etc. in order to save themselves from the death, disease, malnutrition, starvation, and genocide that is currently being inflicted upon them by the Respondents.

52. The General Assembly has the inherent power to create methods and instrumentalities to carry out the Purposes and Principles of the United Nations Charter, the Universal Declaration of Human Rights, the Genocide Convention and the other aforementioned instruments of international law. The Secretary General also possesses inherent powers to carry out these Purposes and Principles. The same is true for the Human Rights Commission, the Sub-Commission on Prevention of Discrimination and Protection of Minorities, as well as for UNESCO and UNICEF, etc.

53. The Respondents represent and constitute a Member State of the United Nations and therefore would be obligated to act in compliance with any determination by any United Nations organ concerning this matter.

VI.

PRAYER FOR RELIEF

54. Applicants pray for the issuance of a Directive by the Secretariat, or the General Assembly, or the Economic and Social Council, or the Human Rights Commission, or the Sub-Commission on Prevention of Discrimination and Protection of Minorities or UNESCO or UNICEF or any other competent organ or agency of the United Nations to hear this Indictment, Complaint, and Petition; to investigate and adjudicate the allegations of genocide by Respondents against Applicants; and to order the termination of all forms of multilateral and bilateral economic sanctions against Iraq.

55. Applicants also pray for the massive provision of international humanitarian relief to Iraq by the United Nations Organizations as a whole, its specialized agencies and affiliated organizations, as well as by all Member States thereof, in order to save them from death, disease, malnutrition, starvation, genocide, and extermination at the hands of the Respondents.

56. Applicants also pray for due compensation to be paid by Respondents to Applicants and their families for the deaths as well as physical and mental injury caused by Respondents' actions in violation of the Genocide Convention and the Universal Declaration of Human Rights, inter alia.

57. Applicants pray that proper sanctions be taken against Respondents for any refusal to comply with any of the orders or decisions that the United Nations or any international organ makes in relation to this matter.

58. Applicants pray that the United Nations authorize a full investigation of the matters presented in this Indictment, Complaint, and Petition and subsequently authorize a complete and public disclosure of all evidence and findings of fact at the conclusion of such investigation.

59. Applicants further pray that the appropriate organs of the United Nations Organization—as well as of all the Member States thereof—institute criminal proceedings against Respondent George Bush for committing the international crime of genocide against the Applicants, as required by the Genocide Convention and the municipal legal systems of all civilized nations, including his own.

VII.

CONCLUSION

THE PEOPLES AND COUNTRIES OF THE WORLD MUST NOT TURN THEIR EYES AWAY IN SHAME FROM IRAQ AS HUMANKIND APPROACHES THE DAWN OF THE NEXT MILLENNIUM OF ITS PARLOUS EXISTENCE. AS IRAQ'S CHILDREN GO, SO GOES THE ENTIRE WORLD!

RESPECTFULLY SUBMITTED
ON BEHALF OF THE APPLICANTS,
THE 4.5 MILLION CHILDREN OF IRAQ,

FRANCIS A. BOYLE
PROFESSOR OF INTERNATIONAL LAW
. . . .

Chapter Five

Humanitarian Intervention Versus International Law

Originally delivered as The Dr. Irma M. Parhad Lecture *at the invitation of the Faculty of Medicine of the University of Calgary in Canada on March 13, 2001, an updated version of this article is included here to respond to the Bush administration's effort—in the wake of its failure to discover WMD in Iraq—to justify its aggression against that country as an effort to liberate the Iraqi people from the yoke of a brutal dictator.*

In the aftermath of the collapse of the Warsaw Pact and the disintegration of the Soviet Union, there has been a great deal of jubilation in the United States and among its European allies organized into the NATO Alliance, supported by their acolytes in the academic world and their hired-guns in the legal profession, enthusiastically promoting "humanitarian intervention." The purpose of this essay is to examine the so-called doctrine of humanitarian intervention in accordance with the requirements of international law in view of its increasing use by the United States and the NATO member states in justification of their intervention into states such as the former Yugoslavia, Afghanistan, Iraq at the time of this writing, with many more such interventions likely to occur under this guise in future. For example, once it became clear that the Bush Jr. administration could not produce any weapons of mass destruction in Iraq, it fell back upon the retroactive application of the doctrine of "humanitarian intervention" in order to somehow justify its war of aggression against Iraq on an ex post facto basis. The pretexts for aggression against Syria, which at the time of this writing appears to be the Bush Jr. administration's next target, have yet to be fully devised.

Under international law, "humanitarian intervention" is a joke and a fraud that has been repeatedly manipulated and abused by a small number of very powerful countries in the North in order to justify wanton military aggression against and prolonged military occupation of weak countries of the South—and typically by developed countries of the North against lesser developed countries in the South—for political, economic, strategic, and military reasons that have absolutely nothing at all to do with considerations of humanity and humanitarianism. History teaches that powerful states do not use military force for reasons of humanity.

State Practice

Obviously the brief space here cannot review the historical record of massive abuse of the doctrine of humanitarian intervention by militarily powerful states of the North. But a few scholarly sources to that effect will be mentioned. The first comprehensive study of humanitarian intervention was published by Antoine Rougier in 1910:[1]

> The conclusion which emerges from this study is that it is neither possible to separate the humanitarian from the political grounds for intervention nor to assure the complete disinterestedness of the intervening States...
>
> ....
>
> Whenever one power intervenes in the name of humanity in the domain of another power, it cannot but impose its concept of justice and public policy on the other State, by force if necessary. Its intervention tends definitely to draw the [other] State into its moral and social sphere of influence, and ultimately into its political sphere of influence. It will control the other State while preparing to dominate it. Humanitarian intervention consequently looks like an ingenious juridical technique to encroach little by little upon the independence of a State in order to reduce it progressively to the status of semi-sovereignty.

During the subsequent course of the twentieth century, nothing in state practice has altered Rougier's sound conclusions.

In *Foundations of World Order* (1999), this author examined the entire history of United States military intervention into the Western Hemisphere and the Pacific Basin from shortly before the Spanish-American War of 1898 up to the so-called Good Neighbor Policy of President Franklin Roosevelt's administration starting in 1932. At the time, almost all of these military interventions were publicly justified on some type of humanitarian grounds by the United States government. But when the actual historical records were later declassified, released, and published, they established that this specious rationale was nothing more than mere propaganda disseminated for the purpose of building public support for military intervention on grounds of geopolitics, economic exploitation, military strategy and hegemonial domination.

To the same effect, writing in 1963, Professor Ian Brownlie of Oxford concluded that "the state practice justifies the conclusion that no genuine case of humanitarian intervention has occurred, with the possible exception of the occupation of Syria in 1860 and 1861."[2] And in a seminal treatise published in 1961, Professor Myres McDougal and Florentino Feliciano of the Yale Law School branded the doctrine of humanitarian intervention as "amorphous."[3] It is noteworthy that forty years ago the world saw a consensus of scholarly opinion against "humanitarian intervention" by the leading proponents of the two most important and competing schools of international legal studies in the West at that time: International Legal Positivism and the New Haven School of policy-oriented jurisprudence.[4] Third World legal scholars have typically been vehement in their denunciation of so-called humanitarian intervention—for reasons too obvious to belabor here.

The latest scholarly book on this subject is by Sean D. Murphy, *Humanitarian Intervention* (1996). This book was written by now Professor Murphy while he was a lawyer working for the United States Department of State. There is only space here to quote two of Professor Murphy's conclusions: "In conclusion, unilateral humanitarian intervention finds little support in the rules of the UN Charter and in state practice in the post Charter era..."[5] Chapter 5 of Professor Murphy's book dealt with incidents of military intervention after the termination of the Cold War on alleged humanitarian grounds: Liberia, Iraq, Bosnia and Herzegovina, Somalia, Rwanda, and Haiti. Later at the very end of his book, Professor Murphy summed up: "Recent events show a striking willingness of states to forego unilateral humanitarian intervention in favor of Security Council authorization, thereby reinforcing the views of those that regard unilateral humanitarian intervention as unlawful."[6] Despite Professor Murphy's prognostication, after his book was published in 1996 the world witnessed the illegal war by the United States and the NATO member states against Serbia over Kosova that was justified on alleged humanitarian grounds. In this regard, the reader is referred to the excellent book by Professor Noam Chomsky of M.I.T., entitled *The New Military Humanism* (1999), which definitively refutes the humanitarian motivations alleged by the United States and the NATO states. Of course this comment is not intended to justify or diminish any of the hideous atrocities that Serbia and the Milosevic regime inflicted upon the Kosovar Albanians, whom this author has advised and assisted in the past *pro bono publico*.

Professor Chomsky has supplemented his viewpoints on the illegal NATO war against Serbia in his book *Rogue States* (2000), where he also sets forth trenchant critiques of United States human rights foreign policies toward East Timor, Colombia, Cuba, Iraq, Turkey, etc. As Professor Chomsky has decisively established in his compendium of publications, humanitarian considerations have absolutely nothing at all to do with the conduct of foreign policy by the United States, the United Kingdom, and Israel except in a mere propagandistic sense.

The reader might also want to read the excellent new book of almost the same name by William Blum, entitled *Rogue State* (2000). As the book makes clear, this title is Blum's reference to the United States of America. Blum is one of those exceedingly rare and truly courageous people who quit the United States Department of State as a matter of principle.

There very well could be some itty-bitty "rogue states" lurking out there somewhere in the Third World. But since the end of the Cold War, the United States of America has become the Rogue Elephant of international relations. And "humanitarian intervention" has become its *crie de guerre*—as witnessed during the illegal U.S./NATO war against Serbia. The world must never again be deluded by the United States and the NATO states to believe that they are using military force against some other state for humanitarian reasons. The longstanding terror bombing campaign against Iraq and its people by the United States and the United Kingdom with the support of

NATO member Turkey, as well as with the support of Saudi Arabia and Kuwait (both of which were "hosting" U.S. armed forces), on the alleged humanitarian grounds of protecting the Kurds in the north, and the Shiite population in southern Iraq, was an excellent example of this ongoing phenomenon.

International Law and Legitimate Military Intervention

Now consider what contemporary international law has to say about the alleged doctrine of humanitarian intervention. While there is not enough space here to discuss all the institutions, procedures, and rules of the international legal regime concerning the transnational threat and use of force that was set up by the United States government, inter alia, as of 1945, its essential component was the United Nations Organization and its Charter. Then came the regional organizations that were brought into affiliation with the United Nations by means of Chapter 8 of the United Nations Charter: *i.e.*, the Organization of American States (OAS), the League of Arab States, the Organization of African Unity (OAU), now the African Union, and perhaps someday the Association of Southeast Asian Nations (ASEAN) as well as the Organization for Security and Cooperation in Europe (OSCE). These institutions were joined by what were proclaimed as collective self-defense agreements concluded under Article 51 of the United Nations Charter, the foremost exemplar of which is NATO. In view of its institutional charter, NATO had absolutely no legal authority whatsoever to wage war against Serbia over Kosova without express authorization from the U.N. Security Council, at a minimum.

As institutionally structured and established under U.S. hegemonic direction, the only legitimate justifications and procedures for the perpetration of violence and coercion by one state against another state became those set forth in the U.N. Charter. The Charter alone contains those rules that have been consented to by the virtual unanimity of the international community that has voluntarily joined the United Nations Organization. Succinctly put, these rules include the U.N. Charter's Article 2(3) and Article 33(1) obligations for the peaceful settlement of international disputes; the Article 2(4) prohibition on the threat or use of force; and the Article 51 restriction of the right of individual or collective self-defense to repel an actual "armed attack" or "*aggression armée,*" according to the French-language version of the U.N. Charter, which is equally authentic with the English.

Related to this right of self-defense are its two fundamental requirements for the "necessity" and the "proportionality" of a state's forceful response to the foreign armed attack or armed aggression. In regard to this first requirement of "necessity," as definitively stated by U.S. Secretary of State Daniel Webster in the famous 1837 case of *The Caroline*, self-defense can only be justified when the "necessity of self-defence is instant, overwhelming, and leaving no choice of means, and no moment for deliberation."[7] The Nuremberg Tribunal later endorsed and ratified this *Caroline* test for self-defense, thus enshrining it as a basic principle of the contemporary international legal order.

Likewise, there exist several institutions and procedures that function as integral parts of this international law regime to prevent, regulate, and reduce the transnational threat and use of force. To mention only the most well-known: (1) "enforcement action" by the U.N. Security Council as specified in Chapter 7 of the Charter; (2) "enforcement action" by the appropriate regional organizations acting with the authorization of the Security Council as required by Article 53 and specified in Chapter 8 of the Charter; (3) the so-called peacekeeping operations and monitoring forces organized under the jurisdiction of the Security Council pursuant to Chapter 6 of the Charter; (4) peacekeeping operations under the auspices of the U.N. General Assembly acting in accordance with its Uniting for Peace Resolution (1950); and (5) peacekeeping operations and monitoring forces deployed by the relevant regional organizations acting in conformity with their proper constitutional procedures. To this list should also be added the "good offices" of the U.N. Secretary General; the International Court of Justice; the Permanent Court of Arbitration; and numerous other techniques and institutions for international arbitration, mediation, and conciliation, etc.

International Law Against "Humanitarian" Intervention

The Corfu Channel Case

In the historical era prior to the conclusion of the United Nations Charter, some Western imperialist powers of the North asserted that there existed supposed principles of customary international law that permitted them to engage in the unilateral threat and use of military force against other states, peoples, and regions of the world. In particular, these "principles" included the so-called doctrines of intervention, protection, and self-help. Yet, these three alleged doctrines were unanimously rejected by the International Court of Justice in the seminal *Corfu Channel Case* (United Kingdom v. Albania) of 1949 as being totally incompatible with the proper conduct of international relations in the post World War II era. Rebutting the British arguments in support of these three atavistic doctrines in order to justify its military intervention into Albanian territorial waters, the World Court ruled:[8]

> The Court cannot accept such a line of defence. The Court can only regard the alleged right of intervention as the manifestation of a policy of force, such as has, in the past, given rise to most serious abuses and such as cannot, whatever be the present defects in international organization, find a place in international law. Intervention is perhaps still less admissible in the particular form it would take here; for, from the nature of things, it would be reserved for the most powerful States, and might easily lead to perverting the administration of international justice itself.
>
> The United Kingdom Agent, ..., has further classified "Operation Retail" among methods of self-protection or self-help.

The Court cannot accept this defence either. Between independent States, respect for territorial sovereignty is an essential foundation of international relations. The Court recognizes that the Albanian Government's complete failure to carry out its duties after the explosions, and the dilatory nature of its diplomatic notes, are extenuating circumstances for the action of the United Kingdom Government. But to ensure respect for international law, of which it is the organ, the Court must declare that the action of the British Navy constituted a violation of Albanian sovereignty.

Even more significantly, the World Court unanimously repudiated these three so-called doctrines—including and especially intervention—without explicitly relying upon the U.N. Charter because Albania was not yet a contracting party thereto while Great Britain was. Hence, the World Court's decision rejecting these three doctrines—including and especially intervention—constituted an authoritative declaration of the requirements of customary international law binding upon all members of the international community irrespective of the requirements of the U.N. Charter. *A fortiori*, when all states parties to an international dispute are members of the United Nations, Charter articles 2(3), 2(4), and 33 absolutely prohibit any unilateral or multilateral threat or use of force that is not specifically justified by the article 51 right of individual or collective self-defense, or else authorized by the United Nations Security Council. To be sure, in regard to this latter point, on February 27, 1998, the International Court of Justice issued two Judgments on Preliminary Objections raised by the United States and the United Kingdom as Respondents (i.e., defendants) in the *Lockerbie* bombing cases filed against them by Libya with the assistance of this author, making it crystal clear that the U.N. Security Council is definitely not the Judge, the Jury, and the Lord-High Executioner of International Law.

Next, three seminal U.N. General Assembly Resolutions have a distinct bearing on the so-called doctrine of humanitarian intervention: the Declaration on the Inadmissibility of Intervention in the Domestic Affairs of States and the Protection of Their Independence and Sovereignty (1965); the Declaration on Principles of International Law Concerning Friendly Relations and Cooperation among States in Accordance with the Charter of the United Nations (1970); and the Definition of Aggression (1974). Considered together, these three resolutions stand for the general proposition that, in the emphatic opinion of the member states of the U.N. General Assembly, non-consensual military intervention by one state into the territorial domain of another state is absolutely prohibited for any reason whatsoever.

Just to quote only one paragraph from this 1970 Declaration on Principles of International Law Concerning Friendly Relations and Cooperation among States in Accordance with the Charter of the United Nations (1970):[9]

No State or group of States has the right to intervene, directly or indirectly, for any reason whatever, in the internal or external affairs of any other State. Consequently, armed intervention and all other forms of interference or attempted threats against the personality of the State or against its political, economic and cultural elements, are in violation of international law.

A specific instance of so-called humanitarian intervention would probably be most properly classified as a "breach of the peace" and an "act of aggression" within the meaning and purpose of U.N. Charter article 39 as interpreted by reference to these three U.N. General Assembly resolutions. Such was the case for the recently concluded U.S./NATO war against Serbia over Kosova on spurious humanitarian grounds.

Nicaragua v. United States of America

In the seminal decision of *Nicaragua v. United States of America* (1986), the International Court of Justice found that this aforementioned 1970 Declaration on Principles of International Law concerning Friendly Relations and Cooperation among States, etc., sets forth rules of customary international law establishing an absolute prohibition against military intervention by one state against another state except in a case of legitimate self-defense at the express request of the victim state itself. The Reagan administration had publicly attempted to justify its Contra/terror war against Nicaragua in substantial part on humanitarian grounds. Consequently, this author spent one week in Nicaragua during the Contra/war from November 16-23, 1985 as part of a Lawyer's Delegation in order to investigate the human rights situation there. This Delegation consisted of former U.S. Attorney General Ramsey Clark, the noted American Civil Rights Attorney Leonard Weinglass, and two French Canadian human rights lawyers from Montreal, Robert Saint-Louis and Denis Racicot. At the request of my colleagues, this author drafted our final Report that was endorsed by the entire Delegation.

To quote only one sentence from this Report that is the most directly relevant here: "...Contrary to press reports in the United States, [we] found that the counterrevolutionary army created by the U.S. Central Intelligence Agency in Honduras constitutes nothing more than a mercenary band of cowards, terrorists and criminals who attack innocent Nicaraguan civilians— old men, women, children, invalids and religious people...."[10] If anything, it was the people and the State of Nicaragua who desperately needed "humanitarian intervention" against the United States and its Contra/terrorist surrogates.

The Reagan administration's Contra/terror war against Nicaragua was soundly condemned by the International Court of Justice in this seminal decision of 1986. Moreover, for technical procedural reasons not relevant here, like unto the *Corfu Channel* case, in the *Nicaragua* case the International Court of Justice had to condemn this U.S. military aggression as a matter of customary international law instead of by directly applying the prohibitions found in the United Nations Charter *per se*. Furthermore, in the *Nicaragua* case the World Court explicitly reaffirmed the above-quoted rulings from the *Corfu Channel* case, and also held: "The Court concludes that acts constituting a breach of the customary principle of non-intervention will also, if they directly or indirectly involve the use of force, constitute a breach of the principle of non-use of force in international relations."[11]

Finally, in the *Nicaragua* case the World Court expressly rejected the assertion by the United States that it had some putative right of military intervention against Nicaragua on the grounds of alleged human rights violations:[12]

> 268. In any event, while the United States might form its own appraisal of the situation as to respect for human rights in Nicaragua, the use of force could not be the appropriate method to monitor or ensure such respect....The Court concludes that the argument derived from the preservation of human rights in Nicaragua cannot afford a legal justification for the conduct of the United States,...

The *Corfu Channel* case and the *Nicaragua* case are the two leading and most conclusive authorities under international law that soundly condemn in no uncertain terms the so-called doctrine of humanitarian intervention.

If one travels all over the world, one will find that the only significant source of opposition to the World Court's decision in the *Nicaragua* case has always come from international lawyers and law professors in the United States—for obvious reasons. Despite United States opposition and opinion to the contrary, it remains the case that the transnational threat or use of military force and military intervention by one state against another state is only permissible in cases of individual or collective self-defense where the victim state of an armed attack has expressly requested such assistance from another state or states or as lawfully authorized by the U.N. Security Council acting within the proper scope of the powers delegated to it by the U.N. member states under the terms of the United Nations Charter.

The Implications of Bosnia and Herzegovina

That being said, what does the world do about major human rights atrocities and catastrophes that undeniably do occur today? Certainly, the world must not accord the great military powers such as the United States, the NATO states, Russia, and China some fictive right of "humanitarian intervention" that these powerful states will only abuse and manipulate in order to justify military intervention against less powerful states and peoples for their own selfish interests. There are more than enough international laws and international organizations to deal with major human rights atrocities and catastrophes going on around the world today without any need to recognize or condone the bogus and dangerous doctrine of "humanitarian intervention." The lack of appropriate response to humanitarian catastrophes on the international level is due to the Great Powers' lack of political will rather than to the unavailability of legal structures and doctrines. Instead, the world has seen in operation the dirty and bloody hands of the Great Powers behind most contemporary major human rights atrocities and catastrophes.

Suffice it to say that pursuant to the self-styled Dayton Peace Agreement, on December 14, 1995, the Republic of Bosnia and Herzegovina— a U.N. member state—was carved-up *de facto* in Paris by the United Nations Organization, the European Union and its member states, the United States, Russia and the other states and dignitaries in attendance, despite the United Nations Charter, the Nuremberg Principles, the 1948 Genocide Convention, the Four Geneva Conventions of 1949 and their two Additional Protocols of 1977, the 1966 Racial Discrimination Convention, the 1973 Apartheid Convention, and the 1948 Universal Declaration of Human Rights, as well as two overwhelmingly favorable protective Orders issued by the International Court of Justice on behalf of the Republic of Bosnia and Herzegovina on April 8, 1993, and September 13, 1993, at the request of this author serving as Bosnia's lawyer before the World Court. This second World Court Order effectively prohibited such a partition of Bosnia and Herzegovina by the vote of 13 to 2.

This latter proposition can be substantiated by reference to the terrible history of outright genocide perpetrated by the rump Yugoslavia (Serbia and Montenegro) and its Milosevic regime against the people and the Republic of Bosnia and Herzegovina from 1992 to 1995, which the Great Powers of Europe, the United States, and the United Nations Organization itself aided, abetted, and facilitated. Bosnia and Herzegovina constituted the worst human rights catastrophe and atrocity in Europe since the genocidal horrors inflicted by the Nazis over a generation ago.[13]

This U.N.-sanctioned execution of a U.N. member state violated every known principle of international law and human rights that had been formulated by the international community in the post World War II era. The Republic of Bosnia and Herzegovina was sacrificed on the altar of Great Power politics to the Machiavellian god of expedience. In 1938 the Great Powers of Europe did the exact same thing to Czechoslovakia at Munich. A generation ago, the Great Power partition of that nation state did not bring peace to Europe then. Today, the Great Power partition of the Republic of Bosnia and Herzegovina will not bring peace to Europe now.

This Great Power elimination of the state known as the "Republic of Bosnia and Herzegovina" at Dayton and Paris stands for the proposition that genocide pays. As this author's client and friend Bosnian Foreign Minister (later Prime Minister) Haris Silajdzic said in reference to the invitation of the genocidaire Radovan Karadzic by the United Nations, the then European Community, and the United States to attend the 1993 Vance-Owen negotiations in New York: "If you kill one person, you're prosecuted. If you kill ten people, you're a celebrity; if you kill a quarter of a million people, you're invited to a peace conference." Almost three years later at the U.S. Air Force Base in Dayton, Ohio, U.S. Envoy Richard Holbrooke, U.S. Secretary of State Warren Christopher, and U.S. President Bill Clinton personally gave the genocidaire Slobodan Milosevic and Serbia 49 percent of the Republic of Bosnia and Herzegovina. And Serbia today still controls, dominates, and strangulates almost one-half the state known only by the purely geographical location of "Bosnia and Herzegovina."

This author currently represents the Mothers of Srebrenica and Podrinja living in Vogosca, Bosnia-Herzegovina, one of the major organizations grouping the women and children survivors of the single greatest massacre in Europe since World War II. In July of 1995 approximately 10,000 Bosnian Muslim men and boys staying at what the U.N. Security Council publicly termed a "safe haven" in Srebrenica were permitted to be taken out and systematically exterminated over just a few days by the Bosnian Serb Army acting at the behest of the Milosevic regime and Serbia. The Great Powers of the world on the U.N. Security Council, the United States, the NATO states, the European Union and its member states, and the United Nations Organization itself allowed this shameful event to happen, their promises of safety thrown to the winds. They deliberately sacrificed Srebrenica and its inhabitants in order to produce the genocidal carve-up of the Republic of Bosnia and Herzegovina that the United States government then later orchestrated and inflicted at Dayton and Paris—"tidying-up the map," as it were. "Christian" Europe and the United States did not want to see another state emerge in Europe where a plurality of the population would be Muslim.

Almost eight years after this horrendous massacre, the Mothers of Srebrenica and Podrinja still cannot even go back to their homes in Srebrenica on the other side of NATO's carve-up line because of dire fear for their lives. Such tragedies mean nothing to the United States, the European Union states, the NATO states, and the United Nations Organization itself. An instance of their heartlessness was clearly manifested when, on Wednesday October 4, 2000, this author met with U.S. Envoy Jacques Klein, then Head of the U.N. Mission in Bosnia-Herzegovina, at the U.N. Headquarters Compound in Sarajevo. Klein repeatedly insulted and berated the Mothers of Srebrenica and Podrinja to my face while their three Presidents sat down the hall patiently waiting for our scheduled appointment with the Prosecutor for the International Criminal Tribunal for the Former Yugoslavia (ICTY), The Honorable Carla Del Ponte, in order to discuss ICTY prosecutions arising out of the Srebrenica "genocide"—her word for it. Acting at our request, she would later indict Milosevic for every crime in the ICTY statute for what was done at his direction in Bosnia and at Srebrenica.

After what happened to the Republic of Bosnia and Herzegovina, it should come as no surprise that the world witnessed outright genocide inflicted by the Hutu government with the connivance of France against the Tutsis in Rwanda in 1994, while the U.N. Security Council stood by and did nothing despite the prophetic warnings by Canadian General Romeo Dallaire. Or that the world saw Russia inflict outright genocide against the Chechens from 1994 to 1996, and then another round from 1999 until today—financed by the Western Powers, which have also acquiesced in Russia's gross violation of the Conventional Forces in Europe Treaty in order to prosecute another genocidal war against this author's clients, the Chechen Republic of Ichkeria and its people. Yet again a nominally Christian European state is wantonly exterminating Muslims while Europe and the United States do nothing to stop this genocide precisely in order to prevent the emergence of yet another Muslim state in Europe.

After Bosnia-Herzegovina, it should have come as no surprise that the world saw outright genocide inflicted by Serbia and the Milosevic regime against the Kosovar Albanians immediately after the United States and the NATO states launched their illegal war against Serbia in March of 1999, a genocide which NATO admittedly anticipated but which in actuality transpired as the direct result of its aggression. Of course the nominally Christian United States and NATO states could not care less about the basic human rights of the Kosovar Albanians, most of whom are Muslims. Soon thereafter, the world witnessed once again outright genocide inflicted by Indonesia against the people of East Timor after decades of military and economic support to the genocidal military dictatorship ruling Indonesia by the United States and Britain—"our kind of guy," as the Clinton administration publicly referred to the genocidaire Suharto when he came to visit the United States.

Likewise, the people of Iraq (most of whom are Muslims) have been dying at extraordinary rates as a direct result of genocidal economic sanctions that have been maliciously imposed upon them now for over a decade at the behest of the United States and the United Kingdom. Approximately 1.5 million Iraqi civilians have died, about 500,000 of whom were children. The termination of these U.S./U.K. genocidal economic sanctions against Iraq and its people became one of the most compelling moral, legal, humanitarian, and medical issues of our time.

Just recently, the world has seen the United Nations Human Rights Commission condemn Israel for inflicting a war crime and a crime against humanity upon the Palestinian people, most of whom are Muslims.[14] The Nuremberg crime against humanity is the historical and legal precursor to the international crime of genocide as defined by the 1948 Genocide Convention. Historically, the "Jewish" state's criminal conduct against the Palestinians has been financed, armed, equipped, supplied, and politically supported by the "Christian" United States. Although the United States is a founding sponsor of, and a contracting Party to, both the Nuremberg Charter and the Genocide Convention, as well as the United Nations Charter, these legal facts have never made any difference to the United States when it comes to its criminal mistreatment of the Palestinians—truly the wretched of the earth.

Finally, the world must never forget that the Indigenous peoples of Canada, the United States, and Latin America have been subjected to continuing acts of genocide for over the past 500 years. How can the United States and its NATO ally Canada talk about "humanitarian intervention" abroad when both states have a long history of practicing "humanitarian extermination" at home? Despite the slogan and the rhetoric of "Never again!," toward the start of the twentieth-first century, genocide has become an increasingly familiar and acceptable tool for powerful states to wield against weaker states and peoples.

CONCLUSION

No state has the right or standing under international law to launch an illegal military attack upon another U.N. member state in the name of "humanitarian intervention". This applies to both the United States and Canada, who are today continuing to extinguish the Indigenous peoples who live within their imperial domains. It applies to Britain's longstanding campaign to exterminate the Irish people and its prolonged colonial occupation of Ireland, as it does to Turkey's efforts to submerge the Kurds. It applied to the outright genocides Italy inflicted against the peoples of Libya and Ethiopia, those perpetrated by Spain and Portugal against the Indigenous peoples of South America, the monstrous genocide committed by Belgium in the Congo, and that committed by France in Algeria. Only the Nazi genocide against the Jews in Germany and elsewhere has been recognized for what it was. The NATO Alliance constitutes the greatest collection of genocidal states ever assembled in the entire history of the world!

Consequently, the world has not yet heard even one word uttered by the United States and its NATO allies in favor of "humanitarian intervention" against Israel in order to protect the Palestinian people. The United States, its NATO allies and the Great Powers on the U.N. Security Council would not even dispatch a U.N. Charter Chapter 6 monitoring force to help protect the Palestinians, let alone even contemplate any type of U.N. Charter Chapter 7 enforcement action against Israel. The doctrine of "humanitarian intervention" has been clearly proved to be a joke and a fraud when it comes to stopping the ongoing Israeli campaign of genocide against the Palestinian people. Rather than rein in the Israelis—which would be possible just by turning off the tap—the United States government, the U.S. Congress, and U.S. taxpayers instead support the Israeli state to the tune of about 4 billion dollars per year. Once again, genocide in today's world pays so long as it is done at the behest of the United States and its de facto or de jure allies.

George Bush, Jr., September 11, and the Rule of Law

George W. Bush was never elected President by the People of the United States of America. Instead, he was anointed for that Office by five Justices of the United States Supreme Court who themselves had been appointed by Republican Presidents. Bush Jr.'s installation was an act of judicial usurpation of the American Constitution that was unprecedented in the history of the American Republic. Had it occurred in a developing country, such a subversion of democratic process would have been greeted with knowing derision throughout the West. What happened in America could only be likened to a judicial coup d'état inflicted upon the American people, Constitution, and Republic. There should now be no doubt that the United States Supreme Court is governed by raw, naked, brutal, power politics. Justice has nothing at all to do with it. This Supreme Court's constitutional sophistry proved a harbinger of the new administration's disrespect for the Rule of Law, whether domestic or international.

Machiavelli Redux

When Bush Jr. came to power in January of 2001, he proceeded to implement foreign affairs and defense policies that were every bit as radical, extreme, and excessive as the Reagan/Bush administrations had starting in January of 1981. To be sure, Bush Jr. had no popular mandate to do anything. Indeed, a majority of the American electorate had voted for his corporate-cloned opponent.

Upon his installation, Bush Jr.'s "compassionate conservatism" quickly revealed itself to be nothing more than reactionary Machiavellianism—as if there had been any real doubt about this during the presidential election campaign. Even the appointees to the Bush Jr. administration were pretty much the same as the original Reagan/Bush foreign affairs and defense "experts," many of whom were called back into service and given promotions for policies ten to twenty years ago that many might argue had been crimes under international law.[1] It was déjà vû all over again, as Yogi Berra aptly put it.

International Legal Nihilism

In quick succession the world saw the Bush Jr. administration repudiate the Kyoto Protocol on global warming, the International Criminal Court, the Comprehensive Test Ban Treaty (CTBT), an international convention to regulate the trade in small arms, a verification Protocol for the Biological Weapons Convention, an international convention to regulate and reduce smoking, the World Conference Against Racism, and the Anti-Ballistic Missile Systems Treaty, inter alia. To date the Bush Jr. administration has not found an international convention that it likes. The only exception to this rule was its shameless exploitation of the 11 September 2001 tragedy in order to get the U.S. House of Representatives to give Bush Jr. "fast-track" trade negotiation authority so as to present the American people and Congress with yet another non-amendable fait accompli on behalf of American multinationals, corporations, banks, insurance companies, the high-tech and biotech industries, etc. The epitome of "globalization," American-style.

More ominously, once into office the Bush Jr. administration adopted an incredibly belligerent posture towards the Peoples' Republic of China (PRC), publicly identifying the PRC as America's foremost competitor/opponent into the 21st Century. Their needlessly pugnacious approach towards the downing of a U.S. spy plane in China with the death of a Chinese pilot only exacerbated already tense U.S./Chinese relations. Then the Bush Jr. administration decided to sell high-tech weapons to Taiwan in violation of the 17 August 1982 Joint Communiqué of the USA and PRC that had been negotiated and concluded earlier by the Reagan/Bush administration. Finally came Bush Jr.'s breathtaking statement that the United States would defend Taiwan in the event of an attack by the PRC irrespective of Article I, Section 8, Clause 11 of the United States Constitution expressly reserving to Congress alone the right to declare war. President Jimmy Carter had long ago terminated the U.S.-Taiwan self-defense treaty.[2]

For twelve years the Constitution and the rule of law—whether domestic or international — never deterred the Reagan/Bush administrations from pursuing their internationally lawless and criminal policies around the world. The same was true for the Clinton administration as well (such as invading Haiti; bombing Iraq, Sudan, Afghanistan, and Serbia). The Bush Jr. administration has behaved no differently from its lineal Machiavellian predecessors. Their bellicose handling of the 11 September 2001 tragedy was no exception to this general rule.

Indeed, the Bush Jr. administration proceeded to start its bombing campaign on the defenseless people of Afghanistan on Sunday, October 7— not allowing the Sabbath to get in their way either, despite the fact that during the presidential election campaign Bush Jr. proudly stated that his favorite philosopher was Jesus Christ. Yet, as Machiavelli taught, the Prince must appear to be "all religion,"[3] especially when he goes to war.

11 September 2001

The Bush Jr. administration's war against Afghanistan cannot be justified on either the facts, a paucity of which have been offered, or the law, either domestic or international. Rather, it is an illegal armed aggression that has created a humanitarian catastrophe for the twenty-two million people of Afghanistan and is promoting terrible regional instability. The longer Bush Jr.'s war against Afghanistan goes on—and at this writing, Secretary of Defense Rumsfeld has stated that U.S. ground troops will remain in Afghanistan until at least the summer—the worse it is going to be not only for the millions of Afghan people but also in the estimation of the 1.2 billion Muslims of the world comprising 58 Muslim states, few of whom really believe the Bush Jr. administration's propaganda that this is not a war against Islam.

In fact, the Bush Jr. war against Afghanistan has been akin to throwing a match into an explosives factory. Among its deleterious results, India and Pakistan, which have already fought two wars before over Kashmir and today are nuclear armed, are now standing "nuclear-eyeball to nuclear-eyeball" over Kashmir. Mimicking the Bush Administration's response to September 11, India has accused internal groups in Pakistan of the December 2001 attack on the Indian parliament, and demanded, without any offer of proof for its accusations, that Pakistan proceed against them or else face military reprisal. The continuing conflict and armed confrontation between India and Pakistan over Kashmir could readily go nuclear.

The Facts

There is not and may never be conclusive proof as to who was behind the terrible bombings in New York and Washington, D.C., on September 11, 2001. No point would be served here by making a detailed review of the facts that have so far emerged into the public record. Suffice it to say that the accounts provided by the United States government simply do not add up.

The October 3 edition of the *New York Times* recounted the definitive briefing by a U.S. ambassador to NATO officials on the alleged facts as follows:

> One Western official at NATO said the briefings, which were oral, without slides or documents, did not report any direct order from Mr. bin Laden, nor did they indicate that the Taliban knew about the attacks before they happened.
>
> A senior diplomat for one closely allied nation characterized the briefing as containing "nothing particularly new or surprising," adding: "It was rather descriptive and narrative rather than forensic. There was no attempt to build a legal case."

In other words, there was no real case against Al Qaeda, bin Laden, and the Taliban government of Afghanistan. Such was the conclusion of senior diplomats from friendly nations who attended the so-called briefing.

The Powell/Blair White Paper

Secretary of State Colin Powell publicly promised that they were going to produce a "White Paper" documenting their case against Osama bin Laden and the Al Qaeda organization concerning September 11. As those of us in the Peace Movement know all too well from previous international trans-gressions, these U.S. government "White Papers" are all too frequently laden with lies, propaganda, half-truths, dissimulation, disinformation, etc. that are usually very easily refuted after a little bit of research and analysis.

What happened here? We never received a "White Paper" produced by the United States government as publicly promised by Secretary Powell, who was later overridden by President Bush Jr. What we got instead was a so-called White Paper produced by British Prime Minister Tony Blair. Obviously, Blair was acting as Bush Jr.'s surrogate or, as the British press routinely referred to him, "Bush's pet-poodle". Tony Blair is neither an elected nor an appointed official of the U.S. government, not even an American citizen. Conveniently, no American official could be brought to task for or even questioned about whatever errors or inadequacies he might purvey.

The Powell/Blair White Paper fell into that hallowed tradition of a "White Paper" based upon insinuation, allegation, rumors, propaganda, lies, half-truths, etc. Even unnamed British government officials on an off-the-record basis admitted that the case against bin Laden and Al Qaeda would not stand up in court. As a matter of fact, the Blair/Powell White Paper was widely derided in the British news media. There was nothing there.

The Cover-Ups

Despite the clear import of the matter, at Bush Jr.'s request the U.S. Congress has so far decided not to empanel a Joint Committee of the House and of the Senate with subpoena power giving them access to whatever hard evidence they want throughout any agency of the United States government—including the National Security Council, FBI, CIA, NSA, DIA—and also to put their respective Officials under oath to testify as to what happened and why under penalty of perjury. Obviously a cover-up is underway for the express purpose of *not* determining (1) who was ultimately responsible for the terrible attacks of 11 September 2001; and (2) why these extravagantly funded U.S. "intelligence" agencies were either unable or unwilling to prevent these attacks despite numerous warnings of a serious anti-American attack throughout the Summer of 2001 – and yet, amazingly, could assert the identity of those responsible with such certainty in the space of hours thereafter so as to preclude any serious investigation of other possible perpetrators. For reasons not necessary to get into here, there is also an ongoing governmental cover-up of the obvious involvement of the Pentagon/CIA, or one of their contractors, in the attacks inflicting U.S.-produced weapons-grade anthrax upon those institutional components of American society that the American right-wing has traditionally viewed with antipathy: the Democratic Congressional leadership, and the media.

The Bin Laden Video

The so-called bin Laden video was miraculously discovered in the rubble of a bombed-out house in the bombed-out city of Jalalabad by the CIA, who undoubtedly turned the video over to the Pentagon's psyops people, who were operating in Afghanistan. The Pentagon then had the tape translated by "outside" experts, one of whom works at the Johns Hopkins School for Advanced International Studies (SAIS), where Deputy Secretary of Defense Paul Wolfowitz had just been his boss as SAIS Dean. The SAIS/Wolfowitz translator has not been giving any interviews.

The text of the translation itself admits it is not a verbatim transcript, but only provides "messages and information flow," whatever that means. Admittedly the tape is disjointed and non-sequential. Since I am not a technical expert, I will not comment upon how easy it would be to falsify this video. I doubt very seriously that any fair, objective and impartial judge would admit this video into evidence for consideration by a jury in a criminal case.

But let us put aside for the time being the long history of U.S. intelligence agencies operating both at home and abroad in order to manufacture "evidence" that suits the party line coming out of Washington, DC.[4] Let us further assume that everything in and about the bin Laden video is true and can be authenticated to the satisfaction of an impartial and objective international court of justice. Even so, the bin Laden video provided no evidence that implicated the Taliban government of Afghanistan in the 11 September 2001 attacks upon the United States. The video provides no justification for the United States to wage war against Afghanistan, a U.N. Member State, in gross violation of the United Nations Charter. The fact that Afghanistan's dysfunctional former President Rabbani was left to occupy the Afghan "Seat" at the United Nations makes no legal difference here. The United Nations Charter protected the State of Afghanistan from aggression by the United States. Indeed, the Clinton administration had already negotiated with the Taliban government over letting it have the U.N. Seat as well as extending it bilateral de jure recognition in return, in part, for the construction of the UNOCAL pipeline across Afghanistan,[5] a negotiation from which—ominously, in light of the onslaught to come—the Taliban government demurred.

Framing a Response to September 11

Terrorism and the Law

So let us now turn to the law. Immediately after the 11 September 2001 attacks President Bush's first public statement characterized these terrible attacks as an act of terrorism. Under United States domestic law there is a definition of terrorism, which clearly qualifies them as such. To be sure, under international law and practice there is no generally accepted definition of terrorism, for reasons that are too complicated to explain in detail here but basically relate to that hackneyed aphorism that "one person's terrorist is another person's freedom fighter."[6] Yet certainly under United States domestic law this qualified as an act or acts of terrorism.

What happened? It appears that President Bush consulted with Secretary Powell and all of a sudden they changed the rhetoric and characterization of these terrible attacks. They now called them an act of war—though clearly this was not an act of war, which international law and practice define as a military attack by one nation state upon another nation state.

There are enormous differences and consequences, however, in how you treat an act of terrorism compared to how you treat an act of war. This nation and others have dealt with acts of terrorism before. Normally acts of terrorism are dealt with as a matter of international and domestic law enforcement—which is, in my opinion, precisely how these terrible attacks should have been dealt with—not as an act of war.

Indeed there is a treaty directly on point to which both the United States and Afghanistan are party: the 1971 Convention for the Suppression of Unlawful Acts Against the Safety of Civil Aviation, the so-called Montreal Sabotage Convention. Article 1(I)(b) thereof criminalizes the destruction of civilian aircraft while in service. It has an entire legal regime specifically designed to deal with this type of situation and all issues related to it, including reference to the International Court of Justice to resolve any disputes that could not be settled by negotiations between the United States and Afghanistan or other contracting parties. The Bush Jr. administration simply ignored the Montreal Sabotage Convention completely, as well as the 12 or so multilateral conventions already on the books that deal with various components and aspects of what people generally call international terrorism, many of which could have been used and relied upon to handle this matter in a lawful, effective, and peaceful manner.

The U.S. Policy Preference: Not Terrorism—War

Instead, proving again the Bush Jr. administration's unwillingness to utilize international conventions which might require the submission of American power to external restraints, and thereby constrain rather than facilitate the realization of overt or covert American objectives, the Bush Jr. administration rejected this entire multilateral approach and called these terrible attacks an act of war. They deliberately invoked the rhetoric of Pearl Harbor, December 7, 1941. It was a conscious decision to escalate the emotions and perceptions of the American people generated on September 11, and thus dramatically escalate the stakes, both internationally and domestically.

The implication was that if this is an act of war, then you do not deal with it by means of international treaties and negotiations: You deal with an act of war by means of military force. You go to war. So a decision was made remarkably early in the process to ignore and abandon the entire framework of international treaties that had been established under the auspices of the United Nations Organization for the past 25 years in order to deal with acts of international terrorism and instead go to war against Afghanistan, a U.N. member state. In order to prevent the momentum towards war from being impeded, Bush Jr. issued an impossible ultimatum, refusing all negotiations with the Taliban government, as well as all the extensive due process protections that are required between sovereign states related to extraditions, etc. The Taliban government's requests for proof and offers to surrender bin Laden to a third party, similar to those which ultimately brought the Libyan Lockerbie suspects to trial, were all peremptorily ignored. Why such haste?

The U.N. Security Council Disagrees: Terrorism, Not War

An act of war has a technical legal meaning: basically, a military attack by one nation state against another nation state. While this is what happened on December 7, 1941, it is not what happened on September 11, 2001. Nonetheless, immediately after September 11, the Bush Jr. administration went to the United Nations Security Council in order to get a resolution authorizing the use of military force against Afghanistan and Al Qaeda. They failed. Indeed, the Security Council resolution that was adopted, instead of calling this an "armed attack" by one state against another state, denominated these events "terrorist attacks."[7] And again there is a magnitude of difference between an armed attack by one state against another state, which is an act of war, and a terrorist attack, which is not. Again, terrorists are dealt with as criminals. Terrorists are not treated like nation states. Terrorists are dealt with by means of international and domestic law enforcement. Terrorists are not given the dignity of special status under international law and practice.

Bush Sr. v. Bush Jr.

What the Bush Jr. administration tried to do in the Security Council was to get a resolution similar to that obtained by the Bush Sr. administration in the run up to the Gulf War in the late Fall of 1990. Bush Sr. got a resolution from the Security Council authorizing U.N. member states to use "all necessary means" in order to expel Iraq from Kuwait.[8] The Bush Sr. administration originally wanted language in there expressly authorizing the use of military force *in haec verba*. The Chinese objected, so the Security Council employed the euphemism by "all necessary means," though everyone knew what that meant. Besides, even if it may have been induced to do so, Iraq had actually invaded Kuwait, which was contrary to international law—a real act of war.[9]

The first Bush Jr. Security Council resolution, on the other hand, provided no authority to use military force at all. That language simply was not in there. A close reading of the Security Council Resolution indicates that Bush Jr. tried but failed to get the authorization to use force that Bush Sr. got. Bush Jr. was defeated at the Security Council. This failure, of course, did not make national headlines; rather, it was subsumed in commentary which dwelt on a U.N. supposedly galvanized behind the Bush Jr. administration to combat terrorism.

No Declaration of War from Congress

Having failed to co-opt the U.N. Security Council for war as his father had, Bush Jr. then went to the United States Congress and exploited the raw emotions of this national tragedy to ram through a congressional authorization to use force. The exact nature of the Bush Jr. proposal to Congress at that time is unknown. However, reading between the lines of a public statement made by Senator Robert Byrd that was reported in the *New York Times*, it appears that Bush Jr. wanted a formal declaration of war along the lines of what President Roosevelt got from Congress after Pearl Harbor.[10] Congress failed to give Bush Jr. that—and for a very good reason. If a formal declaration of war had been passed by Congress, it would have made Bush Jr. a "constitutional dictator" insofar as that, basically, Americans would now all be living under marshal law.[11] Congress might have just as well closed up and gone home for the rest of the duration of the Bush Jr. war against terrorism for all the difference they would have made. Bush Jr./Sr. would have known that full well. Indeed, prior to September 11, President Bush Jr. had publicly opined about becoming a U.S. "dictator."

The Infamy of *Korematsu*

As a direct result of that congressional declaration of war after Pearl Harbor, America made the infamous *Korematsu* mistake, whereby about 100,000 Japanese-American citizens and Japanese immigrants were rounded up and put in concentration camps on the basis of nothing more than an Executive Order that later on turned out to be based upon a gross misrepresentation of the factual allegation that Japanese in America constituted some type of unique security threat different from Germans in America or Italians in American, inter alia.[12] Obviously, in *Korematsu* race made all the difference. Again today, race is making all the difference in the Bush Jr. administration's specific targeting of Arabs and Muslims from the Middle East and Southwest Asia.

Had Bush Jr. received a formal declaration of war from Congress, many groups of American citizens could have been on the exact same legal footing of the terrible *Korematsu* case, which has never been overturned by the United States Supreme Court. We could have witnessed the mass internment of American citizens of Arab, Muslim, Middle Eastern, Asian, and African American (many of whom are Muslims) descent. Instead, to date at least, the Bush Jr. administration has been restricting itself to detaining aliens who fit into these racial and religious categories. Of course such discrimination violates the International Convention on the Elimination of All Forms of Racial Discrimination, to which the United States is a contracting party—yet another international convention that the Bush Jr. administration has set at naught. And we still could be seeing the mass detention and internment of American citizens of whatever ethnicity who may become engaged in civil resistance against administration policies if Bush Jr., Attorney General John Ashcroft, White House Counsel Alberto Gonzales and their reactionary coterie of Federalist Society lawyers can ultimately get their way. They have already instigated a nationwide campaign of illegal profiling against the racial and religious categories of U.S. citizens and aliens mentioned above.

Instead, A Blank Check to Use Military Force

Instead of a formal declaration of war, the U.S. Congress gave Bush Jr. what is called a War Powers Resolution Authorization. The War Powers Resolution of 1973 was passed over President Nixon's veto by a two-thirds majority in both Houses of Congress, and was expressly designed to prevent another Vietnam War.[13] Although the resolution that Bush Jr. did get from Congress is not a formal declaration of war, it was stronger than the Tonkin Gulf Resolution,[14] which served as the legal pretext for President Johnson's massive escalation of the Vietnam War into outright genocide against the Vietnamese People. Only one courageous Member of Congress, Barbara Lee, an African American representative from Oakland, voted against it, as a matter of principle.

This War Powers Resolution authorization basically gives Bush Jr. a blank check to use military force against any individual, organization, or state that he alleges—by means of his own *ipse dixit*—was somehow involved in the attacks on September 11, or else harbored those who were.[15] To date, the number of potential targets has fluctuated from between 30 to 60 nation states, all of which are U.N. Members and thus protected from U.S. aggression by the U.N. Charter. In other words, Bush Jr. has received a blank check from the United States Congress to exert military force pretty much against any state he wants to despite the U.N. Charter. This was then followed by Congress granting Bush Jr. a $20 billion appropriation as a cash down payment on this blank check in order to exert military force against Afghanistan, for starters.

Bush Sr. v. Bush Jr. Redux

Let us compare and contrast this congressional resolution with the War Powers Resolution obtained by Bush Sr. in January of 1991. First, Bush Sr. got the Security Council resolution mentioned above, which he took to the U.S. Congress for authorization under the War Powers Resolution to use military force in order to carry it out. Congress then gave Bush Sr. a very precise authorization to use military force for the express purpose of carrying out the Security Council resolution, that is, only for the purpose of expelling Iraq from Kuwait.[16] And indeed that is what Bush Sr. did. He expelled Iraq from Kuwait, stopping south of Basra, saying that was all the authority he had. This is not to approve what Bush Sr. did in that war, but simply to compare it with Bush Jr.

While Bush Sr. has been criticized on the grounds that he should have marched all the way to Baghdad, he truly had no authority from either the Security Council or from the United States Congress to do so. Compare that to Bush Jr.'s War Powers Resolution that basically gave Bush Jr. a blank check to use military force against anyone he wants to, and with no more than his asserting the need to do so. It is astounding to believe. With such latitude, even more extensive than that of the Tonkin Gulf Resolution, can another Vietnam War be far behind? Has one already commenced, with direct U.S. military re-intervention into the Philippines?

"Ending States"

At this writing, the Bush Jr. administration is publicly debating the "wisdom" of launching yet another massive military attack upon Iraq—only this time for the express purpose of deposing and replacing the Government of Iraq. Needless to say, such an unwarranted and aggressive attack on yet another sovereign state would violate the United Nations Charter, inter alia.

Worse yet, Deputy Secretary of Defense Paul Wolfowitz has publicly bragged about "ending states"[17]—a rhetorical escalation from efforts to designate some as "failed" states, whose institutional and legal structures might thereby be illegally disregarded by the United States. Terminating states, if actually carried out, would violate the 1948 Genocide Convention, to which the United States is a contracting party. Such a reprehensible statement by Wolfowitz acting within the scope of his official duties could be taken to the World Court and filed in order to prove the existence of genocidal intent by the United States government. Indeed, there is a good chance that the first victim of this Wolfowitz threat may be the Republic of Iraq, which has been continuously and illegally bombed by the United States and the United Kingdom since the end of the Gulf War eleven years ago under the pretext of enforcing unauthorized "no-fly zones." In this regard, Bush Jr.'s aggressive threat to Iraq, Iran, and North Korea uttered during the course of his State of the Union Address to Congress on 29 January 2002 does not augur well. It appears from his language that the Bush Jr. administration is deliberately preparing the ground for a bogus claim to "anticipatory self-defense" in order to justify their pre-planned aggression against Iraq.

Honest Nuclear Warmongering

Since the events of September 11, the American people may have been treated to more truth from their government than ever before. In the post-Vietnam era, when the notorious Phoenix program of assassinations finally came to light, public indignation was sufficient to empower investigation by the Church Committee, and a subsequent ban on foreign assassinations. Over the past decade and increasingly under the Bush Jr. administration, however, open talk of intended foreign assassinations, efforts to overthrow the leaders of other sovereign states, or invasions of an unspecified array of nations can reach the daily papers through on-record remarks by elected officials. Secretary of Defense Donald Rumsfeld can call for the apprehension of suspects "dead or alive" or even "preferably dead"—which would happily avoid all the legal difficulties of proving bin Laden guilty in an evidentiary manner, or indeed the possibility of being confronted by a range of legal improprieties or malfeasances committed on the American side, especially by the CIA.[18] Even the *International Herald Tribune,* in its effort to convince European readerships of the longstanding struggle of the U.S. to deal with Al Qaeda, revealed how the comparatively temperate Clinton had signed three highly classified Memorandums of Notification authorizing killing instead of capturing Mr. bin Laden, then added several of Al Qaeda's senior lieutenants to the list, and finally approved the shooting down of private civilian aircraft on which they flew.[19]

It should come as no surprise therefore, in this onslaught of candid revelation of Machiavellian Realpolitik, that the historically covert intent of America's nuclear deterrence policy should come to light through almost off-the-cuff remarks such as those by the omnipresent Deputy Secretary of Defense Wolfowitz appearing in the 9 January 2002 edition of the *New York Times*:

> "We're looking at a transformation of our deterrence posture from *an almost exclusive emphasis on offensive nuclear forces* [italics added] to a force that includes defenses as well as offenses, that includes conventional strike capabilities as well as nuclear strike capabilities, and includes a much reduced level of nuclear strike capability," the deputy secretary of defense, Paul D. Wolfowitz, said.

Well at least he was honest about it.

Wolfowitz admitted that the current U.S. practice of so-called nuclear "deterrence" is in fact really based upon "an almost exclusive emphasis on offensive nuclear forces." To reiterate, since this deserves emphasis: The U.S. Deputy Secretary of Defense has publicly admitted and conceded that "almost" all U.S. nuclear forces are really "offensive" and not really "defenses." Once again, that Statement could be taken to the International Court of Justice and filed against the United States government as an Admission against Interest, Wolfowitz acting within the scope of his official duties. Of course the Peace Movement and informed American public knew this was true all along. Nonetheless, it should be regarded as an ominous sign of the times that the Pentagon has become so brazen that it is publicly admitting U.S. nuclear criminality to the entire world.

The Prostitution of NATO

In furtherance of its quest for war-making pseudo-legitimacy, the Bush Jr. administration also went to NATO headquarters in Brussels to get a resolution of support for the use of force. NATO proceeded to invoke Article 5 of the NATO Pact.[20] Article 5 of the NATO Pact is only intended to deal with an armed attack by a nation state or states against a NATO member state or states. It is not, and has never been, intended to deal with a terrorist attack.

NATO was originally organized as a collective self-defense pact pursuant to Article 51 of the U.N. Charter, recognizing the right of individual and collective self-defense in the event of an armed attack by one nation state against another nation state. In theory, the NATO Pact was supposed to deal with an armed attack upon a NATO member state or states by a member or members of the Warsaw Pact, especially the Soviet Union. But with the collapse of the Warsaw Pact and the disintegration of the Soviet

Union, there was no real justification or excuse anymore for the continued existence of NATO. NATO had lost its supposed raison d'être.

In an effort to keep NATO alive, Bush Sr. then tried to transmute its very nature in order to serve two additional purposes: (1) policing Eastern Europe; and (2) military intervention into the Middle East in order to secure the oil and gas fields. The NATO Council basically approved Bush Sr.'s transmutation of NATO from a lawful collective self-defense agreement into an illegal, offensive interventionary pact.[21] Shades of the 1939 Ribbentrop-Molotov Pact that was the necessary precursor to Hitler's invasion of Poland, thus leading to the commencement of World War II!

A generation later, Bush Sr. would set the political predicate for NATO's illegal war against Serbia over Kosova in 1999 under the criminal leadership of President Bill Clinton. Serbia never attacked a NATO member state; rather, the reverse was true. The NATO Alliance attacked Serbia with no authorization from the U.N. Security Council.[22] But this was what "policing" Eastern Europe was supposed to be all about in the estimation of Bush Sr. and Clinton. As I always asked my law students from 1991 to 2001: Please explain to me the basic difference between Clinton and Bush Sr.?

The main legal problem here is that the NATO Pact provides no authorization to do this at all and indeed should have to be amended by the parliaments of the NATO member states to justify either policing Eastern Europe or as an interventionary force against the Middle East. Furthermore, any such offensive mission for NATO would also have required the express authorization of the U.N. Security Council on a case-by-case basis as clearly required by U.N. Charter Article 53(1). Bush Sr. and Clinton simply wanted a useful tool for collective, offensive military intervention under the predominant control of the United States that would provide a thin veneer of multilateralism for domestic and international propaganda purposes, while at the same time avoiding the supervisory jurisdiction of the U.N. Security Council in accordance with the requirements of the U.N. Charter. The same was true for the Bush Jr. Leaguers in their prostitution of NATO after 11 September 2001.

Immediately thereafter, Bush Jr. simply followed in the illegal pathway that had already been carved out for him by Bush Sr. and Clinton. The Bush Jr. invocation of NATO Article 5 was completely bogus. It is a matter of some irony but little surprise that the United States, which allegedly set up NATO in order to "protect" Europe from an armed attack by the Soviet Union, has become the very first beneficiary of NATO's invocation of Article 5. He who pays the piper calls the tune. Or as Clinton officials readily admitted during their illegal NATO war against Serbia over Kosova: The U.S. *is* NATO! This seeming paradox can be resolved by understanding that the real reason why the United States set up NATO in the first place was to secure American control and domination of the European Continent.[23] That still is NATO's primary purpose, even as Europe struggles to bring into being its own military force for collective self-defense.

Bush Jr.'s Crusade

Today the NATO Member States are readily enlisting in the Bush Jr.

holy war against international terrorism in Afghanistan, Somalia, and other Arab and Muslim countries. We are witnessing another medieval Crusade by the White, European, Christian colonial powers against the 1.2 billion Muslims of the world organized into about 58 countries, most of whom are or are regarded as People of Color in the racist European mindset, and who happen to legally own the massive oil and natural gas resources of the Middle East, Central Asia, and Southeast Asia that the West so desperately craves. That is what is really going on here. And if you have any doubt, remember that it was Bush Jr. himself who publicly called his holy war against international terrorism a "crusade."

Of course the Muslim World knows all about Western Crusades and Western Crusaders. The "clash of civilizations" forecast by my fellow Harvard Ph.D. graduate Samuel Huntington has received intensive discussion in the West,[24] while the Iranian riposte calling for "a dialogue between civilizations" has gone unnoticed. The Muslim world has recently witnessed widespread extermination of Muslim Peoples by Western Crusaders and their surrogates in Bosnia, Chechnya, Iraq, Palestine, Lebanon, and now Afghanistan. It is almost as if the script for the Bush Sr./Jr. New World Order had been lifted from Huntington's clash of civilizations. Ominously, that ponderous tome ends with a prognosticated catastrophic war between the United States and China— bringing to mind again the Bush Jr. administration's reckless hostility towards the PRC in its earliest days.

The U.S./U.N. Ambassador of Death

By going to NATO, the Bush Jr. administration was attempting to get some type of multilateral endorsement for a war against Afghanistan after it had failed to achieve the same at the United Nations Security Council. The Bush Jr. administration then tried once again to get authority for war from the Security Council, but all they got was a Presidential Statement, which legally meant nothing. They then tried yet a third time to get some type of authorization to use military force from the Security Council. This time they did get stronger language but—and it is necessary to emphasize this, since the U.N.stand has not been clearly impressed upon the American public—they still failed to get any authorization from the Security Council to use military force for any reason, let alone a full scale war against Afghanistan, a U.N. Member state.[25]

Then the new U.S. Ambassador to the United Nations, John Negroponte, sent a letter to the U.N. Security Council asserting Article 51 of the United Nations Charter.[26] Some of us in the Peace Movement are familiar with Negroponte, who was the U.S. Ambassador in Honduras during the Reagan/ Bush Contra terror war against Nicaragua, and has the blood of about 35,000 Nicaraguan civilians on his hands—about ten times the number of victims from the terrorist attacks on 11 September 2001. Indeed, because of this, the only way Bush Jr. could get him confirmed by the Senate was to ram Negroponte's name through the Senate "confirmation" process right after the 11 September 2001 attacks. Yet another Machiavellian exploitation of this terrible national tragedy by George W. Bush. In an unwitting tribute to Orwell, the Bush Jr. administration selected Negroponte to lecture the entire world at the U.N. about international terrorism—a subject upon which he is an acknowledged expert by dint of vast personal experience.

Nazi "Self-defense" Resurfaces

Given his "priors", the letter by Negroponte to the Security Council was not surprising. It basically said that the United States reserved its right to use force in self-defense against any state that the Bush Jr. administration felt the need to victimize in order to fight their holy war against international terrorism as determined by themselves. Soon thereafter a reporter from the *San Francisco Chronicle* asked me if there was any precedent for the sweeping position being asserted by Negroponte that the United States is reserving the right to go to war in self-defense against 30 to 60 other states as determined solely by the United States. I responded that there is indeed one very unfortunate precedent, recorded in the Nuremberg Judgment of 1946.

It was striking but not surprising that this mass murderer Negroponte was making an argument similar to that put forth in defense of the Nazi war criminals before the Nuremberg Tribunal with respect to the non-applicability of the Kellogg-Briand Pact of 1928. This "Paris Peace Pact" had formally renounced war as an instrument of national policy. Article 1 provided: "The High Contracting Parties solemnly declare in the names of their respective peoples that they condemn recourse to war for the solution of international controversies, and renounce it as an instrument of national policy in their relations with one another." However, when signing the Pact, Germany entered a reservation to the effect that it reserved the right to go to war in self-defense as determined by itself.

So when in 1945 the Nazi war criminals were prosecuted for crimes against peace on the basis of the Kellogg-Briand Pact, they basically argued that the Second World War was a war of self-defense as determined by the Nazi government, and therefore that the Nuremberg Tribunal had no competence to determine otherwise because of Germany's self-judging reservation. Needless to say, the Tribunal summarily rejected this preposterous argument and later convicted and sentenced to death several Nazi war criminals for the commission of crimes against peace, among other international crimes.[27] Both the United States and Afghanistan are contracting parties to the Kellogg-Briand Pact. Article 6(a) of the 1945 Nuremberg Charter defines "crimes against peace" as follows:

> (a) CRIMES AGAINST PEACE: namely, planning, preparation, initiation or waging of a war of aggression, or a war in violation of international treaties, agreements or assurances, or participation in a common plan or conspiracy for the accomplishment of any of the foregoing;...

The Bush Jr. war against Afghanistan in violation of the Kellogg-Briand Pact of 1928 and the U.N. Charter of 1945 constitutes a Nuremberg Crime

Against Peace. This provides yet another glaring example of precisely why the Pentagon and Bush Jr. have so vigorously opposed the establishment of an International Criminal Court.

Retaliation Is Not Self-Defense

Clearly the Bush Jr. war against Afghanistan is not self-defense. Let us be honest about it. The entire world knows it. At best it may be vengeance, catharsis, or scape-goating. Call it what you want, but it is not self-defense. Retaliation is never self-defense.

Indeed, this truth had always been the official position of the United States government, even during the darkest days of the Vietnam War. In 1973-74, Eugene V. Rostow—who had been Undersecretary of State in the genocidal Johnson administration, and was later to serve as the Director of the Arms Control and Disarmament Agency (ACDA) in the Reagan/Bush administration (truly Orwellian!)—requested that the Department of State change its policy on retaliation and reprisal. Pursuant to Rostow's request, the State Department did look into the matter. But the State Department concluded that there were no good grounds for the United States government to change its longstanding policy that retaliation and reprisal were not legitimate exercises of the right of self-defense and, therefore, were prohibited by international law.[28]

Choosing Violent Resolutions for International Disputes

The Taliban government of Afghanistan had made repeated offers to negotiate a solution to the dispute over bin Laden with the United States. Even before the tragic events of September 11, negotiations were going on between the United States and the Taliban government over the disposition of bin Laden—as well as over the UNOCAL oil pipeline. The Taliban government had offered to have bin Laden tried in a neutral Islamic court by Muslim judges applying the laws of Sharia. Later on, their proposal was modified to simply have him tried before some type of neutral court, which would exclude handing him over to the United States government. Finally, the Taliban government even offered to try bin Laden themselves provided the United States gave them some credible evidence of his involvement in the 11 September attacks, which was never done.

Bush Jr. responded to their overtures in his 20 September 2001 Address before the U.S. Congress by ruling out any type of negotiations and instead issuing the Taliban government an impossible ultimatum. However, Article II of the above-mentioned Kellogg-Briand Pact requires the peaceful resolution of international disputes between contracting parties such as the United States and Afghanistan, as follows:

> *Article II*
> The High Contracting Parties agree that the settlement or solution of all disputes or conflicts of whatever nature or of whatever

origin they may be, which may arise among them, shall never be sought except by pacific means.

To the same effect are Article 2(3) and Article 33(1) of the United Nations Charter:

Article 2
   The Organization and its Members, in pursuit of the Purposes stated in Article 1, shall act in accordance with the following Principles.
   ....
   3. All Members shall settle their international disputes by peaceful means in such a manner that international peace and security, and justice, are not endangered.
   ....
   CHAPTER VI
   PACIFIC SETTLEMENT OF DISPUTES
   Article 33
   1. The parties to any dispute, the continuance of which is likely to endanger the maintenance of international peace and security, shall, first of all, seek a solution by negotiation, inquiry, mediation, conciliation, arbitration, judicial settlement, resort to regional agencies or arrangements, or other peaceful means of their own choice...

Indeed, if you read the ultimatum that President Bush Jr. publicly gave to the Taliban government of Afghanistan, no self-respecting government in the world could have complied with that ultimatum. Quite obviously the Bush Jr. ultimatum was specifically drafted and publicly uttered so that it could not be complied with by the Taliban government of Afghanistan.

Indeed, there are striking similarities between the Bush Jr. public ultimatum to Afghanistan and the ultimatum given in private by U.S. Secretary of State Jim Baker on behalf of Bush Sr. to Tariq Aziz on the eve of the Bush Sr. war against Iraq. That Bush Sr. ultimatum was deliberately designed so as not to be acceptable, which it was not. Why? Because the Bush Sr. administration had already made the decision to go to war against Iraq no matter what. A similar ultimatum had been delivered to Milosevic at Rambouillet prior to the NATO war against Serbia. Bush Jr. thus once again, following his predecessors, trod the path of Machiavelli when he issued his public ultimatum to the Taliban government of Afghanistan.

It appears that the Bush Jr. administration is basically following the same script and scenario that had already been written and successfully carried out over a decade ago by the Bush Sr. Leaguers when they went to war against Iraq for the primary purpose of establishing direct American military control and domination over the Persian Gulf oil and gas fields. Only this time the Bushes were putting a move on the vast energy resources of Central Asia. As is well known, the Bush Family has extensive investments in the

Oil and Gas Business, as does Vice President Cheney, who earlier served as Bush Sr.'s Minister of War. The same is true for other prominent Bush Jr./Sr. officials. Two major grabs for world hegemony and family fortunes.

Humanitarian Catastrophe

Now, all that being said, what then is really going on here? If there is no basis in fact and no basis in law for this war against Afghanistan, why are we doing this? Why are we creating this humanitarian catastrophe for the Afghan people? After all, it was Bush Jr.'s threat to bomb Afghanistan that put millions of Afghans on the move without food, clothing, housing, water, or medical facilities. The result has been a humanitarian catastrophe for anywhere from 5 to 7 million Afghans, particularly as the winter approached in Afghanistan. U.S. responsibility cannot be cloaked by the American media's incessant references to the ravages of Afghanistan's decades-long conflicts.

Indeed, the Bush Jr. administration ordered Pakistan to close the border with Afghanistan so that humanitarian relief supplies could not be shipped by land to its long-suffering people. The starvation of civilians as a method of warfare is prohibited by Article 54(I) of Geneva Protocol I of 1977, and thus a war crime. The so-called U.S. airlifts of food packets—dropped at first in yellow packets similar in color to unexploded bomblets from the cluster bombs it also dropped—was nothing more than an international propaganda campaign, receiving extensive criticism from international NGOs already working on site. The same was true of Bush Jr.'s personal appeal to the Children of America to send in $1 to help the Children of Afghanistan. It would have been better to auction off the payload of one B2 Bomber.

Why War?

Why did we really bomb, attack, and invade Afghanistan? Could one truly say it was even so human a motivation as retaliation—or vengeance—or even atavistic bloodlust? No! The Bush Jr./Sr. Leaguers are cold, calculating, and shrewd Machiavellians. They know exactly what they are doing and why they are doing it. And during the first two weeks of the war it became crystal clear what their ultimate objective really was.

Secretary of Defense Rumsfeld flew over to Uzbekistan and concluded an agreement with their well-known dictator Karimov to the effect that the United States government will protect Uzbekistan—irrespective of the fact that the Secretary of Defense has no constitutional authority to conclude such an agreement. Constitutional authority aside, the Pentagon is now in the process of establishing a long-term military base in Uzbekistan. That base and this war have been in the works for quite some time. U.S. Special Forces have been over there for several years training the Uzbekistan military.

Uzbekistan now wants a Status of Forces Agreement (SOFA) with the United States. A SOFA permits the long-term deployment of significant numbers of U.S. armed forces in another state. The U.S. has SOFAs with Germany, Japan, and South Korea, inter alia, and has had troops in all three of those countries since 1945 in order to control them. When the U.S. gets its military base in Uzbekistan, it will clearly not be leaving anytime soon.

It is obvious that this unconstitutional agreement between Rumsfeld and Karimov is to set the legal predicate for America to stay in Uzbekistan for the next 20 years or so for the alleged purpose of defending this country from Afghanistan, where the U.S. has deliberately created total chaos in the first place. This is exactly the same rationale that has been made for keeping the United States military forces deployed in the Persian Gulf for over eleven years after the Gulf War. Indeed, planning for the Gulf War went all the way back to the Carter administration with its so-called Rapid Deployment Force,[29] later renamed the U.S. Central Command that carried out the war against Iraq and still *de facto* occupies these Persian Gulf countries and their oil fields. The U.S. still retained about 20,000 troops sitting on top of the oil and gas fields in all these countries. It even established a separate naval fleet in Bahrain to police the Persian Gulf oil fields. It never had any intention of leaving the Persian Gulf. It went there to stay.

It's Still the Oil, Stupid!

Today the U.S. Central Command is executing the Pentagon's outstanding war plan against Afghanistan and deploying U.S. military forces to build U.S. military bases in Uzbekistan, Afghanistan, Pakistan, Kyrghyzstan, and Tajikistan. There is more than enough evidence in the public record that the U.S. war against Afghanistan had been planned and prepared well before 11 September 2001.[30] Clearly since at least 11 September 2001, the world has been witnessing the formal execution of a Pentagon war plan that had been in the works for about four years.

Why do we want military bases in Uzbekistan, Kyrghyzstan, Tajikistan, Pakistan, and Afghanistan? Very simple: The oil and natural gas resources of Central Asia, reported to be the second largest deposits in the world after the Persian Gulf. Shortly after the collapse of the Soviet Union and the ascent to independence of its constituent states in 1991, U.S. think-tanks and their respective "thinkers" produced all sorts of studies about how a U.S. presence in Central Asia had suddenly become a "vital national security interest" of the United States because of its vast energy resources. Yet another "vital national interest" the American public had never heard of or even dreamed about before.

Since Central Asia is landlocked, the United States government wanted to find a way to get the oil and natural gas out, while avoiding Iran, Russia, and China. The easiest way to do that was to construct a pipeline south through Afghanistan, into Pakistan and right out to the Arabian Sea. UNOCAL had been negotiating to do this with the Taliban government of Afghanistan for quite some time, still with the full support of the United States government into the summer of 2001, but their negotiations had failed. The U.S. government then tendered a proverbial offer that could not be refused to the Taliban government.

Just as the Persian Gulf War against Iraq was all about oil and natural gas, this war against Afghanistan too is all about oil and natural gas—as well as about strategically outflanking Russia, China, Iran, and India by establishing U.S. military bases throughout Central Asia. The United States is going to be there for quite some time—at least until all that oil and natural gas have been sucked out of Central Asia. This move into Central Asia under the rubric of waging a non-delimited holy war against international terrorism represents yet another major expansion of the American Empire, deep into the sphere of influence of a former super-power, and shoving up against distant emerging world powers such as China and India, none of which can be counted on as friendly to America. Imposing Pax Americana upon Central Asia may, in the end, exemplify the limits of America's power, rather than its range. Not only foreign populations, but the American people themselves, will suffer from this imperial overstretch.

How Empires Rule at Home

Undoubtedly, the further expansion of the American Empire and Pax Americana abroad will require the further imposition of an American police state here at home. As the Romans discovered, an empire is incompatible with a Republic. No point would be served here by reviewing the extensive literature that was generated during the Vietnam War comparing the United States with the demise of the imperial Athenian democracy during what Thucydides first denominated as the "Peloponnesian War" that really extended over 27 years. Yet the Bush Jr. administration is publicly and shamelessly promising us a war against terrorism without a conceivable end in sight. Not even the proverbial light at the end of the tunnel.

Bush Jr.'s Constitutional Coup D'État

From the Supreme Court's installation of Bush Jr. as President to the Ashcroft/Federalist Society post-September 11 regime of police state "laws," the politico-legal functioning of America is increasingly resembling that of a Banana Republic. Since September 11, we have seen one blow against the U.S. Constitution after another. For example, Attorney General John Ashcroft unilaterally instituted the monitoring of attorney-client communications despite the Fourth Amendment ban on unreasonable searches and seizures and the Sixth Amendment right to representation by counsel in criminal cases. He just went ahead and did it, without even bothering to inform anyone.

Over 1100 aliens have been picked up and "disappeared" by Ashcroft and his Department of Injustice. The American people have no idea where most of these people are. They are being held on the basis of immigration law, not criminal law, for a period of detention which has not been defined. Ashcroft proclaimed another ukaze that these immigration proceedings must be held in secret. The phenomenon of "enforced disappearances" is considered to be a crime against humanity by Article 7(I)(i) of the Rome Statute for the International Criminal Court.

It appears that many of these aliens have been deprived of their basic human rights to consular notification and access as set forth in the 1963

Vienna Convention on Consular Relations, to which the United States is a contracting party and which even the U.S. State Department concedes constitutes binding customary international law. Apparently Bush Jr.'s left hand does not care about what his right hand does. Yet another international convention set at naught.

The one characteristic these detained foreigners have in common is that they are mostly Muslims, Arabs, and Asians. Everyone needs a scapegoat for the 11 September tragedy, and it looks like we have one, both at home and abroad. Thousands more such aliens are being moved into the pipeline for the Ashcroft gulag by the FBI.

Ashcroft is now planning to reinstate the infamous COINTELPRO Program, whose atrocities against the civil rights and civil liberties of the American people have been amply documented elsewhere.[31]

It is just a matter of time before the Bush Jr. Leaguers unleash the newly-augmented powers of the FBI, CIA, and NSA directly against the American people. And we already have 2 million Americans rotting away in prison—the highest rate of incarceration in the world, a disproportionate majority of whom are Americans of Color, victims of the Nixon/Ford, Reagan/Bush, and Clinton administrations' racist "war on drugs," which is really a war against people of color.[32] The American police state has already arrived for people of color!

Ashcroft's Police State

This brings the analysis to the Ashcroft Police State Act. There are no other words to describe it. While Bush failed to get a formal declaration of war that would have rendered him a constitutional dictator, clearly Attorney General John Ashcroft and his right-wing Federalist Society lawyers took every piece of regressive legislation off the shelf, tied it all into what they called an anti-terrorism bill, and then rammed it through Congress, giving it the appropriately Orwellian name of the U.S.A. Patriot Act.[33] According to one report, Ashcroft's first draft would have had Congress suspend the ancient Writ of Habeas Corpus—the necessary prerequisite for imposing a police state in the United States of America. Many Members of Congress publicly admitted that they did not even bother to read the Ashcroft Police State Act. Another Congressman said basically: "Right, but there's nothing new about that." Interestingly enough the so-called liberal Democrats in the House and the Senate were willing to give Bush Jr. and Ashcroft more police state powers than the conservative Republicans in the House. But there are no real differences that matter between Republicans and Democrats when it comes to promoting America's self-proclaimed "Manifest Destiny" to control the world and now outer space too.

Bush's Kangaroo Courts

It would take an entire law review article for me to analyze all the legal and human rights problems with Bush Jr.'s proposed military commissions. Here a cabal of Federalist Society lawyers in the White House got President

Bush to sign a Presidential Order on 13 November 2001 which, when implemented, will be widely recognized to constitute a grave breach of the Geneva Conventions and establish a prima facie case of criminal accountability against the President himself. It is emblematic of this particular war that right towards its very outset President George W. Bush personally incriminated himself under both international criminal law and United States domestic criminal law. The Bush Jr. administration has severely undermined the integrity of the Four Geneva Conventions of 1949. By doing this, the Bush Jr. administration has opened up U.S. Armed Forces and civilians around the world to similar reprisals, which has already happened.

As a licensed attorney for 25 years, a law professor for 23 years and someone who has done a good deal of criminal defense work in U.S. federal courts, I am opposed to the insinuation of these Federalist Society lawyers that America's federal courts established by Article III of the U.S. Constitution cannot hold accountable those responsible for the crimes of 11 September 2001. This is an insult to all federal judges, federal prosecutors, federal public defenders and all the lawyers who are officers of these courts.

In one fell stroke these Federalist Society lawyers have besmirched and undermined the integrity of two banches of the United States federal government established by the Constitution—the Presidency and the Judiciary. So far the U.S. Congress has supinely gone along with the Bush Jr. police state agenda. If and when these Bush/Ashcroft police state practices make their way to the U.S. Supreme Court, many of them will probably be upheld. After all, a 5 to 4 majority of the Supreme Court already gave the Presidency to Bush Jr. We need to seriously consider whether they would strike down laws and practices that would give Bush Jr. a Police State as well.

Philosophers have taught that a People get the type of government they deserve. If the American people permit the Bush Jr. Leaguers to impose a Police State at home in the name of furthering Pax Americana abroad, we will have deserved it by abnegating our responsibilities as Citizens living in what is supposed to be a constitutional Republic with a commitment to the Rule of Law. The same thing happened to the Romans and to the Athenians. The United States of America is not immune to the laws of history. Sic transit gloria mundi!

The Bush Jr. Withdrawal from the ABM Treaty

Then, as had been foreshadowed, whispered, hinted at, and finally broadcast over a period of months, came the monumentally insane, horrendous, and tragic announcement on 13 December 2001 by the Bush Jr. administration to withdraw from the ABM Treaty, effective within six months. Of course it was sheer coincidence that the Pentagon released the bin Laden video just as Bush Jr. himself publicly announced his indefensible decision to withdraw from the ABM Treaty in order to pursue his phantasmagorical National Missile Defense (NMD) Program, the lineal successor to the Reagan/Bush Star Wars dream. Predictably, the bin Laden video back-staged this major, pro-nuclear announcement. Once again the terrible national tragedy of 11 September was shamelessly exploited in order to justify a reckless decision that had already been made for other reasons long before then. Then on 25 January 2002, the Pentagon promptly conducted a sea-based NMD test in gross violation of Article 5(I) of the ABM Treaty without waiting for the required six months to expire, thus driving a proverbial nail into the coffin of the ABM Treaty before its body was legally dead.

The Bush Jr. withdrawal from the ABM Treaty, which was originally negotiated by those well-known Realpolitikers Richard Nixon and Henry Kissinger,[34] threatens the very existence of other seminal arms control treaties and regimes such as the Nuclear Non-Proliferation Treaty (NPT) and the Biological Weapons Convention, which have similar withdrawal clauses. The prospect of yet another round of the multilateral and destabilizing nuclear arms race now stares humanity directly in the face, even as the Bush Jr. administration today prepares for the quick resumption of nuclear testing at the Nevada test site in outright defiance of the CTBT regime and NPT Article VI. The entire edifice of international agreements regulating, reducing, and eliminating weapons of mass extermination (WME) has been shaken to its very core. Now the Pentagon and the CIA are back into the dirty business of researching, developing and testing biological weapons and biological agents that are clearly prohibited by the Biological Weapons Convention and its U.S. domestic implementing legislation, the Biological Weapons Anti-Terrorism Act of 1989.[35]

Conclusion

This book comes at a critical time in American history: when an expansionist American administration not only endangers the past century's momentous achievements in international treaty law by crashing through them, but also threatens the very fabric of domestic rights and freedoms cherished by American citizens enshrined in the Rule of Law and the U.S. Constitution itself.[36]

Despite the best efforts by the Bush Jr. Leaguers to the contrary, we American Citizens still have our First Amendment rights: freedom of speech, freedom of association, freedom of assembly, freedom to petition our government for the redress of these massive grievances, civil resistance, etc. We are going to have to start vigorously exercising all of our First Amendment rights right now; we must use them or indeed, as the saying goes, we will lose them. We must act—not only for the good of the people of Afghanistan, for the good of the peoples of Southwest Asia—but for our own future, that of our children, that of our nation as a democratic society committed to the rule of law and the U.S. Constitution, and for all humanity.

1 February, 2002

Chapter Seven

The Bush Jr. Administration's War of Aggression Against Iraq

Neo-Cons, Fundies, Feddies, and Con-Artists

It is now a matter of public record that immediately after being inaugurated as president in January 2001, George Bush, Jr., Vice-President Dick Cheney, Secretary of War Donald Rumsfeld, and his pro-Israeli "Neoconservative" Deputy Paul Wolfowitz began to plot, plan, scheme, and conspire to wage a war of aggression against Iraq. Later, they manipulated the tragic events of September 11 in order to provide a pretext for doing so.[1] The fact that Iraq had nothing at all to do with September 11 or supporting Al-Qaeda—as the CIA itself advised—made no difference to Rumsfeld, Wolfowitz, their Undersecretary of War Douglas Feith, Undersecretary of State John Bolton, and the numerous other pro-Israeli Neo-Cons inhabiting the Bush Jr. administration.

These pro-Israeli Neo-Cons had been schooled in the Machiavellian/Nietzschean theories of Professor Leo Strauss, who taught political philosophy at the University of Chicago in its Department of Political Science. The best exposé of Strauss's pernicious theories on law, politics, government, for elitism, and against democracy can be found in two scholarly books by the Canadian Professor of Political Philosophy, Shadia B. Drury, who wrote:

> . . . According to Strauss, ancient philosophers (such as Plato) were wise and wily, but modern philosophers (such as Locke and other liberals) were foolish and vulgar. The wise ancients thought that the unwashed masses were not fit for either truth or liberty; and giving them these sublime treasures was like throwing pearls before swine. Accordingly, they believed that society needs an elite of philosophers or intellectuals to manufacture "noble lies" for the consumption of the masses. Not surprisingly, the ancients had no use for democracy...
>
> ....
>
> . . . [I]n Strauss's estimation, they were right in thinking that there is only one natural right—the right of the superior to rule over the inferior—the master over the slave, the husband over the wife, and the wise few over the vulgar many. . .[2]

I entered the University of Chicago in September of 1968 shortly after Strauss had retired. But I was trained in Chicago's Political Science Department by Strauss's foremost protégé, co-author, and later literary executor, Joseph Cropsey. Based upon my personal experience as an alumnus of Chicago's Political Science Department (A.B., 1971, in Political Science), I concur completely with Professor Drury's devastating critique of Strauss, as with her penetrating analysis of the degradation of the American political process that has been inflicted by Chicago's Straussian Neo-Con cabal.[3]

The University of Chicago routinely trained me and innumerable other students to become ruthless and unprincipled Machiavellians. That is precisely why so many neophyte Neo-Con students gravitated towards the University of Chicago or towards Chicago Alumni at other universities. Years later, the University of Chicago became the "brains" behind the Bush Jr. Empire and his Ashcroft police state. Attorney General John Ashcroft received his law degree from the University of Chicago in 1967. Many of his lawyers at the Bush Jr. Department of Justice are members of the right-wing, racist, bigoted, reactionary, and totalitarian Federalist Society (aka "Feddies"),[4] which originated in part at the University of Chicago. Feddies wrote the USA Patriot Act (USAPA) I and the draft for USAPA II, which constitute the blueprint for establishing an American police state.[5] Meanwhile, the Department of Justice's own F.B.I. continues to cover up the U.S. governmental origins of the post September 11, 2001 anthrax attack on Washington, D.C. that enabled Ashcroft and his Feddies to stampede the U.S. Congress into passing USAPA I into law in the first place.[6]

Integrally related to and overlapping with the Feddies are members of the University of Chicago "School" of Law-and-Kick-Them-in-the-Groin-Economics, which in turn was founded upon the market fundamentalism of Milton Friedman, long-time Professor of Economics at the University of Chicago, now retired. Friedman and his "Chicago Boys" provided academic cover for right-wing economic policies that have raped, robbed, looted, plundered, and pillaged economies and their respective peoples all over the developing world.[7] This Chicago gang of academic con-artists and charlatans subscribe to the Nazi Doctrine of "useless eaters," the notion that human beings with physical, mental, or emotional impairments are not worth expending the resources necessary to keep them alive. Pursuant to Friedman's philosophy of market fundamentalism, the "privatization" of Iraq and its oil industry are already underway for the primary benefit of the U.S. energy companies (*e.g.*, Halliburton, formerly under Vice President Dick Cheney) that, along with Enron, had already interpenetrated the Bush Jr. administration as well as the Bush Family itself.

Although miseducated[8] at Yale and Harvard Business School, the "Ivies" proved to be too liberal for Bush Jr. and his fundamentalist Christian supporters, whose point man and spear carrier in the Bush Jr. administration was Ashcroft, a Fundie himself. The Neo-Cons and the Fundies contracted an "unholy alliance" in support of Bush Jr. For their own different reasons, both gangs also worked hand-in-hand to support Israel's genocidal Prime Minister Ariel Sharon, an internationally acknowledged war criminal.[9]

According to his own public estimate and boast before the American Enterprise Institute, President Bush Jr. hired about 20 Straussians to occupy key positions in his administration.[10] They intentionally took offices where they could push American foreign policy in favor of Israel and against its chosen enemies such as Iraq, Iran, Syria, and the Palestinians. Most of the Straussian Neo-Cons in the Bush Jr. administration and elsewhere are Israel-firsters: what is "good" for Israel is by definition "good" for the United States— making it questionable sometimes whether even the notion of "dual loyalties" accurately expresses the extent of diluted loyalty to true American interests and values.[11]

It was the Chicago Straussian cabal of pro-Israeli Neo-Cons who set up a special "intelligence" unit within the Pentagon that was responsible for manufacturing many of the bald-faced lies, deceptions, half-truths, and sheer propaganda that the Bush Jr. administration then disseminated to the lap-dog U.S. news media[12] in order to generate public support for a war of aggression against Iraq for the benefit of Israel and in order to steal Iraq's oil.[13] To paraphrase advice Machiavelli once rendered to his Prince in Chapter XVIII of that book: those who want to deceive will always find those willing to be deceived.[14] As I can attest from my personal experience as an alumnus of the University of Chicago Department of Political Science, the Bible of Chicago's Neo-Con Straussian cabal is Machiavelli's *The Prince*. We students had to know our Machiavelli by heart and rote at the University of Chicago.

As for the University of Chicago overall, its biblical Gospel is Allan Bloom's *The Closing of the American Mind* (1987). Of course Bloom was another protégé of Strauss, as well as a mentor to Wolfowitz. In his Bloom-biographical novel *Ravelstein* (2000) Saul Bellow, formerly on the University of Chicago Faculty, outed his self-styled friend Bloom as a hedonist, pederast, and most promiscuous homosexual who died of AIDS. All this was common knowledge at the University of Chicago, where Bloom is still worshiped and his elitist screed against American higher-education still revered on a pedestal.

In *Ravelstein* Wolfowitz appeared as Bloom's protégé Philip Gorman, leaking national security secrets to his mentor during the Bush Sr. war against Iraq. Strauss hovered around the novel as Bloom's mentor and guru Professor Davarr. Strauss/Davarr is really the éminence grise of *Ravelstein*. With friends like Bellow, Bloom did not need enemies. On the basis of *Ravelstein* alone, Wolfowitz warrants investigation by the F.B.I.

Just recently the University of Chicago officially celebrated its Bush Jr. Straussian Neo-Con cabal, highlighting Wolfowitz Ph.D. '72, Ahmad Chalabi, Ph.D. '69 (the CIA's Iraqi puppet), Abram Shulsky, A.M. '68, Ph.D. '72 (head of the Pentagon's special Office of Special Plans "intelligence" unit), Zalmay Khalilzad, Ph.D. '79 (Bush Jr.'s roving pro-consul for Afghanistan and then Iraq), as well as faculty members Bellow, X '39, and Bloom, A.B. '49, A.M. '53, Ph.D. '55, together with Strauss. According to the *University of Chicago Magazine*, Allan Bloom's *The Closing of the American Mind*[15] rant "helped popularize Straussian ideals of democracy."[16] It is correct to assert that Bloom's book helped to popularize Straussian "ideas," but those ideas were blatantly anti-democratic, Machiavellian, Nietzschean, and elitist to begin with. Only the University of Chicago would have the unmitigated Orwellian gall to publicly assert that Strauss and Bloom cared one whit about democracy, let alone comprehended the "ideals of democracy."

Given the core orientation of Leo Strauss indicated above, it should be difficult for anyone to seriously believe that a pro-Israeli Chicago/Strauss/Bloom product such as Wolfowitz could care less about democracy in Iraq. Or for that matter anyone in the Bush Jr. administration, after they stole the 2000 presidential election from the American people both in Florida and before the Republican-controlled U.S. Supreme Court, some of whom were Feddies.[17] As a measure of the extent of Straussian infiltration, Justice Clarence Thomas is a Straussian to boot.[18] At the behest of its Straussian Neo-Con Political Science Department, in 1979 the entire University of Chicago went out of its way to grant the "first Albert Pick Jr. Award for Outstanding Contributions to International Understanding" to Robert "Mad Bomber" McNamara,[19] in an effort to rehabilitate one of the greatest international war criminals in the post-World War II era.[20] Do not send your children to the University of Chicago where they will grow up to become warmongers like Wolfowitz or totalitarians like Ashcroft!

Oil and Gas as the Key to Global Dominance

I will not waste the reader's time here by cataloguing, reviewing, and refuting all the factoids of the Bush Jr.'s pro-Israeli Straussian Neo-Con war propaganda campaign against Iraq,[21] the unraveling of which is already emerging, even through the mainstream media. But there were certainly multiple reasons for this Bush Jr. war of aggression against Iraq besides ensuring the well being of Israel. Notable among them is the Bush Family vendetta against Iraqi President Saddam Hussein and his family, which can now claim to have rubbed out Saddam's two sons and a teenage grandson. Having been born and raised on the Southside of Chicago right near Al Capone's old headquarters as well as the site of his St. Valentine's Day Massacre, I know gangsters when I see them in operation.

These reasons aside, there is no denying that oil was at the top of the Bush Jr./Sr. hit-list and the fact that Iraq possesses about 11% of the world's oil reserves. Indeed, prior thereto it was the thirst and lust for oil and natural gas by the American power elite[22] that really propelled the Bush Jr. administration's aggression against Afghanistan: the need to gain direct access to the rich oil and natural gas fields of Central Asia, which marked the first exploitation of the terrible tragedy of September 11 as public justification for a pre-planned war of aggression under the pretext of "combating international terrorism."[23] Though according to the Bush Jr. administration's version of events, 15 of the 19 hijackers on September 11 were from Saudi Arabia, for some mysterious reason America had to attack, invade, and occupy Afghanistan. Bush administration functionaries continue to lie, cover up, and obstruct investigations into who was ultimately responsible for the terrible tragedy of September 11, and why no one in the Bush Jr. administration acted to prevent it despite numerous, repeated, and widespread warnings beforehand from American as well as European diplomats and agencies. We are witnessing a Pearl Harbor cover-up all over again.[24]

The Bush Jr. wars of aggression against Afghanistan and Iraq must be understood as part of a major grab by the United States government for global energy resources and the attendant power to be derived from controlling about two-thirds of the world's oil and natural gas supplies located around this Eurasian heartland. Such an assault had been contemplated and planned by the U.S. power elite for quite some time, dating back to the Kissinger threat and plan to steal the Arab oil fields in reaction to the 1973 Arab oil embargo of the West for assisting Israel in its war to hold on to the Arab lands Israel had illegally stolen in its 1967 aggressions against the surrounding Arab states and peoples.[25] The collapse of the Warsaw Pact and the disintegration of the Soviet Union provided the U.S. power elite with the opportunity to put their Machiavellian scheme for world economic hegemony into operation.[26]

But the Bush Jr. wars of aggression against Afghanistan and Iraq must be seen as more than the seizure of oil for domestic consumption. Rather, they are components of a longstanding American plan to control and dominate the oil and natural gas supplies for Europe, Japan, and Asia, and thus the future of the world's economy—a project my teacher, mentor, and later friend, the late and great Professor Hans Morgenthau once denominated as "unlimited imperialism"[27] in his classic work *Politics Among Nations*. Tied into this was the subsidiary objective of making sure that oil continues to be paid for in dollars instead of Euros on the open market.

The Bush Sr. 1991 war against Iraq for oil was the first battle in the U.S. quest for world economic hegemony. These subsequent events must be viewed in the same light: the Bush Sr. invasion of Somalia;[28] the Clinton/ Bush Jr. military intervention into Colombia;[29] Bush Jr.'s support for the anti-Chavez failed coup in oil-rich Venezuela;[30] the post-9/11 U.S. military intervention into and occupation of Djibouti in order to control the Suez Canal/ Persian Gulf oil route to Europe, and also to obtain direct military access to the oil and natural gas resources around the Horn of Africa; the August 2003 U.S. military intervention into Liberia, once again to grab direct military access to the oil and natural gas resources located off and on the West Coast of Africa;[31] etc. Whatever the public rhetoric or justification might be, the fact of the matter is that if the reader looks at a map of the world, the United States government has its military, paramilitary, and covert forces converging upon and/or threatening almost every country in the world that possesses significant quantities of oil or natural gas, as well as their transportation supply-lines and the latter's choke-points.

Many of these energy-resource-rich countries just happen to be Muslim. That reveals what Huntington's infamous "Clash of Civilizations" was really all about.[32] Our clash, their civilization. After September 11, Bush Jr. himself proudly boasted that he was going on a Crusade. Certainly that is the way the Muslim world sees it: an American fundamentalist mission to remake "world order" in America's imperialist image—not as democracies, but as client or even failed states—while fomenting world disorder in the process.

In this relentless quest and insatiable lust for oil and gas around the world, the United States power elite is now in the process of destroying the entirety of the international legal order that had been established by a predecessor elitist generation running the United States government in the aftermath of and in reaction to the genocidal horrors of the Second World War.[33] Most particularly and especially, this includes, inter alia, the United Nations Charter, as well as the Nuremberg Charter, Judgment, and Principles, all of which had heretofore been the bedrock upon which the entirety of the post-World War II international legal order rested.[34]

Preventive Warfare: The Nazi Precedent

Iraq had been continuously and illegally bombed by the United States and the United Kingdom since the end of the Bush Sr. Gulf War in 1991 under the pretext of enforcing unauthorized and clearly illegal no-fly zones.[35] But in order to accomplish their objective of seizing Iraq outright, the Bush Jr. warmongers had to articulate another operational rationale for a war of aggression that they could then sell to the American people and Congress that was separate and apart from their fatuous "war against international terrorism."[36] So they resurrected the long-ago discredited Nazi doctrine of "preventive warfare," once again using the terrible tragedy of 11 September 2001 as a pretext for doing so.

The first overt step in their plan was the Bush Jr. aggressive threat to Iraq uttered during the course of his State of the Union Address to the United States Congress on 29 January 2002, in which he branded Iraq as part of a so-called "axis of evil" along with Iran and North Korea.[37] By means of employing this provocative language harkening back to the World War II "axis" of Nazi Germany, Fascist Italy, and Imperial Japan, the Bush Jr. administration was deliberately preparing the ground for bogus claims to launch preventive wars against all three of these U.N. member states. Iraq was at the top of the Bush Jr. hit list. Having been materially and psychologically debilitated by over a decade of genocidal economic sanctions imposed upon its people by the United Nations Security Council acting at the behest of the United States and the United Kingdom, Iraq and its oil fields were finally ripe for the imperial picking by Bush Jr. and his right-hand henchman, Tony Blair. By contrast, North Korea and Iran could be expected to defend themselves by inflicting enormous casualties against an aggressor. As on the Southside of Chicago, bullies prefer to pick upon hapless victims.

The Nazi doctrine of preventive warfare was publicly articulated by President Bush Jr. in his 1 June 2002 commencement address at the West Point Military Academy. Then in late August of 2002, Vice President Cheney signaled the formal commencement of the Bush Jr. war of aggression against Iraq by giving two public speeches before the Veterans of Foreign Wars (Aug. 26) and the Korean War Veterans (Aug. 29) in which he too publicly touted the Nazi doctrine of preventive warfare against Iraq. The U.S. news media were too obeisant to observe that though warmongering for a war against Iraq before these former soldiers who had actually gone to war, Cheney had ducked out of the Vietnam War, as had Bush, Jr. Wolfowitz and the rest of the Bush Jr. administration's Straussian Neo-Con cabal were too busy studying Machiavelli and Nietzsche with Strauss, Bloom, and their acolytes from the University of Chicago. Unlike the WWII American power elite, many of whose sons actually fought in combat (*e.g.,* Bush Sr.), the contemporary American power elite prefers to send the children of poor blacks, Latinos, and whites off to kill and be killed in Afghanistan, Iraq, and elsewhere, as did their elitist predecessors a generation ago in Vietnam, Cambodia, and Laos. Class war, indeed.

Finally, in September 2002 the Bush Jr. administration officially approved and adopted the "National Security Strategy of the United States," fully embracing this reprehensible, criminal, and Nazi doctrine of preventive warfare, and transmitted it to the U.S. Congress as a declaration of official policy by the United States of America.[38] I will not waste the reader's precious time here analyzing this criminal document *in extenso*, but it reads like a Nazi war-planning document that could have been introduced into evidence before the Nuremberg Tribunal. Certainly its most odious language is: ". . . we recognize that our best defense is a good offense. . ." In other words, the United States government has publicly admitted in an official government document that it is now prepared to wage offensive warfare against adversaries of its choosing around the world irrespective of the requirements of, inter alia, the United Nations Charter, the Kellogg-Briand Peace Pact, as well as the Nuremberg Charter, Judgment, and Principles.

This official U.S. government document could be filed with the International Court of Justice in The Hague as proof-positive that it is now the official policy of the United States government to wage criminal wars of aggression against other U.N. member states in violation of the most elementary principles of the contemporary international legal order that would be too numerous to list here. The document is nothing less than what lawyers call an "Admission Against Interest." In brief, the Bush Jr. administration has officially incriminated the United States of America under international law and practice. Such is the arrogance of Power—which usually spells its downfall!

Even more disturbingly, while it was publicly campaigning for a war of aggression against Iraq, in December 2002 the Bush Jr. administration released its so-called "National Strategy to Combat Weapons of Mass Destruction," which was published on the web-page for the White House itself. This supplementary Nazi war plan calls for the first use of weapons of mass destruction (WMD)—chemical, biological, and nuclear—by the United States government under the justification of waging a preventive or preemptive war. Of course this Nazi Doctrine of Preventive Warfare is nothing more than a pretext for waging a war of aggression in the first place. So the Bush Jr. administration officially signaled that it is fully prepared to be the first to use WMD. It would do so against its chosen adversaries around the world as part of an offensive military operation, or even to launch a full-scale war itself, thereby evoking shades of Hiroshima and Nagasaki![39] North Korea took notice and responded accordingly to defend itself.[40]

The Judgment of Nuremberg

Suffice it to say here that the Nazi Doctrine of Preventive Warfare was rejected by the Nuremberg Tribunal when the Nazi defendants attempted to make this reprehensible argument in order to justify their invasion of Norway.[41] Instead, the Nuremberg Tribunal explicitly endorsed the well-known *Caroline Case* (1837), thus enshrining this test as a basic principle of the post-World War II international legal order: "It must be remembered that preventive action in foreign territory is justified only in case of 'an instant and overwhelming necessity for self-defense, leaving no choice of means, and no moment of deliberation' (The *Caroline Case*)."

Moreover, in order to further justify their preventive war against Norway, the Nazi defendants had argued that in accordance with reservations on self-defense made at the time of the conclusion of the Kellogg-Briand Peace Pact of 1928, Germany alone could decide whether preventive action was a necessity, and also that in making such a decision, Germany's judgment was conclusive. In rejecting this Nazi self-judging argument on self-defense, the Nuremberg Tribunal emphatically ruled: "But whether action taken under the claim of self-defense was in fact aggressive or defensive must ultimately be subject to investigation and adjudication if international law is ever to be enforced."

The Legal Determination of Guilt For War

Today the basic test for self-defense recognized by the international legal order is set forth in Article 51 of the United Nations Charter: "Nothing in the present Charter shall impair the inherent right of individual or collective self-defence if an armed attack occurs against a Member of the United Nations, until the Security Council has taken measures necessary to maintain international peace and security." Contrary to conventional wisdom and the framing of this event constructed by Bush administration officials and reinforced by widespread propaganda through the mainstream media, it was the Bush Jr. administration and the Tony Blair government which perpetrated an "armed attack" against Iraq, and thus triggered Iraq's "inherent right" of individual and collective self-defense under U.N. Charter Article 51. Despite the fact, then, that Iraq was clearly the victim, and had a legitimate right under international law both to self-defense and to seek U.N. assistance in deterring aggression against it, no U.N. Member State came to the defense of Iraq. Rather, Iraq became the first victim of this Nazi Doctrine of Preventive Warfare propounded by Bush Jr. and Tony Blair.

From the perspective of international legal history, it is Bush Jr. and Blair who constitute the real "axis-of-evil" along the lines of Hitler and Mussolini. In this regard, Article 6 of the 1945 Nuremberg Charter provides in relevant part as follows:

. . . .
The following acts, or any of them, are crimes coming within the jurisdiction of the Tribunal for which there shall be individual responsibility:

Crimes against peace: namely, planning, preparation, initiation or waging of a war of aggression, or a war in violation of international treaties, agreements or assurances, or participation in a common plan or conspiracy for the accomplishment of any of the foregoing;

. . . .

Leaders, organizers, instigators and accomplices participating in the formulation or execution of a common plan or conspiracy to commit any of the foregoing crimes are responsible for all acts performed by any persons in execution of such plan.

To the same effect is the Sixth Principle of the Principles of International Law recognized in the Charter of the Nuremberg Tribunal and in the Judgment of the Tribunal, which were adopted by the International Law Commission of the United Nations in 1950:

PRINCIPLE VI
The crimes hereinafter set out are punishable as crimes under international law:
Crimes against peace:
(i) Planning, preparation, initiation or waging of a war of aggression or a war in violation of international treaties, agreements or assurances;
(ii) Participation in a common plan or conspiracy for the accomplishment of any of the acts mentioned under (i).
. . . .

Pursuant to this Nuremberg Doctrine, the Bush Jr./Blair war against Iraq clearly qualified as an "aggression" and an "act of aggression" within the meaning of customary international law as set forth, for example, by the United Nations General Assembly in its Resolution 3314 (XXIX) on the Definition of Aggression (1974), and therefore a Crime against Peace. Furthermore, in addition to being a war of aggression, the Bush Jr./Blair war against Iraq also violated "international treaties, agreements or assurances," such as and most importantly the United Nations Charter and the Kellogg-Briand Peace Pact, to both of which Iraq, the United States and the United Kingdom are contracting parties. In other words, the Bush Jr./Blair war against Iraq constituted a Nuremberg Crime against Peace on both counts.

Finally, U.S. Department of the Army Field Manual FM 27-10, The Law of Land Warfare (1956), expressly incorporates this Nuremberg Doctrine of Crimes under International Law as follows:

Section II. CRIMES UNDER INTERNATIONAL LAW

498. Crimes Under International Law

Any person, whether a member of the armed forces or a civilian, who commits an act which constitutes a crime under international law is responsible therefor and liable to punishment. Such offenses in connection with war comprise:

1.   Crimes against peace.
2.   Crimes against humanity.
3.   War crimes.

Although this manual recognizes the criminal responsibility of individuals for those offenses which may comprise any of the foregoing types of crimes, members of the armed forces will normally be concerned only with those offenses constituting "war crimes."

499. War Crimes

The term "war crime" is the technical expression for a violation of the law of war by any person or persons, military or civilian. Every violation of the law of war is a war crime.

500. Conspiracy, Incitement, Attempts, and Complicity

Conspiracy, direct incitement, and attempts to commit, as well as complicity in the commission of, crimes against peace, crimes against humanity, and war crimes are punishable.

Naming the Guilty

These prohibitions of U.S. Army Field Manual 27-10 (1956) apply directly to President Bush Jr. in his constitutional capacity as "Commander-in-Chief of the Army and Navy of the United States" under Article 2, Section 2, Clause 1 of the United States Constitution. They also apply to his subordinates in the military chain-of-command: Vice President Cheney, Secretary of Defense Rumsfeld, Deputy Secretary of Defense Wolfowitz, etc. Even in accordance with the terms of U.S. Army Field Manual 27-10 itself, Bush Jr., Cheney, Rumsfeld, and Wolfowitz, inter alia, are guilty of committing a Nuremberg Crime against Peace for their war of aggression against Iraq in violation of the United Nations Charter and the Kellogg-Briand Peace Pact, at a minimum.

The same conclusion applies to Secretary of State Colin Powell, National Security Adviser Condoleezza Rice, C.I.A. Director George Tenet, the pro-Israeli Neo-Con Straussian cabal, and other high-level Bush Jr. administration officials dealing with foreign affairs, "defense" and "intelligence," who plotted, planned, conspired, promoted, incited, as well as aided and abetted this criminal war against Iraq. U.S. Army Field Manual 27-10 (1956) makes it quite clear that these prohibitions of international criminal law apply to everyone, whether civilians or military personnel. Nazi civilian government officials were convicted and hanged at Nuremberg too.[42]

An Ongoing Criminal Conspiracy

Notice that in accordance with paragraph 500 of U.S. Army Field Manual 27-10 (1956), pursuant to the now officially promulgated Bush Jr. Doctrine of Preventive Warfare, the above-named individuals are also currently engaging in an ongoing criminal conspiracy to commit more Nuremberg Crimes against Peace which are "punishable." While the actual aggression against Iraq was a crime against the peace, the official Bush Jr. Doctrine of Preventive Warfare itself constitutes in fact and in law an ongoing Nuremberg Crime against Peace in its own right. From the perspective of international legal history, the United States government itself is now mimicking the Nazi government. This raises the specter of Austria, Czechoslovakia, and Poland of World War II having resurfaced today as Serbia,[43] Afghanistan, Iraq, and next—North Korea, or Iran, or Syria? Can World War III be far behind?

On 18 June 2003 the Bush Jr. administration illegally attacked and invaded but withdrew from Syria.[44] There is no international legal doctrine justifying "hot pursuit" across land borders. This was aggression pure and simple. Then on 26 August 2003 President Bush Jr. told the American Legion Convention that he was fully prepared to launch more "preemptive" attacks against his chosen enemies around the world.[45] Next, Bush Jr. repeatedly approved Ariel Sharon's blatant act of aggression against Syria on 5 October that could prove to be a harbinger for Israeli wars of aggression against Syria, Lebanon, and Palestine, inter alia, which could readily degenerate into a general Middle Eastern war along the lines of 1948, 1967, and 1973. The latter conflict could have gone nuclear. Would World War III be far behind?

At the very opening of his 2004 presidential election campaign, Bush Jr. has clearly sketched out the prospect on the horizon of more acts of aggression. Will Bush Jr. further exploit aggression and warfare in order to actually win his very first U.S. presidential election? Or will he steal the U.S. Presidency from the American people as he did in 2000? Or perhaps some combination of both strategies? His Rasputin, Karl Rove, will know for sure.

Belligerent Occupation

When the Bush Jr. administration's aggression against Iraq was over, the United States and the United Kingdom became the "belligerent occupants" of Iraq in accordance with, and subject to the requirements of, the laws of war. Bush Jr.'s May 1, 2003 "end of major combat operations" speech on the deck of a U.S. aircraft carrier was nothing more than a cheap campaign and legally deceptive propaganda stunt. Succinctly put, these legal rules of war can be found in the Fourth Geneva Convention of 1949, its Additional Protocol One of 1977, the Hague Regulations of 1907, and U.S. Army Field Manual 27-10 (1956), which require, inter alia, the preservation of Iraq's constitutional and domestic legal order. Nevertheless, the Bush Jr. administration made it crystal clear that they were going to remake Iraq in their own image and thus not pay the least bit of attention to the laws of war. This has entailed a range of policies which would further U.S./U.K. interests while seeking to drastically curtail future Iraqi options, *e.g.*, "privatization" of the Iraqi economy, including and especially its oil industry; drafting a new constitution for Iraq to determine the nature and extent of its democracy; re-writing Iraq's laws; establishing ad hoc war crimes tribunals along the lines of the Bush Jr. kangaroo courts in Guantanamo; de-Baathification; indoctrinating Iraqi schoolchildren with American propaganda through extensive "reform" of its education system; etc. All of this serves to put the future of Iraq up for sale to the lowest American (and then British and Israeli) bidders. Such violations of the laws of war are war crimes, establishing the legal predicate for a legitimate Iraqi government in the future to repudiate them all.

The U.N. Fails to Observe Its Charter—Again

Even worse yet, the Bush Jr. administration then went to the United Nations Security Council where it procured Resolution 1472 (28 March 2003) effectively ratifying the status quo of the United States and the United Kingdom as the belligerent occupants of Iraq, irrespective of their evident non-compliance with obligations related to the laws of belligerent occupancy. Pursuant to the requirements of the United Nations Charter, the United Nations Security Council should have soundly condemned the United States and the United Kingdom for their naked aggression against Iraq, and have demanded their immediate withdrawal from that victim U.N. member state, together with the payment of reparations to Iraq for their joint and severable aggression. Chapter VII of the United Nations Charter mandates that the Security Council act immediately and effectively to prevent, repress, and reverse "threats to the peace, breaches of the peace, and acts of aggression." By contrast, from August 2002 through March 2003 the Member States of the U.N. Security Council only lifted rhetorical and linguistic fingers to save Iraq from the obviously oncoming U.S./U.K. aggression. Indeed, Security Council Resolution 1441 of 8 November 2002 was originally drafted to facilitate the U.S./U.K. aggression against Iraq by issuing a diktat to Iraqi President Saddam Hussein that was deliberately designed to be almost impossible to comply with.[46] This has been a standard operating procedure for the United States government going all the way back to its instigation of the 1898 War against Spain in order to steal the latter's colonial empire.[47]

The government of the United States of America commenced the 19th century by stealing a western empire from the American Indians and then ethnically cleansing them—"manifest destiny."[48] The American government started the 20th century by stealing a colonial empire from Spain and then conducting a near genocidal war against the Filipino people– "a place in the sun." The U.S. government opened the 21st century by trying to steal a hydrocarbon empire from the Muslim states and peoples of Eurasia– "a war against international terrorism." But this latest transgression could very well prove to be the definitive step of "imperial overstretch" that will break the back of the American Empire both abroad and at home.[49] In 1991 the mighty Soviet Empire collapsed like a house of cards after a decade of "imperial overstretch" in Afghanistan. Like the former Soviet Union, the United States of America itself is an imperial house of cards built upon the backs of indigenous peoples, African Americans, Latinos, other peoples of color and a melting pot of non-Anglo-European descendants whose communities, after decades of assimilationist policies, still resemble more closely a stew. The Bush Jr. administration's aggressions against and occupations of Afghanistan and Iraq could very well generate a reverse domino effect: ". . . they all fall down."[50] The United States of America is not immune to the laws of history.

Prostitution of and by the United Nations

To the same effect was Security Council Resolution 1500 of 14 August 2003, which "Welcomes the establishment of the" U.S. puppet-council in Iraq under the leadership of the CIA asset Chalabi, and established the so-called United Nations Assistance Mission for Iraq (UNAMI), whose head-quarters in Baghdad was promptly car-bombed five days later.[51] Even worse was the unanimously adopted U.N. Security Council Resolution 1511 of 16 October 2003, which ludicrously determined that Paul Bremer's puppet "Governing Council" under the leadership of the pro-Israeli Chicago Neo-Con Straussian C.I.A. asset Chalabi "embodies the sovereignty of the State of Iraq during the transitional period. . ." To the contrary, according to the laws of war (which cannot be validly contravened by the U.N. Security Council), the establishment of a regime of belligerent occupation cannot affect the sovereignty of the occupied state, let alone somehow fraudulently transfer this residual state sovereignty into the hands of a puppet government set up by the belligerent occupying power. Security Council Resolutions 1441 (2003), 1500 (2003), and 1511 (2003) just go to prove how subservient the United Nations Organization itself has become to the imperialist enterprises of the United States government, [52] which corrupts and corrodes world order wherever it goes.

Throughout this sordid affair, U.N. Secretary-General Kofi Annan basically operated as little more than an errand-boy for the United States government despite the requirements of Chapter XV of the U.N. Charter establishing the U.N. Secretariat as one of the six independent organs of the United Nations Organization, and in particular, of Charter Article 100, paragraph 1 mandating the absolute independence of the Secretary-General and the U.N. Secretariat from taking instructions by any U.N. Member State:

In the performance of their duties the Secretary-General and the staff shall not seek or receive instructions from any government or from any other authority external to the Organization. They shall refrain from any action which might reflect on their position as international officials responsible only to the Organization.

Kofi Annan is no Dag Hammarskjold, who when he was U.N. Secretary-General moved heaven and earth in order to promote peace, prevent wars and terminate ongoing conflicts, and who died during the process of doing so while on a peace mission to the war-ravaged Congo.[53] For example, U.N. Charter Article 99 gives the U.N. Secretary-General the power to convene an emergency meeting of the United Nations Security Council: "The Secretary-General may bring to the attention of the Security Council any matter which in his opinion may threaten the maintenance of international peace and security." From August of 2002 through March of 2003, Kofi Annan should have repeatedly convened emergency meetings of the U.N. Security Council in order to prevent the threatened Bush Jr./Blair war of aggression against Iraq, a U.N. Member State. Instead Kofi Annan did not lift more than a rhetorical finger to save Iraq from the oncoming U.S./U.K. aggression. In fact, before the start of this war of aggression, the United Nations bureaucracies began to plot, plan, and conspire in secret with the Pentagon and other agencies of the United States government in order to relieve the Pentagon of its obligation under the laws of war to feed the population of an occupied Iraq, thus enabling the Pentagon to concentrate its resources on better promoting the aggression itself. In other words, the United Nations bureaucracies and Kofi Annan were complicit in the U.S./U.K. war of aggression against Iraq.[54]

For these reasons, the United Nations Organization was quickly perceived to be aiding and abetting the criminal U.S./U.K. belligerent occupation regime in Iraq and thus an appropriate target for attack by Iraqi resistance forces. Hence the 19 August 2003 car bombing of the U.N. Headquarters in Baghdad with its horrendous loss of human lives should have come as no surprise to anyone. While Bush Jr. and Kofi Annan publicly shed some crocodile tears for the U.N. personnel victims of that tragedy, for which the former bear joint and several responsibility with the perpetrators. In point of fact, the U.N. Secretary-General and the U.N. Secretariat have operated as proxies for the United States government for at least the past decade since the collapse of the Soviet Union.[55] The complicity of the United Nations Secretariat in the administration of the genocidal economic sanctions against Iraq was well known to the long-suffering Iraqi people.[56]

Tearing Up the Kellogg-Briand Peace Pact

Today the United Nations Organization has become about as functionally ineffectual at stopping naked aggression by the United States and its hench-state the United Kingdom as the League of Nations had become in stopping Nazi Germany, Fascist Italy, Imperial Japan, and Stalinist Russia during the 1930s. Indeed, from a comparative historical perspective, under U.S. hegemonic imperialism the legal, institutional, and political situation is far worse. For Security Council Resolution 1472 (2003) on Iraq constituted the outright repudiation of 75 years of formal international legal condemnation of wars of aggression by the world community of states.

Between World War I and World War II, at the initiative of France and the United States, the then world community of states concluded the Kellogg-Briand Peace Pact of 1928.[57] Article 1 thereof repudiated war as an instrument of national policy: "The High Contracting Parties solemnly declare in the names of their respective peoples that they condemn recourse to war for the solution of international controversies, and renounce it as an instrument of national policy in their relations with one another." This prohibition countermanded the so-called Von Clausewitz Doctrine to the effect that war was a continuation of diplomacy by other means. At the time it was generally believed that the Von Clausewitz Doctrine had been responsible for the precipitation of the First World War by Imperial Germany and its imperialist allies. Today the Von Clausewitz Doctrine has become the operational dynamic of the Bush Jr. administration's foreign policy. Again, can World War III be far behind?

Article II of the Kellogg-Briand Peace Pact mandated the exclusively peaceful resolution of all international disputes: "The High Contracting Parties agree that the settlement or solution of all disputes or conflicts of whatever nature or of whatever origin they may be, which may arise among them, shall never be sought except by pacific means." Iraq, the United States, and the United Kingdom are all contracting parties to the Kellogg-Briand Peace Pact. Not that it mattered to the Bush Jr. administration, which now openly preaches and promotes the violent resolution of international disputes, as had Nazi Germany, Fascist Italy, and Imperial Japan during the 1930s.

Despite Axis powers' abrogation of these two fundamental requirements of the inter-war international legal order set forth in the Kellogg-Briand Peace Pact, their absolute necessity for a peaceful international system led to their later incorporation into Article 2, paragraph 4, and Article 2, paragraph 3 of the United Nations Charter, respectively, by means of the following language:

Article 2

The Organization and its Members, in pursuit of the Purposes stated in Article 1, shall act in accordance with the following Principles.

. . . .

3. All Members shall settle their international disputes by peaceful means in such a manner that international peace and security, and justice, are not endangered.

4. All Members shall refrain in their international relations from the threat or use of force against the territorial integrity or political independence of any state, or in any other manner inconsistent with the Purposes of the United Nations.

Iraq, the United States, and the United Kingdom are all Founding Members of the United Nations Organization. Not that it mattered to the United States and the United Kingdom.

Reversing the Stimson Doctrine

When imperial Japan invaded China in 1931 in order to loot and plunder Manchuria, the United States government adopted what came to be known as the Stimson Doctrine, after then U.S. Secretary of State Henry Stimson: namely, that the United States government would not recognize any legal consequences flowing from a violation of the Kellogg-Briand Peace Pact, otherwise known as the Pact of Paris.[58] Despite the fact that the United States was not a Member of the League of Nations, nevertheless the League of Nations endorsed the Stimson Doctrine with respect to the Japanese aggression against China and in order to secure the non-recognition of Japan's establishment of its puppet-state of "Manchuko" in Manchuria. Furthermore, on 11 March 1932 the League of Nations Assembly passed a Resolution officially adopting the Stimson Doctrine in the following language: "[I]t is incumbent upon the members of the League of Nations not to recognize any situation, treaty, or agreement which may be brought about by means contrary to the Covenant of the League of Nations or to the Pact of Paris."

The Stimson Doctrine and its subsequent endorsement by the League of Nations became the origins of the elemental international legal principle that the world community of states will not recognize any fruits flowing from aggression. Yet that is precisely what the U.N. Security Council did in its Resolution 1472 (2003) on Iraq. Historically it would be as if the League of Nations had adopted a resolution ratifying Japan's belligerent occupation of Manchuria; or Hitler's belligerent occupation of Czechoslovakia and Poland; or Mussolini's belligerent occupation of Ethiopia; or Stalin's belligerent occupation of Lithuania, Latvia, and Estonia; etc. For all of its ineffectiveness, even the League of Nations did not stoop so low as the United Nations Security Council did in its Resolution 1472 (2003) on Iraq. In accepting the U.S. diktat rather than fulfilling its systemic function as a promoter and protector of world peace, multinationalism, and harmonious development, the U.N. has not avoided irrelevance, but embraced it, thereby threatening the post World War II international order with disintegration.

Sabotaging the International Criminal Court

In order to justify the Bush Jr. war of aggression against Iraq, one contemporary U.S. Machiavellian argued that since the Kellogg-Briand Peace Pact was a phantasm to begin with, so too must the same now be true for the United Nations Charter itself because the Bush Jr. administration wantonly violated it in the run-up to their war of aggression against Iraq.[59] What is this, but the Gangster Theory of international law, modified in present circumstances to read: U.S. might is right. Or as President Bush Sr. quaintly put it concerning his Gulf War I: ". . .what we say goes." The Nazis had their law professors too. While Hitler only envisioned a "New Order" for Europe, the Bush Family projects a New World Order.[60] Not surprisingly, Bush Jr.'s grandfather Prescott Herbert Bush had supported and facilitated the rise to power of Hitler and the Nazis in Germany.[61] As an indicator of Bush Family values at work, under their governorships, Texas and Florida became state execution hubs for the country.

Despite their transgression by Bush Jr., both the Kellogg-Briand Peace Pact and the United Nations Charter remain solemn and binding "treaties" to which the United States of America is a contracting party and thus "the supreme Law of the Land" according to Article VI of the U.S. Constitution. At the Nuremberg prosecution, the gist of the charge against the Nazi leaders for committing a Crime against Peace was based upon their wanton violation of the Kellogg-Briand Peace Pact, to which Germany was a party. Several Nazi leaders were later condemned and hanged at Nuremberg for violating the Kellogg-Briand Peace Pact. In other words, the governments of the United States and the United Kingdom hanged Nazis at Nuremberg for engaging in the same type of reprehensible behavior that Bush Jr. and Blair committed against Iraq. To be sure, I personally oppose the imposition of the death penalty upon any person for any reason, no matter how monstrous their crimes might be—including Bush Jr., Blair, Bush Sr., McNamara, Kissinger,[62] Saddam Hussein, Slobodan Milosevic,[63] Sharon, etc.

So much for the Kellogg-Briand Peace Pact being conveniently categorized as a "phantasm" and Nuremberg being pejoratively labeled as "soft law" by imperialist American international lawyers and professors. Dead Nazis at Nuremberg disproved those propositions. Since that time, the Nuremberg Charter, Judgment, and Principles have served as the legal core of, and precedent for establishing, the International Criminal Tribunal for the Former Yugoslavia in 1993, the International Criminal Tribunal for Rwanda in 1994, and now the International Criminal Court in 2002.[64]

Therefore, it came as no surprise that immediately upon their coming to power in 2001, the Bush Jr. Leaguers did everything humanly possible to sabotage the International Criminal Court (ICC) precisely because they were then currently planning, preparing, and conspiring to commit criminal wars of aggression around the world. The highest level civilian officials of the Bush Jr. administration did not want the International Criminal Court looking over their shoulders while they were committing wanton aggression, crimes against humanity, and war crimes against the peoples and states of Afghanistan, Iraq, Iran, North Korea, Syria, and elsewhere. The Bush Jr. Leaguers' concerted efforts to sabotage the ICC represent what criminal lawyers call an example of their "consciousness of guilt."

What Is To Be Done: Iraq for the Iraqis

Foreign troops should stay out of Iraq at the behest of the Bush Jr. administration for any reason whatsoever. Otherwise, they too will become legitimate targets of attack by an Iraqi resistance movement to foreign occupation forces that are actively aiding and abetting the U.S./U.K. criminal war of aggression against Iraq for oil and Israel, which was in violation of the United Nations Charter and the Kellogg-Briand Peace Pact as well as the Nuremberg Charter, Judgment, and Principles—a crime against peace. Iraq should immediately be placed under the direct control and supervision of a United Nations Trusteeship under Chapter XII of the U.N. Charter.

A real and independent United Nations Peacekeeping Force should be deployed to Iraq under the auspices of the U.N. General Assembly (not the U.S.-co-opted U.N. Security Council) pursuant to its powers under the Uniting for Peace Resolution (1950). The U.S. and U.K. aggressors' military occupation forces should be removed immediately from Iraq. This is exactly what happened in the 1956 Middle East "war" when the U.N. General Assembly deployed the United Nations Emergency Force (UNEF) to the Sinai in order to facilitate the withdrawal of aggressor military forces by the United Kingdom, France, and Israel that had illegally attacked and invaded Egypt in their joint and severable Nuremberg Crime against Peace for the purpose of inflicting "regime change" against Egyptian President Nasser.[65]

The Bush Jr. pro-consul in Iraq, Paul Bremer III, and his Iraqi puppet council under the pro-Israeli Chicago Straussian Neo-Con CIA asset Chalabi should be replaced by a U.N. Transitional Authority reporting directly to the U.N. Trusteeship Council (not the U.S.-co-opted U.N. Security Council) in accordance with Chapter XIII of the U.N. Charter. The Iraqi people can then proceed to exercise their international legal right to self-determination for themselves in order to decide their own political, economic, constitutional and legal future as they see fit—not one pre-selected for them by the pro-Israeli Straussian Neo-Cons and the Big-Oil operatives of the Bush Jr. administration, who were responsible for fomenting this criminal war of aggression against Iraq in the first place.

America for the Americans

Failure to do this may mean the U.S., U.K., and allied foreign military occupation forces will be facing a situation similar to the Vietnam War. Iraq could readily become a combination of Tonkin Gulf, L.B.J., Vietnam, Nixon, Cambodia, Watergate, and Impeachment[66] all over again, rolled into one, and accelerated, where history repeats itself as both a tragedy and a farce.[67]

But this time the American Peace Movement is ready. We have seen this elitist "game" of Machiavellian power politics before. Once again, it is up to the common sense and decency of the American people to stop it. Our alternative is an American Empire in Eurasia and an American police state at home. The Thousand Year Nazi Reich was purportedly defending its "homeland" too.[68]

Chapter Eight

A Guide to Impeaching President George W. Bush

"We the People of the United States, in Order to form a more perfect Union, establish Justice, insure domestic Tranquility, provide for the common defence, promote the general Welfare, and secure the Blessings of Liberty to ourselves and our Posterity, do ordain and establish this Constitution for the United States of America."

Preventive Impeachment

When the most recent United States aggression against Iraq began to be publicly put into motion during August of 2002, it was obvious that the Bush Jr. administration was using exactly the same strategy that the Bush Sr. administration had employed from August 1990 through January 1991 to justify its first war of aggression against Iraq for oil. Consequently, I went back to my old file cabinets full of legal work performed in resistance to the Bush Sr. imperialist oil venture and pulled out those documents that would prove to be particularly useful for opposing the upcoming Bush Jr. version. One of the most important documents was the Bill to Impeach President George Bush, Sr. over the Gulf War that was introduced into the United States House of Representatives by the late and great Congressman Henry B. Gonzalez of Texas on 16 January 1991,[1] together with his most eloquent speech in support thereof.[2]

As expected, on rereading the texts of the Gonzalez Bill of Impeachment against Bush Sr. and his speech, I found the language almost directly on point with respect to President Bush Jr. Basically all one had to do was change the names from Bush Sr. to Bush Jr. Therefore, I concluded that, similarly, a self-styled "preventive war" against Iraq by the Bush Jr. administration required a preventive impeachment campaign to be launched against the Bush Jr. administration as soon as possible in order to head off this second Bush Family war of aggression against Iraq. So at a peace rally held on the campus of the University of Illinois at Urbana-Champaign on Monday, October 7, I launched the National Campaign to Impeach President George Bush Jr., Vice President Dick Cheney, Secretary of Defense Donald Rumsfeld, and Attorney General John Ashcroft. It would be modeled upon the same impeachment campaign that the American Peace Movement had launched against President Bush Sr.

Impeaching Bush Sr.

On 14 January 1991, pursuant to the terms of the 1973 War Powers Resolution, the United States Congress authorized President Bush Sr. to use military force against Iraq in order to expel Iraq from Kuwait in accordance with U.N. Security Council Resolution 678 of 29 November 1990. In direct reaction thereto, Congressman Gonzalez, former U.S. Attorney General Ramsey Clark, and I agreed to set up a National Campaign to impeach Bush Sr. if he went to war against Iraq, initially for the purpose of deterring him from doing so. It was agreed that I would write the Bill of Particulars against President Bush Sr. to serve as the basis for drafting the Articles of Impeachment comprising the Gonzalez Bill. We launched the Bush Sr. impeachment campaign on 15 January 1991.

Nevertheless the war started, and the very next day Congressman Gonzalez appeared on the floor of the House of Representatives to introduce his Bill of Impeachment against President Bush Sr. It was my great honor and privilege to serve as Counsel to Congressman Gonzalez on the subsequent course of this impeachment effort that he so courageously and tenaciously investigated and pursued in his capacity as Chairman of the House Banking Committee, a position he held until the Democrats lost control of the House of Representatives in the 1994 congressional elections. In response, President Bush Sr. even unleashed the C.I.A. on this beloved Congressman known affectionately to his friends as "Henry B."

Constitutional Grounds for Impeachment

Article II, Section 4 of the United States Constitution provides that: "The President, Vice-President and all civil Officers of the United States, shall be removed from Office on Impeachment for, and Conviction of, Treason, Bribery, or other high Crimes and Misdemeanors." In his classic work on impeachment, Professor Raoul Berger of the Harvard Law School established that this constitutional term of art "other high Crimes and Misdemeanors" did not require that the subject of impeachment proceedings must actually have committed a violation of the United States Federal Criminal Code or state criminal laws.[3] According to the proceedings of the 1787 Constitutional Convention it appears that the litmus test for "other high Crimes and Misdemeanors" was "Attempts to subvert the Constitution. . ."[4]

Consistent with the Constitution's overall design of separation of powers, the Founders divided the impeachment power between the House and the Senate of the United States Congress. Basically, the House would function like a grand jury bringing an indictment against an official. Thereafter the Senate would try that official in a judicial proceeding. According to Article I, Section 2, Clause 5 of the U.S. Constitution, the House of Representatives "shall have the sole Power of Impeachment." Should a civil Officer of the United States government be impeached by the House of Representatives, according to Article I, Section 3, Clause 6 of the U.S. Constitution, the Senate "shall have the sole Power to try all Impeachments." Conviction by the U.S.

Senate requires "the Concurrence of two thirds of the Members present." According to Article I, Section 3, Clause 7 of the U.S. Constitution: "Judgment in Cases of Impeachment shall not extend further than to removal from Office, and disqualification to hold and enjoy any Office of Honor, Trust, or Profit under the United States; but the Party convicted shall nevertheless be liable and subject to Indictment, Trial, Judgment, and Punishment, according to Law." Once removed from Office, a former President could be criminally prosecuted for conduct that led to his or her impeachment provided such conduct also violated federal or state criminal laws.

Impeaching Bush Jr.

The Bill of Impeachment I drafted against President Bush Jr. was modeled upon the Gonzalez Impeachment Resolution against President Bush Sr. I made some very minor technical corrections to the original Gonzalez Impeachment Resolution, which had been produced in a remarkable hurry under the enormous pressures of trying to stop an imminently pending war. But for all intents and purposes, this draft Bill of Impeachment against President Bush Jr. was almost the same as the original Gonzalez Bill of Impeachment against President Bush Sr.—except for a new Article I added to deal with what can only be called the Ashcroft Police State.[5] It was published by *CounterPunch.org.* on January 17, 2003, and immediately put into public circulation—just in time to be available for review by the newly-elected and incoming Members of the 108th Congress, in the hope that an equivalent, one decade later, to the courageous Congressman Gonzalez might be found to introduce it. The draft Resolution follows.

108th Congress H.Res.XX
1st Session
Impeaching George Walker Bush, President of the United States,
for high crimes and misdemeanors.

IN THE HOUSE OF REPRESENTATIVES
January __, 2003

Mr./Ms. Y submitted the following resolution; which was referred to the Committee on Judiciary.

A RESOLUTION
Impeaching George Walker Bush, President of the United
States, for high crimes and misdemeanors.

Impeaching George Walker Bush, President of the United States, for high crimes and misdemeanors.

Resolved, That George Walker Bush, President of the United States be impeached for high crimes and misdemeanors, and that the following articles of impeachment be exhibited to the Senate:

Articles of Impeachment exhibited by the House of Representatives of the United States of America in the name of itself and of all of the people of the United States of America, against George Walker Bush, President of the United States of America, in maintenance and support of its impeachment against him for high crimes and misdemeanors.

ARTICLE I

In the conduct of the office of President of the United States, George Walker Bush, in violation of his constitutional oath faithfully to execute the office of President of the United States and, to the best of his ability, preserve, protect, and defend the Constitution of the United States, and in violation of his constitutional duty to take care that the laws be faithfully executed, has attempted to impose a police state and a military dictatorship upon the people and Republic of the United States of America by means of "a long Train of Abuses and Usurpations" against the Constitution since September 11, 2001. This subversive conduct includes but is not limited to trying to suspend the constitutional Writ of Habeas Corpus; ramming the totalitarian U.S.A. Patriot Act through Congress; rounding up and incarcerating foreigners en masse; establishing kangaroo courts; depriving at least two United States citizens of their constitutional rights by means of military incarceration; interfering with the constitutional right of defendants in criminal cases to lawyers; violating and subverting the Posse Comitatus Act; conducting unlawful and unreasonable searches and seizures; violating the First Amendment rights of the free exercise of religion, freedom of speech, peaceable assembly, and the right to petition the government for redress of grievances; packing the federal judiciary with hand-picked judges belonging to the totalitarian Federalist Society[6] and undermining the judicial independence of the Constitution's Article III federal court system; violating the Third and Fourth Geneva Conventions and the U.S. War Crimes Act; violating the International Covenant on Civil and Political Rights and the International Convention on the Elimination of All Forms of Racial Discrimination; reinstituting the infamous

"Cointelpro" Program; violating the Vienna Convention on Consular Relations, the Convention Against Torture, and the Universal Declaration of Human Rights; instituting the totalitarian Total Information Awareness Program; and establishing a totalitarian Northern Military Command for the United States of America itself.

In all of this George Walker Bush has acted in a manner contrary to his trust as President and subversive of constitutional government, to the great prejudice of the cause of law and justice and to the manifest injury of the people of the United States.

Wherefore George Walker Bush, by such conduct, warrants impeachment and trial, and removal from office.

ARTICLE II

In the conduct of the office of President of the United States, George Walker Bush, in violation of his constitutional oath faithfully to execute the office of President of the United States and, to the best of his ability, preserve, protect, and defend the Constitution of the United States, and in violation of his constitutional duty to take care that the laws be faithfully executed, has violated the Equal Protection Clause of the Constitution. U.S. soldiers in the Middle East are overwhelmingly poor White, Black, and Latino and their military service is based on the coercion of a system that has denied viable economic opportunities to these classes of citizens. Under the Constitution, all classes of citizens are guaranteed equal protection of the laws, and calling on the poor and minorities to fight a war for oil to preserve the lifestyles of the wealthy power elite of this country is a denial of the rights of these soldiers. In all of this George Walker Bush has acted in a manner contrary to his trust as President and subversive of constitutional government, to the great prejudice of the cause of law and justice and to the manifest injury of the people of the United States.

Wherefore George Walker Bush, by such conduct, warrants impeachment and trial, and removal from office.

ARTICLE III

In the conduct of the office of President of the United States, George Walker Bush, . . . has violated the U.S. Constitution, federal law, and the United Nations Charter by bribing, intimidating and threatening others, including the members of the United Nations Security Council, to support belligerent acts against Iraq. In all of this George Walker Bush has acted . . . .

ARTICLE IV

In the conduct of the office of President of the United States, George Walker Bush, . . . has prepared, planned, and conspired to engage in a massive war and catastrophic aggression against Iraq by employing methods of mass destruction that will result in the killing of tens of thousands of civilians, many of whom will be children. This planning includes the threatened use of nuclear weapons, and the use of such indiscriminate weapons as well as massive killings by aerial bombardment, or otherwise, of civilians, in violation of the Hague Regulations on land warfare, the rules of customary international law set forth in the Hague Rules of Air Warfare, the Four Geneva Conventions of 1949 and Protocol I thereto, the Nuremberg Charter, Judgment, and Principles, the Genocide Convention, the Universal Declaration of Human Rights, and U.S. Army Field Manual 27-10 (1956). In all of this George Walker Bush has acted . . . .

ARTICLE V

In the conduct of the office of President of the United States, George Walker Bush, . . . has committed the United States to acts of war without congressional consent and contrary to the United Nations Charter and international law. From September 2001 through January 2003, the President embarked on a course of action that systematically eliminated every option for peaceful resolution of the Persian Gulf crisis. Once the President approached Congress for consent to war, tens of thousands of American soldiers' lives were in jeopardy—rendering any substantive debate by Congress meaningless. The President has not received a Declaration of War by Congress, and in contravention of the written word, the spirit, and the intent of the U.S. Constitution has declared that he will go to war regardless of the views of the American people. In failing to seek and obtain a Declaration of War, George Walker Bush has acted . . . .

ARTICLE VI

In the conduct of the office of President of the United States, George Walker Bush . . . has planned, prepared, and conspired to commit crimes against the peace by leading the United States into an aggressive war against Iraq in violation of Article 2(4) of the United Nations Charter, the Nuremberg Charter, Judgment, and Principles, the Kellogg-Brand Pact, U.S. Army Field Manual 27-

10 (1956), numerous other international treaties and agreements, and the Constitution of the United States. In all of this George Walker Bush has acted . . . .

The above draft Articles II, III, IV, V, and VI were taken almost verbatim from Articles I, II, III, IV, and V of Congressman Gonzalez's Bill of Impeachment against President Bush Sr. that he introduced into the House of Representatives on January 16, 1991 as House Resolution 34, 102nd Cong., 1st Sess., which he later re-introduced as House Resolution 86 on February 21, 1991. The above draft Article I on the Ashcroft Police State must now be supplemented by adding a reference to Bush Jr.'s proposed draft USA Patriot Act II.[7] In other words, the civil rights, civil liberties, and human rights of all American citizens (let alone resident foreigners) are now in truly dire straits!

Impeaching Clinton For the Right Reasons

No point would be served here by extensively comparing and contrasting the 1998 Bill of Impeachment against President Bill Clinton with the original Gonzalez Impeachment Resolution against President Bush Sr. and the above draft Bill of Impeachment against President Bush Jr.—which might be reduced to: sex and lying about sex versus war and lying about war. According to our Founding Fathers, the most awesome decision the Republic of the United States of America could ever take would be to go to war. That is precisely why America's Founders put the "Power... to declare War" into the hands of both Houses of Congress acting together by means of Article I, Section 8, Clause 11 of the U.S. Constitution after having considered, debated and rejected other alternatives.[8] Thereafter, Article II, Section 2, Clause 1 of the U.S. Constitution determined that: "The President shall be the Commander in Chief of the Army and Navy of the United States and of the Militia of the several States, when called into the actual Service of the United States . . ."

However, on 20 November 1998 this author had started a National Campaign to "Impeach Clinton for the Right Reasons": his illegal bombings of Sudan, Afghanistan, and Iraq, compounded by his motivation for so doing—to distract public attention from the Ken Starr-interrelated Monica Lewinsky/Paula Jones sex scandals, and thus avoid impeachment by the House of Representatives over the latter.[9] This document follows:

Impeach Clinton for the Right Reasons

20 November 1998

An excellent example of impeachable offenses, high crimes and misdemeanors, and abuses of power by President Clinton are his gratuitous bombings of Sudan and Afghanistan and his aborted attack on Iraq. In the 1991 impeachment resolution against President Bush for going to war against Iraq, there were five articles. The general test set forth in each article was that the President "acted in a manner contrary to his trust as President and subversive of constitutional government to the great prejudice of the cause of law and justice and to the manifest injury of the people of the United States." That language was taken from the impeachment resolution against President Nixon. This test requires much more than sexual escapades by a President—remember John Kennedy. You need presidential conduct that is "subversive of constitutional government."

For President Clinton to go to war against two states, to launch military attacks on them in the middle of the night, without any authorization by Congress, to destroy the civilian pharmaceutical factory in Sudan killing at least one person—and we still do not know how many people Clinton killed and exactly what he destroyed in Afghanistan while also hitting Pakistan—subverts our constitutional system of government. First comes the War Powers Clause of the United States Constitution, Article I, Section 8 that expressly requires authorization by Congress before the President can engage in acts of war, unless there is a direct attack upon the United States.

Second comes the War Powers Resolution of 1973 that was enacted by Congress over President Nixon's veto in order to prevent a repetition of the Vietnam War scenario, which America gradually entered because of repeated presidential lies, misrepresentations, deceits, and falsehoods at every step of the way. During the summer of 1995 the Republican-controlled Congress made an attempt to repeal the War Powers Resolution, which failed. So the War Powers Resolution still remains the "supreme Law of the Land" under Article VI of the Constitution, which Clinton also violated. In addition, President Clinton violated his constitutional oath required by Article II, Section 1 to faithfully execute the Office of President of the United States and, to the best of his ability, preserve, protect, and defend the Constitution of the United States. President Clinton also violated his constitutional duty to take care that the laws be faithfully executed under Article II, Section 3.

There are also impeachable abuses of presidential power present here. President Clinton manipulated these gratuitous assaults on Sudan, Afghanistan, and Pakistan in order to deflect public attention from his Monica Lewinsky scandal. It was no coincidence that these attacks came on the exact same day that Ken Starr recalled Lewinsky to testify before the Washington grand jury where Clinton had just appeared. It was also no coincidence that Clinton scheduled an extended bombing campaign of Iraq to commence the weekend before Congress was to open impeachment hearings against him. Only the courageous and timely intervention by U.N. Secretary General Kofi Annan prevented the mass extermination of at least 10,000 Iraqis—a gross and deliberate underestimate of the human carnage involved by the Pentagon.

Based upon repeated prior experience, if the impeachment proceedings go against Clinton, he will orchestrate another genocidal bombing campaign against the People of Iraq. All the indications are that Clinton and his henchmen intend to do this in any event. The second aircraft carrier task force organized around the *Enterprise* arrives in the Persian Gulf on Monday, November 23, 1998. Bombing Iraq is just a matter of opportunistic timing. For these reasons, then, Clinton must be impeached. The sooner the better.

Shortly after I wrote this essay, circulated it on the internet, and started this campaign, on 15 December 1998 the Clinton administration effectively ordered the United Nations to remove its UNSCOM weapons inspectors from Iraq. President Clinton then unilaterally commenced the start of a massive bombing campaign against Iraq that was code-named "Operation Desert Fox" as part of an ultimately unsuccessful effort to stave off a vote of impeachment by the U.S. House of Representatives that was already scheduled to be held that very week over the Ken Starr-interrelated Lewinsky/Jones sex scandals.[10] Predictably the Democrats in the House and elsewhere aided and abetted Clinton's nefarious scheme and unconstitutional subterfuge by publicly arguing that "we" cannot impeach "our" Commander-in-Chief while "our" Republic was at war—proving once again that they were indeed the sons and the daughters of the "Best and the Brightest" from the President John F. Kennedy administration who gave the American people and Republic the Vietnam War.[11] As George Santayana prophesied: "Those who cannot remember the past are condemned to repeat it."[12] Of course those who lie about and misrepresent the past are equally likely to repeat it.[13]

Notwithstanding, Clinton was ultimately impeached by the House and tried but acquitted by the Senate on the basis of two Articles of Impeachment related to the Lewinsky/Jones sex scandals: lying before a Federal Grand Jury over "sex" with Monica Lewinsky; and obstruction of justice in the Paula Jones case.[14] These two Articles of Impeachment against President Clinton over the Lewinsky/Jones sex scandals generally averred that: "In doing this, William Jefferson Clinton has undermined the integrity of his office, brought disrespect on the Presidency, has betrayed his trust as President, and has acted in a manner subversive of the rule of law and justice, to the manifest injury of the people of the United States."

By comparison, the five Articles of Impeachment in the 1991 Gonzalez Bill of Impeachment against President Bush Sr. all generally averred that his war-related offenses were "subversive of constitutional government, to the great prejudice of the cause of law and justice and to the manifest injury of the people of the United States." Clinton's Lewinsky/Jones sex scandals could not meet that higher standard for impeachment that was set forth in the Gonzalez Impeachment Resolution against President Bush Sr. Of course I realize that there were some people of good faith and good will who believed that Clinton should have been impeached, convicted, and removed from Office over the Lewinsky/Jones sex scandals.[15]

A fortiori, however, Clinton's bombings of Sudan, Afghanistan, and Iraq, together with his precipitations and manipulations of these criminal attacks in order to stave off impeachment by the U.S. House of Representatives, certainly constituted "high Crimes and Misdemeanors" that warranted President Clinton's impeachment by the House, conviction by the Senate, and removal from Office—precisely because these war-related offenses truly were "subversive of constitutional government, to the great prejudice of the cause of law and justice and to the manifest injury of the people of the United States." The same was true for President Bush Sr., and is currently true for President Bush Jr. All three presidents were or are impeachable in relation to their commission of acts of war.

Bush Jr. Impeachment Debate

With another Bush war of aggression against Iraq staring the American people, Congress and the Republic in their face, on Tuesday, 11 March 2003, Congressman John Conyers of Michigan, the Ranking Member of the House Judiciary Committee (which would have jurisdiction over any Bill of Impeachment) convened an emergency meeting of forty or more of his top advisors, most of whom were lawyers. The purpose of the meeting was to discuss and debate immediately putting into the House of Representatives Bills of Impeachment against President Bush Jr., Vice President Cheney, Secretary of Defense Rumsfeld, and Attorney General Ashcroft in order to head off the impending war.[16] Congressman Conyers kindly requested that Ramsey Clark and I come to the meeting and argue the case for impeachment. Ramsey had launched his own campaign to impeach Bush Jr. et al. in mid-January 2003 at a peace rally held in Washington, D.C.

This impeachment debate lasted for two hours. It was presided over by Congressman Conyers, who quite correctly did not tip his hand one way or the other on the merits of impeachment. He simply moderated the debate between Clark and I, on the one side, favoring immediately filing Bills of Impeachment against Bush Jr. et al. to stop the threatened war, and almost everyone else there, who were against impeachment. Obviously no point would be served here by attempting to digest a two-hour-long vigorous debate among a group of well-trained lawyers on such a controversial matter at this critical moment in American history. But at the time I was struck by the fact that this momentous debate was conducted at a private office right down the street from the White House.

Suffice it to say that most of the "experts" there opposed impeachment not on the basis of enforcing the Constitution and the Rule of Law, but on the grounds that it might hurt the Democratic Party effort to get their presidential candidate elected in the year 2004. As a political independent, I did not argue that point. Rather, I argued the merits of impeaching Bush Jr., Cheney, Rumsfeld, and Ashcroft under the United States Constitution, U.S. Federal Laws, U.S. Treaties and other International Agreements to which the United States was a contracting party. Article VI of the U.S. Constitution provides that Treaties "shall be the supreme Law of the Land." This so-called Supremacy Clause of the U.S. Constitution also applies to International Executive Agreements concluded under the auspices of the U.S. President such as the 1945 Nuremberg Charter.

Congressman Conyers was so kind as to allow me the closing argument in the debate. Briefly put, the concluding point I chose to make was historical: The Athenians lost their democracy. The Romans lost their Republic. And if we Americans did not act now we could lose our Republic! The United States of America is not immune to the laws of history!

After two hours of most vigorous debate among those in attendance, the meeting adjourned with a second revised draft Bill of Impeachment sitting on the table:

At the end of accompanying remarks
expressly provides for impeachment:
Article II, Section 4 of the Constitution of the
United States of America

"The President, Vice President and all civil Officers of the United States, shall be removed from Office on Impeachment for, and Conviction of, Treason, Bribery, or other High Crimes and Misdemeanors."

[Note: This is really all presented as one Article. See the Nixon articles voted out of committee, which stated two or three broad descriptions of the impeachable conduct. These were each followed by the phrase: "This conduct has included one or more of the following: Then the specific act, as illustrations, were listed under each of these Articles.

That form is followed below. But it lists all of the number items 1-22 as specific acts under the one omnibus, general charge stated at the outset. They need to be split up and grouped under two or three different Articles.]

Articles of Impeachment
of
President George W. Bush
and
Attorney General John David Ashcroft

President George W. Bush, Attorney General John David Ashcroft have committed violations and subversions of the Constitution of the United States of America; have assumed powers of an imperial executive unaccountable to law; and have usurped powers of the Congress and the Judiciary. This has included an attempt to carry out with impunity crimes against peace and humanity, war crimes, threats of aggression and deprivations of the civil rights and civil liberties of the people of the United States by the following acts:

1) Threatening Iraq with a military attack which is not an act of self defense, and therefore is a war of aggression including specific threats to use nuclear weapons.

2) Authorizing, ordering or condoning direct attacks on civilians, civilian facilities and locations where civilian casualties are unavoidable.

3) Threatening the independence and sovereignty of Iraq by proclaiming an intention to change its government by force.

4) Planning and preparing to wage a war against Iraq without a Declaration of War by Congress, or its functional equivalent.

5) Authorizing, ordering or condoning assassinations, summary executions, kidnapping, secret and other illegal detentions of individuals.

6) Authorizing, ordering or condoning torture and other unlawful treatment of prisoners in order to obtain false statements concerning acts and intentions of governments and individuals.

7) Authorizing, ordering or condoning actions, within the United States or by U.S. forces and agents elsewhere, that violate the rights of individuals under the First, Fourth, Fifth, Sixth and Eighth Amendments to the Constitution of the United States, the Universal Declaration of Human Rights and the International Covenant on Civil and Political Rights.

8) Making, ordering or condoning false statements and improper propaganda about the conduct of foreign governments and individuals, and the conduct by U.S. government personnel, in order to deceive and manipulate: the Congress, the Judiciary, the American public, foreign governments and the media.

9) Making, ordering or condoning the withholding, concealing or falsifying of information needed by the Congress, the Judiciary, the American public and the media, including information concerning acts, intentions and possession, or efforts to obtain weapons of mass destruction in order to falsely create a

climate of fear and destroy opposition to U.S. wars of aggression and first strike attacks.

10) Violations and subversions of the Charter of the United Nations and international law, both a part of the "Supreme Law of the land" under Article VI, paragraph 2, of the Constitution, and others and usurping powers of the United Nations, its Member nations and the peoples of its nations by bribery, coercion and other corrupt acts.

11) Rejecting treaties, committing treaty violations and frustrating compliance with treaties in order to destroy any means by which international law and institutions can prevent, affect, or adjudicate the exercise of U.S. military and economic power against the international community.

12) Acting to strip United States citizens of their constitutional and human rights, ordering indefinite detention of citizens without access to counsel, without charge, and without opportunity to appear before a civil judicial officer to challenge the detention, based solely on the discretionary designation by the Executive of a citizen as an "enemy combatant."

13) Ordering indefinite detention of non-citizens in the United States and elsewhere, and without charge, at the discretionary designation of the Attorney General or the Secretary of Defense; and violation of the Geneva Convention for prisoners taken or held by the U.S. Government, including those currently held at Guantanamo Bay.

14) Ordering and authorizing the Attorney General to override judicial orders of release of detainees under INS jurisdiction, even where the judicial officer after full hearing determines a detainee is wrongfully held by the government.

15) Authorizing secret military tribunals and summary execution of persons who are not citizens, and who are designated as subject to the jurisdiction of such tribunals solely at the discretion of the Executive who acts as indicting official, prosecutor and as the only avenue of appellate relief.

16) Refusing to provide public disclosure of the identities and locations of persons who have been arrested, detained and imprisoned by the U.S. government in the United States, including in response to Congressional inquiry.

17) Use of secret arrests of persons within the United States and elsewhere and denial of the right of public trials.

18) Authorizing the monitoring of confidential attorney-client privileged communications by the government, even in the absence of a court order and even where an incarcerated person has not been charged with a crime.

19)   Ordering and authorizing the seizure of assets of persons in the United States, prior to hearing or trial, for lawful or innocent association with any entity that at the discretionary designation of the Executive has been deemed "terrorist."

20)   Institutionalization of racial and religious profiling and authorization of domestic spying by federal law enforcement on persons based on their engagement in noncriminal religious and political activity.

21)   Refusal to provide information and records necessary and appropriate for the constitutional responsibilities of the Congress to legislate and oversee executive functions.

22)   Abrogation of the obligations of the United States under, and withdrawal from, international treaties and obligations without consent of the legislative branch, including termination of the ABM treaty between the United States and Russia.

{NOTE: The opening paragraph cites Bush and Ashcroft. While all of the items charged could be attributed to Bush, most of the foreign affairs ones cannot be reasonably related to Ashcroft. So that has to be sorted in the text.]

Despite these efforts, President Bush Jr. started his war of aggression against Iraq on the evening of Wednesday 19 March 2003 with an attempt to assassinate Iraqi President Saddam Hussein by means of a so-called "decapitation" strike, which was clearly illegal and criminal, a consideration once again ignored by the American media.   Since then, Clark and I have accelerated our respective grassroots campaigns to impeach President Bush Jr. et al.

Presidential Fears of Impeachment

Don Quixotes tilting at windmills?[17] Not at all! In the run-up to his 1991 Gulf War, President Bush Sr. feared impeachment. Writing in his diary on 20 December 1990 about the impending war against Iraq, President Bush Sr. recorded his fears of impeachment as follows: "But if it drags out, not only will I take the blame, but I will probably have impeachment proceedings filed against me."[18]   There are thus good grounds to believe that fear of impeachment compelled Bush Sr. to terminate the war early on 28 February 1991 with Iraqi President Saddam Hussein still in power, thus avoiding innumerable and horrendous casualties for Americans and even more so for Iraqis.

Thirteen years later, after President Bush Jr.'s invasion of Iraq, flush with "victory" and the arrogance of power, members of the Bush Jr. administration publicly threatened to attack Iran, Syria, and North Korea. In direct reaction to these threats, on 13 April 2003 former U.S. Secretary of

State (under President Bush Sr., no less!) Lawrence Engleburger told the BBC:

> If George Bush [Jnr] decided he was going to turn the troops loose on Syria and Iran after that he would last in office for about 15 minutes. In fact if President Bush were to try that now even I would think that he ought to be impeached. You can't get away with that sort of thing in this democracy.[19]

Almost immediately after Eagleburger's BBC broadside against them, the Bush Jr. warmongers cooled their public rhetoric and threats against Iran and Syria—but not North Korea.

So the Bush Jr. administration has already stood down for the time being from two further aggressions at least partially due to the influence of one public threat of impeachment. But as of this writing U.S. military, political and economic preparations are underway for a Bush Jr. war of aggression against North Korea. The American People and Congress must put the fear of impeachment into the highest levels of the Bush Jr. administration in order to prevent such a catastrophic war that could readily go nuclear.[20]

Epilogue

Certainly, if the U.S. House of Representatives can impeach President Clinton for sex and lying about sex, then a fortiori the House can, should, and must impeach President Bush Jr. for war, lying about war, and threatening more wars. All that is needed is one Member of Congress with the courage, integrity, and principles of the late and great Congressman Henry B. Gonzalez of Texas. Failing this, the alternative is likely to be an American Empire abroad, a U.S. police state at home, and continuing wars of aggression to sustain both—along the lines of George Orwell's classic novel *1984* (1949). Despite all of the serious flaws demonstrated by United States governments that this author has amply documented elsewhere during the past quarter century as a Professor of Law, the truth of the matter is that America is still the oldest Republic in the world today.[21] We, the People of the United States, must fight to keep it that way![22] And for the good of all humanity, we must terminate America's Imperial Presidency and subject it to the Rule of Law.[23]

Chapter Nine

Can World War III
Be Far Behind?

With the collapse of the Soviet Union and the impoverishment of Russia leaving the United States as the world's "only superpower" or "hyperpower," we are getting to the point, if we are not there already, where only the United States has the capability to launch an offensive first-strike strategic nuclear weapons attack upon any adversary. For that precise reason, deploying the so-called "national missile defense" (NMD) has become a critical objective of the Bush Jr. administration. NMD is not really needed to shoot down a stray missile from some so-called "rogue state." Rather U.S. NMD is essential for taking out any residual Russian or Chinese strategic nuclear weapon that might survive a U.S. offensive first-strike with strategic nuclear weapons systems.

The successful deployment of NMD will finally provide the United States with what it has always sought: the capacity to launch a successful offensive first-strike strategic nuclear attack, coupled with the capability to neutralize a Russian and/or Chinese retaliatory nuclear response. At that point, the United States will proceed to use this capability to enforce its hegemonial will upon the rest of the world. Strategic nuclear "thinkers" such as Harvard's Thomas Schelling call this doctrine "compellence" as opposed to "deterrence." With NMD the world will become dominated through this U.S. "compellence" strategy.

In the March 10, 2002 edition of the *Los Angeles Times*, defense analyst William Arkin revealed the leaked contents of the Bush Jr. administration's Nuclear Posture Review (NPR) that it had just transmitted to Congress on January 8. The Bush Jr. administration ordered the Pentagon to draw up war plans for the first use of nuclear weapons against seven states: the so-called "axis of evil" –Iran, Iraq, and North Korea— plus Libya, Syria, Russia, and China, of which the latter two and possibly the DPRK are nuclear armed. This component of the Bush Jr. NPR incorporated the Clinton administration's 1997 nuclear war-fighting plans against so-called "rogue states" set forth in Presidential Decision Directive 60. These warmed-over nuclear war plans targeting non-nuclear weapons states expressly violated the so-called "negative security assurances" given by the United States as an express condition for the renewal and indefinite extension of the Nuclear Non-Proliferation Treaty (NPT) by all of its non-nuclear weapons states parties in 1995.

Equally reprehensible from a legal perspective was the NPR's additional call for the Pentagon to draft nuclear war-fighting plans for first nuclear strikes (1) against alleged nuclear/chemical/biological "materials" or "facilities"; (2) "against targets able to withstand non-nuclear attack"; and (3) "in the event of surprising military developments," whatever that may subsequently be interpreted to mean. According to the NPR, the Pentagon must also draw up nuclear war-fighting plans to intervene with nuclear weapons in wars (1) between China and Taiwan; (2) between Israel and the Arab states; (3) between North Korea and South Korea; and (4) between Israel and Iraq. It is obvious upon which side the United States will actually plan to intervene with the first-use nuclear weapons.

In this regard, Article 6 of the 1945 Nuremberg Charter provides in relevant part as follows:

> ....
> *The following acts, or any of them,* are crimes coming within the jurisdiction of the Tribunal for which there shall be individual responsibility:
>
> (a) *Crimes against peace:* namely, *planning, preparation,* initiation or waging *of a war of aggression, or a war in violation of international* treaties, agreements or *assurances,* or participation in a common plan or conspiracy for the accomplishment of any of the foregoing;
>
> ...
>
> Leaders, organizers, instigators and accomplices participating in the formulation or execution of a common plan or conspiracy to commit any of the foregoing crimes are responsible for all acts performed by any persons in execution of such plan. [Emphasis added.]

To the same effect is the Sixth Principle of the Principles of International Law Recognized in the Charter of the Nuremberg Tribunal and in the Judgment of the Tribunal, which were adopted by the International Law Commission of the United Nations in 1950:

> PRINCIPLE VI
> The crimes hereinafter set out are punishable as crimes under international law:
> (a) Crimes against peace:
> (i) *Planning, preparation,* initiation or waging *of* a war of aggression *or a war in violation of international* treaties, agreements or *assurances*;
> (ii) Participation in a common plan or conspiracy for the accomplishment of any of the acts mentioned under (i).... [Emphasis added.]

Notice that both of these elemental sources of public international law clearly provide that the "planning" or "preparation" of a war in violation of international "assurances" such as the aforementioned U.S. negative security assurance constitutes a Nuremberg Crime against Peace. To the same effect are paragraphs 498, 499, 500, and 501 of U.S. Army Field Manual 27-10 (1956). Such is the Bush Jr. NPR—prima facie evidence of an international crime!

The Bush Jr. administration is making it crystal clear to all its chosen adversaries around the world that it is fully prepared to cross the threshold proscribing further use of nuclear weapons that has prevailed since the U.S. criminal bombings of Hiroshima and Nagasaki in 1945—yet more proof of the fact that the United States government has officially abandoned "deterrence" for "compellence" in order to rule the future world of the Third Millenium. Clearly, the Bush Jr. administration has become a "threat to the peace" within the meaning of U.N. Charter Article 39. For the future good of all humanity, the Bush Jr. administration must be restrained by both the international community and the American people.

Despite the fact that it is an Imperial Republic and despite the fact that full citizenship rights were only extended to its people of color and women in the twentieth century, the United States of America is touted as the world's oldest constitutional democracy with a commitment to the Rule of Law both at home and abroad. American foreign policy decision-making has been subjected to the Rule of Law by the United States Constitution. This much is true whether the "realists," the "neo-realists," the "neo-liberals," and the "neo-conservatives" like it or not. The American people have never been willing to provide sustained popular support for a foreign policy that has flagrantly violated elementary norms of international law precisely because they have habitually perceived themselves to constitute a democratic political society governed by an indispensable commitment to the Rule of Law in all sectors of their national endeavors.

America's self-styled "realist" or "neo-realist" or "neo-liberal" or "neo-conservative" geopolitical practitioners of power politics such as Kennedy, Johnson, McNamara, Nixon, Kissinger, Brzezinski, Haig, Kirkpatrick, Shultz, Bush Sr., Baker, Clinton, and now Wolfowitz and his Neo-Cons will not and cannot possibly construct a water-tight compartment around their exercise of Machiavellianism in international relations. Inevitably, there are deleterious spillover effects into the domestic affairs of the American people that are counter to and can even threaten the integrity of the American legal, political, and constitutional system. As the Bush Jr. administration bankrupts America to pursue a hydrocarbon empire and global dominance, Attorney General Ashcroft will be compelled to install a police state at home in order to cloak the repression of domestic dissent; this will be done in the guise of protecting Americans from terrorist attacks.

In international legal terms, the Bush Jr. administration should be viewed as constituting an ongoing criminal conspiracy under international criminal law in violation of the Nuremberg Charter, the Nuremberg Judgment, and the Nuremberg Principles, due to its formulation and undertaking of war policies which are legally akin to those perpetrated by the Nazi regime in pre-World War II Germany. As a consequence, American citizens possess the basic right under international law and United States domestic law, including our own Constitution, to engage in acts of nonviolent civil resistance in order to prevent, impede, thwart, or terminate ongoing criminal activities perpetrated by U.S. government officials in their conduct of foreign affairs policies and operations purported to relate to defense and counter-terrorism.

This same right of civil resistance extends *pari passu* to all citizens of the world community of states. Everyone around the world has both the right and the duty under international law to resist ongoing criminal activities perpetrated by the Bush Jr. administration and its foreign accomplices by all nonviolent means possible. If it is not so restrained, the Bush Jr. administration could very well precipitate a Third World War.

The time for preventive action is now. Civil resistance is the way to go. People power can overcome power politics. Popular movements have succeeded in toppling tyrannical, dictatorial and authoritarian regimes throughout former Communist countries in Eastern Europe, as well as in Asia, and most recently in Latin America. It is time once again to exercise People Power in the United States of America:

> We hold these Truths to be self-evident, that all Men are created equal, that they are endowed by their Creator with certain unalienable Rights, that among these are Life, Liberty and the Pursuit of Happiness—That to secure these Rights, Governments are instituted among Men, deriving their just Powers from the Consent of the Governed, that whenever any Form of Government becomes destructive of these Ends, it is the Right of the People to alter or to abolish it, and to institute new Government, laying its Foundation on such Principles, and organizing its Powers in such Form, as to them shall seem most likely to effect their Safety and Happiness. Prudence, indeed, will dictate that Governments long established should not be changed for light and transient Causes; and accordingly all Experience hath shewn, that Mankind are more disposed to suffer, while Evils are sufferable, than to right themselves by abolishing the Forms to which they are accustomed. But when a long Train of Abuses and Usurpations, pursuing invariably the same Object, evinces a Design to reduce them under absolute Despotism, it is their Right, it is their Duty, to throw off such Government, and to provide new Guards for their future Security. Such has been the patient Sufferance of these Colonies; and such is now the Necessity which constrains them to alter their former Systems of Government.
>
> . . . .

Endnotes

Foreword

1. Michael Dougherty, To Steal a Kingdom (1992). *But see* Francis A. Boyle, *The Restoration of the Independent Nation State of Hawaii under International Law,* 7 St. Thomas L. Rev. 723 (1995).
2. Lutz Kleveman, *The 'War on Terror' Is Being Used as an Excuse to Further U.S. Energy Interests in the Caspian,* The Guardian, Oct. 20, 2003.
3. St. Augustine, 2 The City of God Against the Pagans 17 (Harvard: 1963). *See* Gary Wills, Saint Augustine (1999). *See also* Noam Chomsky, Pirates & Emperors (1986).
4. Project for the New American Century (PNAC), Rebuilding America's Defenses (Sept. 2000).
5. *See, e.g.,* Charles A. Beard, An Economic Interpretation of the Constitution of the United States (1935 ed.).
6. Juliet E.K. Walker, *Whither Liberty, Equality or Legality? Slavery, Race, Property and the 1787 American Constitution,* 6 N.Y.L. Sch. J. Hum. Rts. 299-352 (1989).
7. USA on Trial: The International Tribunal on Indigenous Peoples' and Oppressed Nations in the United States (Alejandro Luis Molina: 1996 Editorial el Coquí) (the Verdict and Video are also available). *See also* Noam Chomsky, Year 501: The Conquest Continues (1993).
8. *See, e.g.,* Bruce M. Russett, No Clear and Present Danger (1972); Robert B. Stinnett, Day of Deceit (2000).
9. Manley O. Hudson, *A Design for a Charter of the General International Organization,* 38 A.J.I.L. 711 (1944).
10. Federation of American Scientists, Military Analysis Network, *Iran-Iraq War (1980-1988)* (21 Dec. 1999).
11. Francis A. Boyle, World Politics and International Law 183-203 (1985).
12. Ramsey Clark et al., War Crimes: A Report on United States War Crimes Against Iraq (1992).
13. *See* Can't Jail the Spirit: Political Prisoners in the U.S. (3d ed. 1992); Verdict of the Special Tribunal on the Violation of Human Rights of Political Prisoners and Prisoners of War in United States Prisons and Jails (New York: Dec. 7-10, 1990).
14. Francis A. Boyle, *Biowarfare, Terror Weapons and the U.S.: Home Brew?, Counterpunch.org,* April 25, 2002; Kevin Merida & John Mintz, *Rockville Firm Shipped Germ Agents to Iraq, Riegle Says,* Washington Post, Feb. 10, 1994, at AO8. *See also* Francis A. Boyle, *The Legal Distortions Behind the Reagan Administration's Chemical and Biological Warfare Buildup,* in my The Future of International Law and American Foreign Policy 277-316 (1989).
15. *See generally* George J. Annas, *Mengele's Birthmark: The Nuremberg Code in United States Courts,* 7 J. Contemp. Health L. & Pol'y 17 (1991).
16. Edward Pearce, *Death and Indecency in a Time of Cholera,* The Guardian, Oct. 25, 1991.
17. *See* Ramsey Clark, FAO Report, and Others, The Children Are Dying (World View Forum, Inc.: 1996).
18. *See* 5/12/96 60 Minutes, 1996 Westlaw 8064912.
19. *See also* Francis A. Boyle, Palestine, Palestinians and International Law (2003).
20. Francis A. Boyle, Defending Civil Resistance Under International Law (1987).

Chapter One

1. U.S. Congress, Neutrality Act of June 5, 1794, ch. 50, 3rd Cong., 1st sess., 1 *United States Statutes at Large* [hereinafter *Stat.*] 381.
2. U.S. Congress, Act of March 2, 1797, ch. 5, 4th Cong., 2d sess., 1 *Stat.* 497.

3.   U.S. Congress, Act of April 20, 1818, ch. 88, 15th Cong., 1st sess., 3 *Stat.* 447 (currently reissued as 18 U.S.C.A. §967).

4.   Ibid., 447-450.

5.   Ibid., sec. 8, 449.

6.   Treaty of Washington, May 8, 1871, 17 *Stat.* 863, T.S. No. 133.

7.   Ibid., 865.

8.   Final Act of the International Peace Conference, July 29, 1899, reprinted in American Journal of International Law [hereinafter Am. J. Int'l L.] 1 (Supp. 1907):106.

9.   Convention Respecting the Rights and Duties of Neutral Powers and Persons in Case of War on Land, Oct. 18, 1907, 36 *Stat.* 2310.

10.   Convention Concerning the Rights and Duties of Neutral Powers in Naval War, Oct. 18, 1907, 36 *Stat.* 2415, T.S. No. 545.

11.   Convention Relative to the Laying of Automatic Submarine Contact Mines, Oct. 18, 1907, 36 *Stat.* 2332, T.S. No. 541.

12.   Convention Relative to Certain Restrictions with Regard to the Exercise of the Right of Capture in Naval War, Oct. 18, 1907, art. 1, 36 *Stat.* 2396 at 2408, T.S. No. 544.

13.   See 36 *Stat.* at 2310, 2332, 2396, 2415.

14.   "Neutrals have the right to continue during war to trade with the belligerents, subject to the law relating to contraband and blockade. The existence of this right is universally admitted, although on certain occasions it has been in practice denied." John B. Moore, A Digest of International Law (Washington, D.C.: Government Printing Office, 1906) 7:99-103.

15.   Francis Boyle, *The Law of Power Politics*, University of Illinois Law Forum, 1980:936-937.

16.   Convention with Respect to the Law and Customs of War on Land, July 29, 1899, Annex, art. 46, 32 *Stat.* 1803, 1822, T.S. No. 403; Convention with Respect to the Law and Customs of War on Land, Oct. 18, 1907, Annex, art. 46, 36 *Stat.* 2277, 2306-07, T.S. No. 539.

17.   Joseph H. Choate, The Two Hague Conferences (Princeton: Princeton University Press, 1913), 74-77; Calvin D. Davis, The United States and the Second Hague Peace Conference (Durham: Duke University Press, 1975), 138-140, 171-72, 227-33; William I. Hull, The Two Hague Conferences and Their Contribution to International Law (Boston: Ginn & Co., 1908), 126-41; Charles H. Stockton, "Would Immunity from Capture During War of Non-Offending Private Property Upon the High Seas Be in the Interest of Civilization?", *Am. J. Int'l L.* 1 (1907):932-933.

18.   Barbara J. Fuschholz and John M. Raymond, *Lawyers Who Established International Law in the United States, 1776-1914*, Am. J. Int'l L. 76 (1982):806-07.

19.   Christian L. Wiktor, ed., *Declaration of London, Feb. 26, 1909*, Unperfected Treaties of the United States of America (Dobbs Ferry, N.Y.: Oceana Publications, Inc., 1976) 4:129.

20.   James B. Scott, The Declaration of London February 26, 1909 (New York, Oxford University Press, 1919), v; id., T*he Declaration of London of February 26, 1909*, Am. J. Int'l L. 8 (1914):274.

21.   Charles H. Stockton, *The International Naval Conference of London 1908-1909*, Am. J. Int'l L. 3 (1909):614.

22.   Ethel C. Phillips, *American Participation in Belligerent Commercial Controls 1914-1917*, Am. J. Int'l L. 27 (1933):675-693.

23.   William C. Morey, *The Sale of Munitions of War*, Am. J. Int'l L. 10 (1916):467.

24.   Philip M. Brown, *The Theory of the Independence and Equality of States*, Am. J. Int'l L. 9 (1915):305; Malbone W. Graham, *Neutrality and the World War,* Am. J. Int'l L. 17 (1923):704; *Neutralization as a Movement in International Law*, Am. J. Int'l L. 21 (1927):79; Amos S. Hershey, *Projects Submitted to the American Institute of International Law*, Am. J. Int'l L. 11 (1917):390; Elihu Root, *The Outlook for International Law*, Am. J. Int'l L. 10 (1916):1; *The Organization of International Force*, Am. J. Int'l L. 9 (1915):45; George G. Wilson, *Sanction for International Agreements*, Am. J. Int'l L. 11 (1917):387.

25.   Ruhl J. Barlett, The League to Enforce Peace (Chapel Hill: University of North

Carolina Press, 1944), 215-218.

26.   Alfred E. Zimmern, The League of Nations and the Rule of Law, 1918-1935 (New York: Russell & Russell, 1936), 515-516.

27.   G.A. Res. 377, 5 U.N. GAOR, Supp. (No. 20) at 10, U.N. Doc. A/1775, 1950.

28.   *Whose Interest?*, Economist, 27 Sept. 1980, 42; Mansur (pseud.), *The Military in the Persian Gulf: Who Will Guard the Gulf States from Their Guardians?*, Armed Forces Journal International, Nov. 1980, 44; "Dangerous Game," Nation, 231 (1980):395; *Who Will Police These Shores?* The Middle East, Oct. 1980, 26; David Shipler, *Israeli Says U.S. Is Secretly Supplying Arms to Iraq*, New York Times, Oct. 29, 1981, sec. A, p. 10, col. 1.

29.   Treaty of Friendship, Feb. 26, 1921, R.S.F.S.R.-Persia, art. 5 and 6, *League of Nations Treaty Series* 9:403.

30.   William M. Reisman, Editorial, *Termination of the U.S.S.R.'s Treaty Right of Intervention in Iran*, Am. J. Int'l L. 74 (1980):144; Huschfeld, *Moscow and Khomeini Soviet-Iranian Relations in Historical Perspective*, Orbis (1980):219.

31.   Champaign-Urbana News Gazette, 18 Aug. 1980, sec. A, p. 4, col. 4; id., 19 Aug. 1980, sec. A, p. 4, col. 4; id., 21 Aug. 1980, sec. A, p. 4, col. 1; id., 22 Aug. 1980, sec. A, p. 4, col. 4; Washington Post [hereinafter Wash. Post], 22 Sept. 1980, sec. D, p. 13, col. 3; Washington Star, 21 Sept. 1980, p. 6; Jack Anderson, *Why I Tell Secrets*, Wash. Post, 30 Nov. 1980, sec. Parade, p. 20-25; Wash. Post, 23 Oct. 1981, sec. B, p. 17; id., 28 June 1983, sec. C, p. 15.

32.   Claudia Wright, *Implications of the Iraq-Iran War*, Foreign Affairs, 59 (1980-81):275; Adeed I. Dawisha, *Iraq: The West's Opportunity*, Foreign Policy, Winter 1980-81, No. 41:134.

33.   See e.g. Wash. Post, 27 Aug. 1981, sec. 6, p. 31, col. 3; New York Times, 7 Mar. 1982, p. 1, col. 3; see also The Middle East, 24 Aug. 1980, 24; New York Times, 18 July 1983, p. 3, col. 1.

34.   Jim McGuish and Antony Terry, *How U.S. Sky Spies Help Iraq's War*, Sunday Times (London), 7 March 1985, sec. 1, p. 21.

35.   David Alpern et al., *America's Secret Warriors*, Newsweek, 10 Oct. 1983, 38-45; Jay Peterzell, *Can Congress Really Check the C.I.A.?*, Wash. Post, 24 April 1983, 61.

36.   Mansour Farhang, *The Iran-Iraq War*, World Policy Journal 2 (1985):671.

37.   Under the provisions of the Export Administration Act of 1979, the Secretary of Commerce in consultation with the Secretary of State can review and adjust the list of restricted countries. 50 *U.S.C.A. App.* §2405 (West, 1985).

38.   David Ignatius, *Iraq is Turning to U.S., Britain For Armaments*, The Wall Street Journal [hereinafter Wall St. J.], 5 March 1982, p. 22, col. 1.

39.   Bureau of National Affairs, U.S. Export Weekly, 6 June 1982, 312.

40.   *A Tilt Towards Baghdad?*, The Middle East, June 1982, 7; New York Times, 18 July 1983, p. 3, col. 1.

41.   *U.S. Licenses Sale to Iraq of Small Jet*, Wash. Post, 14 Sept. 1982, p. 12, col. 1.

42.   Don Oberdorfer, *U.S. Moves to Avert Iraqi Loss*, Wash. Post, 1 Jan. 1984, p. 1, col. 1; David Ignatius, *U.S. Tilts Towards Iraq to Thwart Iran*, Wall St. J., 6 Jan. 1984, p. 20, col. 1.

43.   Middle East Policy Survey, No. 102 (20 April 1984):1.

44.   Jack Anderson, *Reagan Urged to Take Sides in Persian Gulf*, Wash. Post, 1 Dec. 1983, 17; Philip Marfleet, *Calling the Iranian Bluff*, The Middle East, July 1984, 16-17.

45.   Amos Perlmutter, *Squandering Opportunity in the Gulf*, Wall St. J., 13 Oct. 1983, p. 32, col. 3.

46.   Roy Gutman, *U.S. Willing to Use Air Power to Keep Iran From Beating Iraq*, Long Island Newsday, 20 May 1984, 3; David Ignatius and Gerald Seib, *U.S. Tilts Toward Iraq to Thwart Iran*, Wall St. J., 5 Jan. 1984.

47.   David Seib, *Textron's Bell Unit and Iraq Seen Near Final Agreements on Sale of 45 Helicopters*, Wall St. J., 28 Feb. 1985, p. 32, col. 5.

48.   David Ottaway, *U.S. Copter Sales to Iraq Raises Neutrality Issue*, Wash. Post, 13 Sept. 1985, p. 1, col. 6.

49.   Bernard Gwertzman, *Iran's Navy Stops U.S. Ship in Search Near Persian Gulf,* New York Times, 13 Jan. 1986, p. 1, col. 6.

50.   Treaty on International Borders and Good Neighborly Relations, June 13, 1975, Iran-Iraq, International Legal Materials, 14 (1975):1133.

51.   Philip Marfleet, *Economic Warfare in the Gulf,* The Middle East, Sept. 1983, 79.

52.   35 U.N. SCOR (2248th mtg.) at 1 U.N. Doc. S/RES 479 (1980); 36 U.N. SCOR (2288th mtg.) at 1 U.N. Doc. S/RES1487 (1981); 37 U.N. SCOR (2388d mtg.) at 1 U.N. Doc. S/RES 514 (1982).

53.   Judith Miller, *6 Nations to Form Joint Gulf Force,* New York Times, 30 Nov. 1984, p. 7, col. 1; John D. Anthony, *The Gulf Cooperation Council,* Orbis 28 (1984):447.

54.   See e.g. *U.S.C.,* 22 (1976):sec. 2302, 2314(d), 2753(c), 2754.

55.   Jeffrey Record, *Persian Gulf--Defending the Indefensible,* Los Angeles Times, 9 Nov. 1981, sec. A, p. 12.

56.   Jack Anderson, *R.D.F. Predicted to Have High Casualty Rate,* Wash. Post, 7 Aug. 1981, sec. C, p. 15; George Wilson, *U.S. Response Force Would Face Heavy Losses Guarding Mideast Oil,* Wash. Post, 28 Oct. 1980, p.1.

57.   War Powers Act of 1973, P.L. No. 93-148, 87 *Stat.* 555.

58.   1958 Geneva Convention, on the High Seas (April 29, 1958); 13 U.S.T. 2312, T.I.A.S. 5200, 450 U.N.T.S. 82, Art. 5.

59.   *Liechtenstein v. Guatemala,* [1955] I.C.J. Rep. 4.

60.   *United Kingdom v. Albania,* [1949] I.C.J. Rep. 4.

61.   *Id.* at 35.

62.   The Complete Writings of Thucydides: The Peloponnesian War (Madean Library ed. 1951), p. 332

63.   42 U.N.S.C.O.R. (2750th Mtg.), at 1 U.N. Doc. S/RES/598 (1987), *reprinted in* 26 I.L.M. 1479 (1987).

64.   *See generally* Noam Chomsky, Hegemony or Survival (Metropolitan Books: 2003); Tariq Ali, Bush in Babylon (Verso: 2003).

Chapter Two

1.   *See* Ramsey Clark, *Planning U.S. Dominion over the Gulf,* in his The Fire This Time 3-37 (1992). *See also* Ramsey Clark & Others, War Crimes: A Report on United States War Crimes Against Iraq (Maisonneuve Press: 1992).

2.   *See* Ramsey Clark, The Fire This Time 23-24 (1992); Hamdi A. Hassan, The Iraqi Invasion of Kuwait 37, 47-51 (1999); *The Glaspie-Hussein Transcript,* Beyond the Storm 391-96 (Phyllis Bennis & Michel Moushabeck eds. 1991).

3.   Francis A. Boyle, *The U.S. Invasion of Panama: Implications for International Law and Politics,* 1 East African J. Peace & Human Rights 80 (Uganda: 1993).

Chapter Three

1.   *See* Francis A. Boyle, Defending Civil Resistance Under International Law 114-18 (1987).

Chapter Five

1.   Louis B. Sohn and Thomas Buergenthal, International Protection of Human Rights (Indianapolis: Bobbs-Merrill Co., 1973), pp. 140-141.

2.   *Ibid.,* p. 179.

3.   Francis A. Boyle, World Politics and International Law (Durham: Duke University Press, 1985), p. 315 note 43.

4   Yale Law School, Myres Smith McDougal: Appreciations of an Extraordinary *Man* (New Haven, Conn.:Yale Law School, 1999).

5.   Sean D. Murphy, Humanitarian Intervention (Philadelphia: University of Pennsylvania Press, 1996), p. 387.

6.   *Ibid.,* p. 393.

7.   Bartram S. Brown, *Humanitarian Intervention at a Crossroads,* William and Mary Law Review, Vol. 41, No. 5 (May 2000), p. 1714.

8.   1949 International Court of Justice Reports, p. 35.

9.   American Society of International Law, International Legal Materials, Vol. 9., p. 1292, 1970.
10.   Francis A. Boyle, Defending Civil Resistance under International Law (Dobbs Ferry, N.Y.: Transnational Publishers Inc., 1987), p. 198.
11.   1986 International Court of Justice Reports, pp. 106-112, par. 209.
12.   *Ibid.,* pp. 134-135.
13.   Since this author has already recounted the depressing story of Serbia's genocidal destruction of Bosnia in my book The Bosnian People Charge Genocide (Putnam-Valley, NY: Aletheia Press, 1996) that went to press just before the 1995 Dayton Accord, there is no need or space to repeat it here. *See also* my *Is Bosnia the End of the Road for the United Nations?*, 6 Periodica Islamica, No. 2, at 45-59 (1996).
14 .   Francis A. Boyle, Palestine, Palestinians, and International Law (Atlanta, Ga.: Clarity Press. Inc., 2003), pp. 127-129.

Chapter Six

1.   *See* Francis A. Boyle, Defending Civil Resistance Under International Law (1987).
2.   *See Goldwater* v. *Carter*, 444 U.S. 996 (1979).
3.   *See* Nicolo Machiavelli, *The Prince* 149 (Mark Musa trans. & ed. 1964): " . . . all religion. And nothing is more essential than to appear to have this last quality."
4.   *See, e.g.,* William Blum, Killing Hope (1995). *See also* William Blum, Rogue State (2000).
5.   *See* Ahmed Rashid, Taliban (2000).
6.   *See* Francis A. Boyle, World Politics and International Law 75-167 (1985); Francis A. Boyle, The Future of International Law and American Foreign Policy 79-112 (1989).
7.   U.N. Security Council Resolution 1368 (12 Sept. 2001).
8.   U.N. Security Council Resolution 678 (29 Nov. 1990).
9.   *See* Ramsey Clark, The Fire This Time (1992).
10.   *See* Adam Clymer, *Senator Byrd Scolds Colleagues for Lack of Debate After Attack*, N.Y. Times, *Oct. 2, 2001.*
11.   *See* Arthur S. Miller, Presidential Power (1977).
12.   *See Korematsu* v. *United States*, 323 U.S. 214 (1944).
13.   The War Powers Resolution, 50 U.S.C.A. §§ 1541-1548 (1973).
14.   H.J. Res. 1145 (7 Aug. 1964).
15.   Public Law No. 107-40 (18 Sept. 2001).
16.   Public Law No. 102-1 (14 Jan. 1991).
17.   *See, e.g.,* Bill Keller, *The World According to Powell, N.Y.Times*, Nov. 25, 2001.
18.   *See* John K. Cooley, Unholy Wars (2d ed. 2000).
19.   International Herald Tribune, Online Edition, Dec. 9, 2001.
20.   Statement by the North Atlantic Council, Press Release (2001) 124 (12 Sept. 2001).
21.   *See* NATO Press Communiqué S-1(91) 86, Rome Declaration on Peace and Cooperation (8 Nov. 1991).
22.   *See* Noam Chomsky, The New Military Humanism (1999); Noam Chomsky, Rogue States (2000).
23.   See Noam Chomsky, What Uncle Sam Really Wants (1992).
24.   See Samuel P. Huntington, The Clash of Civilizations and the Remaking of World Order (1996).
25.   U.N. Security Council Resolution 1373 (28 Sept. 2001).
26.   S/2001/946 (7 Oct. 2001), 40 I.L.M. 1281 (2001).
27.   *See* Boyle, Future of International Law and American Foreign Policy, *supra*, at 87-88.
28.   *Id.* at 240-42.
29.   *See* Boyle, World Politics and International Law, *supra*, at 215-17.
30.   *See, e.g.,* BBC Online Edition, Sept. 18, 2001.
31.   *See* M. Wesley Swearingen, FBI Secrets (1995).
32.   *See* Alexander Cockburn & Jeffrey St. Clair, Whiteout (1998).
33.   Public Law No. 107-56.

34.   *See* Gerard Smith, Doubletalk (1980).
35.   *See* Judith Miller, Stephen Engelberg & William Broad, Germs (2001).
36.   *See* Francis A. Boyle, Foundations of World Order (1999)

Chapter Seven

1.   *See, e.g.*, Rahul Mahajan, Full Spectrum Dominance 108 (2003).
2.   Shadia B. Drury, Saving America, Evatt Foundation Paper, Sept. 10, 2003. *See* Shadia B. Drury, The Political Ideas of Leo Strauss (1988); Leo Strauss and the American Right (1999). *See also* Alain Frachon & Daniel Vernet, *The Strategist and the Philosopher: Leo Strauss and Albert Wohlstetter*, Le Monde, April 16, 2003, translated into English by Norman Madarasz on Counterpunch.org., June 2, 2003; Khurram Husain, *Neocons*, Bulletin of Atomic Scientists, Nov./Dec. 2003, at 62.
3.   *See also* David Brock, Blinded by the Right (2002).
4.   George E. Curry & Trevor W. Coleman, *Hijacking Justice*, Emerge, October 1999, at 42; Jerry M. Landay, *The Conservative Cabal That's Transforming American Law*, Washington Monthly, March 2000, at 19; People for the American Way, The Federalist Society (August 2001); Institute for Democracy Studies, The Federalist Society and the Challenge to a Democratic Jurisprudence (January 2001).
5.   Francis A. Boyle, *Bush's Banana Republic*, Counterpunch.org, Oct. 11, 2002.
6.   Francis A. Boyle, *Biowarfare, Terror Weapons and the U.S.: Home Brew?*, Counterpunch.org, April 25, 2002.
7.   *See* Greg Palast, *The Best Democracy Money Can Buy* (2003), at 5 et seq.
8.   *See* Chomsky on Mis-Education (Donald Macedo ed. 2000).
9.   Francis A. Boyle, *Take Sharon to The Hague*, Counterpunch.org, June 6, 2002.
10.   White House Press Release, *President Discusses the Future of Iraq*, Washington Hilton Hotel, Feb. 26, 2003.
11.   Nasser H. Aruri, Dishonest Broker, 193-216 (2003). *See also* Tanya Reinhart, Israel/Palestine (2002); Cheryl A. Rubenberg, The Palestinians (2003).
12.   Norman Solomon, The Habits of Highly Deceptive Media (1999); Noam Chomsky, Media Control (1997).
13.   Seymour M. Hersh, *Selective Intelligence*, New Yorker, May 8, 2003; Michael Lind, *The Weird Men Behind George W. Bush's War*, New Statesman – London, April 7, 2003; Julian Borger, *The Spies Who Pushed for War*, The Guardian, July 17, 2003.
14.   Machiavelli, The Prince 147 (M. Musa trans. & ed. 1964): ". . . and men are so simple-minded and so dominated by their present needs that one who deceives will always find one who will allow himself to be deceived." This Bilingual Edition of The Prince by Mark Musa was the one preferred by Joseph Cropsey to teach us students.
15.   *But see* Lawrence W. Levine, The Opening of the American Mind (1996).
16.   *Between the Lines*, University of Chicago Magazine, June 2003, at 54.
17.   Vincent Bugliosi, The Betrayal of America (2001); Greg Palast, The Best Democracy Money Can Buy 11-81 (2003).
18.   Gerhard Sporl, *The Leo-Conservatives*, Der Spiegel, Aug. 4, 2003.
19.   *McNamara Receives Pick Award Amid Protests*, University of Chicago Magazine, Summer 1979, at 4.
20.   Noam Chomsky, Rethinking Camelot (1993); Robert S. McNamara, In Retrospect (1995).
21.   *See, e.g.*, Rahul Mahajan, Full Spectrum Dominance 118-40 (2003).
22.   C. Wright Mills, The Power Elite (1956).
23.   *See, e.g.*, Jean-Charles Brisard & Guillaume Dasqué, Forbidden Truth (2002).
24.   Robert B. Stinnett, Day of Deceit (2000).
25.   Robert Dreyfuss, *The Thirty-Year Itch*, MotherJones.com, March 1, 2003.
26.   Zbigniew Brzezinski, The Grand Chessboard (1997).
27.   Hans J. Morgenthau, Politics Among Nations 52-53 (4th ed. 1967). This fourth edition of the book is the one I studied personally with Morgenthau.

28. William Blum, Rogue State 158 (2000); John Pilger, The New Rulers of the World 127-29 (2003).
29. Noam Chomsky, Rogue States 62-81 (2000).
30. Greg Palast, The Best Democracy Money Can Buy 192-99 (2003).
31. Roger Morris, *Hurtful Hand on Liberia*, L.A. Times, Aug. 31, 2003.
32. Samuel P. Huntington, The Clash of Civilizations and the Remaking of World Order (1996). *But see* Edward W. Said, *Afterword* (1994) to Orientalism (1978).
33. Dean Acheson, Present at the Creation (1969).
34. Francis A. Boyle, Foundations of World Order 155-68 (1999).
35. Jules Lobel & Michael Ratner, *Bypassing The Security Council: Ambiguous Authorizations to Use Force, Cease-Fires, and the Iraqi Inspection Regime*, 93 Am. J. Int'l L. 124 (1999).
36. Francis A. Boyle, Palestine, Palestinians and International Law 132-52 (2003).
37. Dilip Hero, Iraq 178-80 (2002).
38. *See Full Text: Bush's National Security Strategy*, N.Y. Times, Sept. 20, 2002.
39. Francis A. Boyle, The Criminality of Nuclear Deterrence 55-91 (2002).
40. Leon V. Sigal, *Negotiating with the North*, Bulletin of Atomic Scientists, Nov./Dec. 2003, at 19.
41. *The Nuremberg Trial,* 6 Federal Rules Decisions 69, 99-101 (1946).
42. Joseph E. Persico, Nuremberg 416-30 (1994).
43. Noam Chomsky, The New Military Humanism (1999).
44. Seymour M. Hersh, *The Syrian Bet*, New Yorker, July 28, 2003; Richard Sale, *U.S. Syria Raid Killed 80*, Washington Times, July 17, 2003.
45. David Stout, *Bush, Speaking to Veterans, Says Iraq May Not be Last Strike*, NYTimes.com, Aug. 26, 2003.
46. Geoff Simons, *The Making of Iraq*, 35 The Link, No. 5, at 12-13 (Dec. 2002); Institute for Public Accuracy, United Nations Security Council Resolution 1441: An Analysis 12 November 2002.
47. Francis A. Boyle, Foundations of World Order 1-24, 86-102 (1999).
48. USA On Trial: The International Tribunal on Indigenous Peoples and Oppressed Nations in the United States (Alejandro Luis Molina ed.1996); Noam Chomsky, Year 501: The Conquest Continues (1993).
49. Paul Kennedy, The Rise and Fall of the Great Powers (1987).
50. James Podgers, *Greetings from Independent Hawaii*, ABA Journal, June 1997, at 74.
51. *See* U.N. Security Council Resolution 1502 (2003).
52. James Petras, *The Politics of the U.N. Tragedy*, Rebelión, Aug. 24, 2003.
53. Dag Hammarskjold, Markings (1964).
54. Steve Stecklow, *The U.N.: Searching for Relevance*, Wall Street Journal, Sept. 26, 2003, at A1.
55. Francis A. Boyle, *Is Bosnia the End of the Road for the United Nations?*, 6 Periodica Islamica, No. 2, at 45 (1996).
56. Denis Halliday, *The U.N. Failed the Iraqi People*, Socialist Worker, Sept. 5, 2003. See *also* Karima Bennoune, *'Sovereignty vs. Suffering'? Re-examining Sovereignty and Human Rights Through the Lens of Iraq*, 13 European Journal of International Law, No. 1, at 243-62 (2002).
57. Cynthia D. Wallace, *Kellogg-Briand Pact (1928)*, 3 Encyclopedia of Public International Law 236 (1982).
58. Werner Meng, *Stimson Doctrine*, 4 Encyclopedia of Public International Law 230 (1982).
59. Michael J. Glennon, *Why the Security Council Failed*, Foreign Affairs, May/June 2003, at 16.
60. Jack Nelson-Pallmeyer, Brave New World Order (1992).
61. Webster G. Tarpley & Anton Chaitkin, *Bush Family Ties to Nazi Germany–the Legacy of Prescott Herbert Bush*, Global Outlook, No. 5, at 54 (Summer/Fall 2003); John Buchanan, *Bush-Nazi Link Confirmed*, New Hampshire Gazette, Vol. 248, No. 1, Oct. 10, 2003.
62. Christopher Hitchens, The Trial of Henry Kissinger (2002).

63.   Francis A. Boyle, The Bosnian People Charge Genocide (1996).
64.   *See generally* Young Sok Kim, The International Criminal Court (2003).
65.   Louis B. Sohn, Cases on United Nations Law 527-609 (2d ed. 1967).
66.   Leon Jaworski, The Right and the Power (1977); Bob Woodward & Carl Bernstein, The Final Days (1976).
67.   Howard Zinn, The Future of History (1999); Michael Parenti, History as Mystery (1999).
68.   William L. Shirer, The Rise and Fall of the Third Reich (1960).

Chapter Eight

1.   House Resolution 34, 102nd Congress, 1st Sess, Jan. 16, 1991, later reintroduced as House Resolution 86, Feb. 21, 1991.
2.   Congressional Record, January 16, 1991 at H520.
3.   Raoul Berger, Impeachment: The Constitutional Problems (1973).
4.   Charles L. Black, Jr., Impeachment: A Handbook 27-33, at 28 (1974).
5.   Francis A. Boyle, *Bush's Banana Republic*, CounterPunch.org, October 11, 2002.
6.   George E. Curry & Trevor Coleman, *Hijacking Justice*, Emerge, Oct. 1999, at 42.
7.   David Cole, *Patriot Act's Big Brother*, The Nation, March 17, 2003, at 6.
8.   David Gray Adler *The Constitution and Presidential Warmaking*, in The Constitution and the Conduct of American Foreign Policy 183 (David Gray Adler & Larry N. George eds. 1996).
9.   Nat Hentoff, *An Entirely New Impeachment Case*, Washington Post, March 6, 1999, at A21.
10.   Dilip Hiro, Iraq: In the Eye of the Storm 129-32 (2002).
11.   David Halberstam, The Best and the Brightest (1969). *See also* Noam Chomsky, Rethinking Camelot (1993); Seymour M. Hersh, The Dark Side of Camelot (1997); Robert S. McNamara, In Retrospect: The Tragedy and Lessons of Vietnam (1995).
12.   G. Santayana, The Life of Reason 284 (1905).
13.   *Cf.* E. May, "Lessons" of the Past (1973).
14.   *Impeachment Articles That the House Approved*, N.Y. Times, Dec. 22, 1998.
15.   Christopher Hitchens, No One Left To Lie To (1999).
16.   Ethan Wallison, *Time to Impeach?*, Roll Call, March 13, 2003, at 1.
17.   Liz Halloran, *Wartime Snapshots of American Life: Tilting at Presidents*, Hartford Courant, March 30, 2003, at A3.
18.   Laura Myers, *Bush Describes Gulf War Quandary*, Associated Press, Sept. 10, 1998, quoting from Bush's memoir A World Transformed (1998), which he co-authored with his National Security Adviser Brent Scowcroft. *See also Bush: Worried about Impeachment for Gulf War*, The Hotline, Sept. 10, 1998; Institute for Public Accuracy, *Bush Worried About Impeachment, Too*, 28 Sept.1998 Press Release.
19.   Ben Russell, *U.S. Warns Syria Not to Provide Haven for Wanted Iraqis*, The Independent (UK), April 14, 2003; *Former Sec.of State Lawrence Engleburger: Bush Should Be Impeached If He Invades Syria or Iran*, Antiwar.com, April 14, 2003 (link to audio).
20.   Francis A. Boyle, The Criminality of Nuclear War Deterrence: Could the U.S. War on Terrorism Go Nuclear? (2002).
21.   *See* Akhil Reed Amar & Alan Hirsch, For the People (1998).
22.   Francis A. Boyle, Defending Civil Resistance Under International Law (1987; Special Paperback ed. 1988).
23.   Arthur M. Schlesinger Jr., The Imperial Presidency (1989). *See also* Michael Parenti, Against Empire (1995); John Pilger, The New Rulers of the World (2003); Chalmers Johnson, Blowback (2000); Daniel Berrigan, Lamentations (2002); International Law and Interventionism in the "New World Order": from Iraq to Yugoslavia (Arab Cause Solidarity Committee ed: Spain, 2000).

INDEX

ABM Treaty, 119, 138–39, 171
Admission against interest, 19,128, 146
Afghanistan, 11, 19, 20, 37, 38, 40,
    76,106, 119–20, 122–124, 126,
    130–35, 139, 142,143–44, 146,
    150, 152, 156,164, 165, 167
African Union, 109
aggression, 6, 11, 12, 16, 19, 20, 30, 32,
    34, 35, 37–38, 40, 43, 49, 50–51,
    54, 56, 57, 83, 91, 106, 109,
    111,112, 116, 119, 122, 126–27,131,
    140, 142–57, 158, 163, 167, 169–
    72, 174
Al Qaeda, 120–21, 124, 127–28, 140.
    See also Osama bin Laden
Albania, 48, 110–11
Albright, Madeline, 18–19
Alexander the Great, 12
Algeria, 117
American Enterprise Institute, 141
American Indian Movement, 13
Amnesty International, 71
Anderson, Jack, 33–34
Annan, Kofi, 152–53, 166
anthrax, 68, 87–88, 121, 141
Anti-Ballistic Missile SystemsTreaty. *See*
    ABM Treaty
Apartheid Convention, 114
Arab League, 109
armed attack, 32, 33, 40, 109, 113, 124,
    128–29, 147
arms control, 13, 139, 166 arms trans-
    fers, 16, 36–38, 40–41,43
Ashcroft, John, 20, 125, 136–38, 141,
    143, 158, 160, 164, 167–69, 171,
    175
assassination, 61, 75, 127, 169, 171
Association of Southeast Asian Nations
    (ASEAN), 109
Augustine of Hippo, St. 11–12
Aung San Suu Kyi, 17
Austria, 28, 150
Ayatollah Khomeini. *See* Khomeini,
    Ruhollah
Aziz, Tariq, 133

Baathist Party, 36, 151
Bahrain, 40, 63, 135
Baker, James, 53, 62, 64, 68, 82–83, 133,
    175
Belgium, 29, 117
Belligerent occupation, 150–53,155

Bellow, Saul, 142
Berger, Raoul, 159
Berger, Robert, 67
Biological Weapons Anti-Terrorism Act
    (1989), 87,139
Biological Weapons Convention, 17, 119,
    139
Bishop, Steven, 68
Blair, Tony, 19, 120–21, 145,147–48, 153,
    156
Bloom, Alan, 142–43, 146
Blum, William, 108
Bolton, John, 140
Borserine, Mark, 69
Bosnia-Herzegovina, 108, 113–16, 130
Botulin, 87–88
Bradford, William, 12
Bremer, Paul, 152, 157
Brownlie, Ian, 107
Brzezinski, Zbigniew, 16, 23,175
Buening, Lawrence, 69
Burger, Robert, 70
Bush, George H. W., 16, 17–18, 20, 22,
    53, 55–64, 68, 83–84, 87, 92, 93,
    95, 98, 99–100, 104, 118, 119, 124–
    25,126, 129, 130, 132, 133,134,
    137, 138, 142, 143,144, 145, 146,
    155,156, 158, 159–160, 164,
    165,166–67, 171, 172, 175
Bush, George W., 15, 16, 17, 19,20, 21,
    22, 52, 106, 118–39,140–57, 158,
    160–65, 167–72, 173–76
Bush, Prescott Herbert, 156
Byrd, Robert, 125

Caroline case, 47–48, 109, 147
Carter, Jimmy, 16, 20, 33–34, 38, 41–42,
    55, 56, 76–77, 84, 86, 119, 135
Catholic Relief Service, 95
Central Intelligence Agency, 20, 35, 36,
    53, 56, 112, 121,122, 127, 137,
    139, 140, 142, 149, 152, 157, 159
Chalabi, Ahmad, 142, 152, 157
Chechnya, 115, 130
Cheney, Richard, 17, 20, 53, 64, 68, 77,
    80–82, 134, 141,145, 149, 158,
    167, 168
Chicago, University of, 140–43,146, 152,
    157
Children's Convention, 93, 94,103
China, 15, 32, 40, 113, 119, 130, 135,
    136, 155, 173, 174

France, 28, 32, 43, 115, 117, 154, 157
Franklin, Miles, 67, 68, 71, 78, 90, 91
Friedman, Milton, 141
fundamentalism, 35, 38, 43, 141, 144

General Framework Agreement for
    Peace in Bosnia and Herzegovina
    (1995). *See* Dayton Peace
    Agreement
Geneva Conventions (1949), 54, 73, 74,
    93, 94, 103, 114, 138, 150, 161,
    163, 170
    Additional Protocols (1977), 54, 61,
    76, 93, 94, 103, 114, 134, 150, 163
genocide, 6, 11, 12, 13, 16, 17, 18, 19,
    54, 60–63, 92–105, 114–16, 117,
    126, 127, 132, 141, 145, 151, 153,
    166
Genocide Convention, 18, 19, 54, 93, 94–
    95, 97–98, 99, 100, 103, 104, 114,
    116, 127, 163
Genocide Convention Implementation Act
    (1987), 54, 98–99
Germany, 28, 29–30, 63, 117, 131, 134,
    145, 147, 153, 154, 156, 175
Glaspie, April, 56
global warming, 76, 119
Gonzales, Alberto, 125
Gonsalez, Enrique, 70
Gonzalez, Henry, 64, 158, 159, 160, 164,
    172
Good Neighbor Policy, 107
Graham, Bob, 20
Guantanamo Bay, 151, 170
Gulf Cooperation Council, 40
Gulf War Syndrome, 17

Habeas corpus, 18, 137, 161
Hague Conventions (1907), 25– 28, 54,
    73, 74, 75, 77, 80, 83, 90, 150, 163
Haig, Alexander, 23, 34–35, 39, 41, 175
Haiti, 108, 119
Hammarskjold, Dag, 153
Havel, Vaclav, 17
Highway of Death, 61
Hiroshima, 18, 32, 146, 175
Hitler, Adolf, 63, 129, 147, 155, 156
Holbrooke, Richard, 114
Honduras, 112, 130
Hooper, Deborah, 65
Hormuz, Straits of, 37, 39, 45, 46, 47
Horna, Frank, 68, 69
Huet-Vaughn, Dr. Yolanda, 16–18, 65–91
humanitarian intervention, 19, 106–17
Huntington, Samuel, 130, 144
Hussein, Saddam, 15–16, 17, 18, 38, 44,

50, 51, 56, 57, 61, 62, 75, 143, 151,
    156, 171

illegal orders, 73, 75, 79, 89
imperialism, 11–13, 16, 21, 49, 55, 110,
    136–38, 141, 144, 151–54, 156,
    157, 158, 172, 175
impeachment, 20, 58, 64, 158–72
inchoate crimes, 13, 20, 55, 63, 77–78,
    83, 90, 98, 131, 140, 148, 149, 150,
    153, 156, 163, 174-75
India, 41, 120, 136
Indigenous peoples, 11–13, 116, 117, 151,
    152
Indonesia, 116
International Convention on the Elimination
    of All Forms of Racial Discrimination
    (1966). *See* Racial Discrimination
    Convention
International Convention on the Preven-
    tion and Punishment of the Crime of
    Genocide (1948). *See* Genocide
    Convention
International Convention on the Rights of
    the Child (1989). *See* Children's
    Convention
International Convention on the Suppres-
    sion and Punishment of the Crime
    of Apartheid (1973). *See* Apartheid
    Convention
International Court of Justice, 13, 15, 19,
    31, 45, 48–49, 72, 90, 100, 110–11,
    112–13, 114, 122, 123, 127, 128,
    146
International Covenant on Civil and
    Political Rights (1966), 161, 169
International Criminal Court, 119, 132, 136,
    155–56
International Criminal Tribunal for
    Rwanda, 156
International Criminal Tribunal for the
    Former Yugoslavia, 115, 156
International Physicians for Prevention of
    Nuclear War, 70
International War Crimes Tribunal, 16, 53,
    54, 59, 64
Iran, 15–16, 17, 33–39, 40, 41, 42, 43–47,
    49, 50–52, 55, 56, 62, 83, 84, 127,
    130, 135, 136, 142, 145, 150, 156,
    171–72, 173
Iraq, 6, 11, 15–16, 17, 18–19, 20, 33–39,
    40, 43–47, 49, 50–52, 53, 54, 55–
    64, 65, 67–68, 70, 73, 75, 76, 77,
    79–80, 81, 83–84, 85, 86, 87, 88,
    91, 95–97, 99, 100, 103, 104, 106,
    108–09, 116, 119, 124, 126, 127,
    130, 133, 135, 140, 141, 142, 143,